Promoting Cognitive Growth
Over the Life Span

Promoting Cognitive Growth
Over the Life Span

Edited by

Milton Schwebel
Charles A. Maher
Nancy S. Fagley
Rutgers University

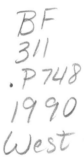

LAWRENCE ERLBAUM ASSOCIATES, PUBLISHERS
1990   Hillsdale, New Jersey   Hove and London

Lawrence Erlbaum Associates, Inc., Publishers
365 Broadway
Hillsdale, New Jersey 07642

Library of Congress Cataloging-in-Publication Data

Promoting cognitive growth over the life span/edited by Milton
Schwebel.
      p.   cm.
   ISBN 0-8058-0663-6
   1. Cognition. 2.   Developmental psychology.   3. Educational
psychology.   I. Schwebel, Milton.
BF311.P748   1990
153.4– dc20   89-77877
                                                                        CIP

Printed in the United States of America
10 9 8 7 6 5 4 3 2 1

CONTENTS

Chapter 3

A LIFE-SPAN PERSPECTIVE
ON THINKING AND PROBLEM-SOLVING   **47**
Jacqui Smith and Paul B. Baltes

Chapter 4

NEGOTIATING SENSE IN THE ZONE
OF PROXIMAL DEVELOPMENT   **71**
James V. Wertsch and Norris Minick

Chapter 5

THINKING AND FEELING – THE ELEPHANT'S TAIL   **89**
Michael Lewis

PART II
PROGRAMS TO PROMOTE COGNITIVE GROWTH
AND PROGRAMMATIC ISSUES   111

_____ *Chapter 9*

PRACTICAL PERSPECTIVES ON CHANGING SCHOOLS
TO STIMULATE COGNITIVE DEVELOPMENT   193
Willy De Coster, Armand De Meyer, and Roger Parmentier

_____ *Chapter 10*

ON COGNITIVE DEVELOPMENT   211
Jerome Kagan

LIST OF CONTRIBUTORS

Paul B. Baltes
Max Planck Institute
for Human Development
and Education, Berlin

Penelope Brooks
Vanderbilt University

Willy De Coster
University of Ghent, Belgium

Armand De Meyer
Educational Center
of Ghent City, Belgium

Nancy S. Fagley
Rutgers University

Reuven Feuerstein
Bar Ilan University, Ramat Gan
Director, Hadassah-Wizo-Canada
Research Institute, Jerusalem

Howard E. Gruber
University of Geneva
(now at Teachers College,
Columbia University)

H. Carl Haywood
Vanderbilt University

Mildred B. Hoffman
Hadassah-Wizo-Canada
Research Institute, Jerusalem

Jerome Kagan
Harvard University

Deanna Kuhn
Teachers College,
Columbia University

Michael Lewis
Institute for the Study
of Child Development,
University of Medicine
and Dentistry of New Jersey,
Robert Wood Johnson Medical
School

Charles A. Maher
Rutgers University

Norris Minick
Frances L. Hiatt
School of Psychology,
Clark University

Roger Parmentier
University of Ghent, Belgium

Lucien Richard
University of Geneva

Milton Schwebel
Rutgers University

Jacqui Smith
Max Planck Institute
for Human Development
and Education, Berlin

James V. Wertsch
Frances L. Hiatt
School of Psychology,
Clark University

PREFACE

This book is about fostering critical and creative thinking and problem solving. Necessarily, it is also about the nature of those cognitive processes and their relationship to feelings. These are matters of interest to psychologists, educators, and public policy makers.

The content of the book contributes to the knowledge base about promoting cognitive growth in two separate yet interrelated ways. One has to do with whether and to what extent education can enhance and sustain cognitive functioning from infancy through old age. The other has to do with the viability of programs, methods, and procedures designed to enhance and sustain intellectual vitality.

In our view, research and scholarship in this area have a high social value and can in no sense be characterized as "academic." We believe knowledge about cognition and its facilitation may be one of the essential keys to clarifying and resolving the seemingly unyielding problems of educating varied populations in diverse societies, in established as well as developing nations. Those enduring problems have been a source of distress to countless millions for many years.

After World War II many nations confronted the challenge of educating entire populations for the first time. School systems that had effectively provided elementary and secondary education primarily to children of middle class or upwardly mobile families, now floundered in their attempts to gain a modicum of success with other children. As if that were not enough, the problems were further complicated by new waves of immigrants, "guestworkers," chronically unemployed, homeless, welfare-supported single parent families, and rural poor transplanted to cities.

Because of repeated failures to make a breakthrough in the education of perhaps 40% to 50% of the population, some psychologists began to question the assumption that all or even most children enter school with the prerequisites to learning. They knew that while the more favored preschool children are read to each day and given a wide variety of stimulating experiences like story-telling, painting, visiting zoos, playing with construction toys, and engaging in conversation with adults and other children, the less advantaged have many fewer opportunities for the kind of stimulation and guidance that prepares one for school. Unless they can be given what they need, children lacking those prerequisites are like sheep being led to academic slaughter. Their need is considerable and cannot be supplied in a summer or a year and, it appears, cannot be satisifed by traditional methods of schooling.

The prerequisites to education are not the experiences just enumerated but their presumed products—the perceptual and mental competences that are the building blocks of human cognition. Psychologists and educators have come to believe that societies committed to mass education must find ways to help children develop those competences and help adults retain them over the course of the life span. That means they must find ways to facilitate intellectual development throughout life.

At the same time, nations are faced with other demands. Critics deplore the quality of elementary, secondary, higher, and adult education available to the population at large, especially for education's failure to cultivate the imaginative and reflective sensibilities. Education is also criticized for its failure to encourage independent thinking in students of all ages. Besides those challenges, nations confront still another problem as the elderly become an ever-larger segment of the population—to help them retain an adequate level of mental functioning.

The assistance available from science to address these problems is all too limited. Although psychology is a century old, its involvement in promoting rather than just studying cognition is fairly recent. For that reason we decided to bring together in one volume the theoretical, research and developmental work of some of the leading psychologists in the world. Our aim was not to focus on a single stage in life or a single aspect of development or a particular type of intervention, but rather to get a sweeping picture over the life span. We expected that we would obtain cohesiveness and continuity in our projected book from common use by our authors of concepts that transcend specific life stages and intervention approaches.

We invited psychologists to write papers on aspects of the topic closest to their present work for a symposium at Rutgers University in 1987. They were later asked to write a critique of another participant's paper. The content of the symposium consisted of paper presentations, prepared critiques, and additional comments by other participants and members of the audience, and rejoinders by the original presenters. The subjects were serious, the exchanges vigorous, sometimes heated, sometimes humorous, and typically provocative. The result was that the contributors to this book were advantaged, in revising their papers, by the thinking of many of their colleagues at the symposium. Later, as editors, we offered suggestions to help clarify and expand some of their ideas. Almost all the papers were revised by the authors at least once, and reviewed, and some updated, in 1989.

An undertaking of the kind entailed in bringing this volume to fruition is understandably demanding and succeeded in no small part because of the generous support we received from many people. We would like to express our gratitude at least to a few of them. Financial support was provided by a grant from the New Jersey Department of Higher Education and a gift from Luella Buros. Special thanks are due to Anthony D. Lutkus, Director of the Basic Skills Assessment Program in the Department of Higher Education, for his interest in our project and his administrative management of the funding. The gift from Mrs. Buros was offered in memory and honor of her late husband, Oscar Krisen Buros, founder of the *Mental Measurement Yearbooks* and for much of his life a member of the Rutgers University faculty. We are far more grateful to Mrs. Buros for her friendly encouragement and generous support than this brief note can express. Our thanks go to others as well. University Professor Nathaniel Pallone, then academic vice president of Rutgers University, a consistent supporter, provided us with university facilities. Professor Cynthia P. Deutsch of New York University offered valuable advice, and so did Professor Edith Neimark, a colleague at Rutgers. Diane Crino served as manager of the conference, the success of which can be attributed in no small part to her patience, good humor, and administrative skill. Charlotte Schulman, secretary to the Dean, as always, was supportive in countless ways. Finally, and with deep-felt gratitude, we acknowledge the consistent, unwavering support and discerning editorial advice of our colleague and friend, Donald Peterson, then Dean of the Graduate School of Applied and Professional Psychology at Rutgers, now Professor Emeritus.

M.S.

C.A.M.

N.S.F.

Piscataway, New Jersey

Many are of the opinion that [people] do not like to think; that they will do much to avoid it; that they prefer to repeat instead. But in spite of many factors that are inimical to real thinking, that suffocate it, here and there it emerges and flourishes. And often one gets the strong impression that [people], even children, long for it.

Max Wertheimer (1959). *Productive thinking.* New York: Harper & Brothers

Chapter 1

INTRODUCTION: THE SOCIAL ROLE IN PROMOTING COGNITIVE GROWTH OVER THE LIFE SPAN

Milton Schwebel
Charles A. Maher
Nancy S. Fagley
Rutgers University

Collectively, the authors and editors of this book are interested in the ongoing development of cognition over the life span. Some of us focus our attention on the early years of life, others on young adulthood, and still others on the later years. Apart from those differences, we are united in our concern with the conditions that promote growth in the abilities to achieve, use, and create knowledge at all ages. We are especially interested in conditions that foster thinking, problem solving, and creativity.

Those who confront issues about promoting cognitive growth are faced with two complex problems:

1. What experiences stimulate cognitive growth and effectively involve individuals in their own intellectual development?
2. How can these be incorporated into their lives, through such agents as family, school, university, or senior citizen center?

Looking at past accomplishments in modifying educational institutions for the purpose of promoting cognitive growth, one could become discouraged. When Jean Piaget (1970) examined the methods of teaching in schools in 1965 and compared his observations with those in 1935, he was impressed by the lack of change. A "force feeding" kind of instruction, not calculated to stimulate thought, was characteristic at both points 30 years apart. Very likely, if he were to make observations today, he would find little change in most classrooms. However, at about the time he made his second set of observations, a decisive change in outlook began to emerge. Fueled by social demands and influenced by the newly popular theories of Piaget,

Vygotsky, Bruner, and McV. Hunt (and later, of cognitive psychology), psychologists and educational researchers confronted learning and developmental problems with a different perspective from that of the past. Before, children were assessed in order to place them in classes suited to their current ability level, the assumption being that their observed performance was an approximate reflection of their academic potential. Now, assessment was made for the purpose of identifying gaps in the cognitive domain—the structures and skills that were absent or not sufficiently developed, the assumption being that programs could be designed to enable the children to achieve them. As a result, programs to facilitate cognitive development and academic achievement were introduced. These efforts were capped by the federal government's introduction of Head Start for preschoolers and, later, of Follow Through for children in the primary grades. By those actions the government endorsed a policy of innovation consistent with the new thinking about intervention, accompanied by evaluation, to initiate desired programmatic changes.

Later, but still within the decade of the sixties, social pressures in high schools and on college and university campuses led to an extension of concern to those educational and age levels. Concomitantly, the increasing proportion of older adults in the population, with their problems of memory, and of intellectual functioning in general, spawned a growing interest in and research literature on gerontological issues. For them, too, the ultimate objective was to design experiences to halt, reverse, or at least ameliorate some of the vicissitudes of aging.

Many programs and experimental methods of intervention have been evaluated and the results suggest that were he making an assessment today of potential for change in the schools, Piaget would not be so pessimistic as he was in 1965. He would find settings at all age levels that were not engaged in "force feeding," although he would recognize them to be all too few in number. He would also find some of the results gratifying; for example, Datta's (1986) painstaking analysis of the cognitive effects of early childhood programs reveals their positive outcomes, especially the long-term educational and career benefits. There have been comparable advances in knowledge about cognition over the life span, although so far as cognitive functioning is concerned, the years between young and old adulthood remained a largely unexplored area until very recently. In the 1980s psychologists turned from their almost total preoccupation with "academic intelligence," which is represented by tasks called for both on IQ tests and in school assignments, to "everyday cognition" and "practical intelligence" (Rogoff & Lave, 1984; Sternberg & Wagner, 1986), which involve the demands of coping with life's situations.

The new thinking about promoting cognitive growth has emerged in many countries besides the United States, including Belgium, Holland,

Iceland, Israel, Venezuela, and West Germany. UNESCO commissioned a state of the art report on cognitive development and its facilitation (Schwebel, 1983) and its journal on education, *Prospects,* features articles on that topic. In sum, the subject of this book—understanding how to help individuals construct the foundations of critical and creative thinking and to encourage its expression thereafter—is very much on the international agenda. And, being on the cutting edge of the behavioral and educational sciences, it is an enterprise filled with challenge, the excitement of new ideas, and the inescapable clash of conflicting views.

The following three sections are intended to set the stage for the remaining chapters. The section on the social role in cognitive growth elaborates concepts that are central to our topic and appear in subsequent chapters. The second section deals with implementation aspects of the social role. The final section, on the chief features of the book, examines several major issues discussed by the authors, including some on which they differ.

THE SOCIAL ROLE IN COGNITIVE GROWTH

In recent years we have come to appreciate that cognitive development involves a partnership between an individual and the social environment. This idea derives from the well-known fact that individuals and their social e...vironments play indispensable parts in cognitive (and other) growth. There are, in other words, both individual and social roles that must be performed in the process of the individual's development, and these roles operate over the entire life span. A social environment is indispensable, for in its absence individual development, and survival itself, are inconceivable. The quality of that environment is, as we would expect, a sensitive factor. Highly inadequate social environments lead to irreversible cognitive deficiences, as in the well-known case of the animal-nurtured child known as the "feral child" (Itard, 1894/1932) or of the brutally deprived one called "Genie" (Curtis, 1977).

The use of the term *social role* has a functional purpose. In studies to facilitate development the independent variable is usually referred to as an *intervention.* And so it is, but it is something more as well. We prefer to think of the independent variable as the social role in a partnership devoted to the individual's fullest possible realization of intellectual potential. Hence, the difference between intervention and social role is more than rhetorical. Intervention implies that A acts or impacts upon B. After thoughtful consideration as an uninvolved observer A determines B's needs and seeks to satisfy them by means of the intervention. By implication, at least, A is uninvolved with and unaffected by B. (In fact, we know that in reality many interveners do not maintain such a remote relationship.) In a partnership the relationship between A and B is reciprocal. Each has its own role to perform, both roles are essential, and the two interact with each other.

Such a partnership exists between parent and child. For example, mother's cooing may have been elicited in the first place by baby's action or expression and, in any event, will be continued or replaced by other behavior depending on the response she gets from the infant, as well as her own needs. The partnership also exists in the teacher–student relationship where the operating definition of the social role determines whether the chief activity will be the teacher's force-feeding (to borrow from Piaget) of disinterested if acquiescent students, who could be 6, 16, or 60 years of age, or on the other hand, thought-provoking experience involving students and teacher. One other form of partnership deserves to be mentioned, that between the innovator of a program (e.g., a psychologist) and those who are expected to introduce it (usually teachers). Too often in the latter case, failure to recognize this relationship as a partnership has led to resistance and even rejection of the program and, in any event, unsatisfactory conditions to evaluate its effectiveness.

In each instance in the previous paragraph the individual would traditionally be thought of as being on the receiving end of an intervention: the child (with mother), the student (with teacher), and the teacher (with innovator). That is not so in the case of a partnership, even when the partnership is unequal as it surely is between mother and baby. The participation of the other person, who might appropriately be called "senior partner" at the outset, is recognized as a necessary step to elevating and accelerating the participation of the individuals in their own cognitive growth. It is probably fair to say that no other objective is more significant in promoting all-around intellectual growth than that of individuals actively participating in and regulating their own development. In that sense, the purpose of the social role in the promotion of cognitive growth is to strengthen individuals' roles in advancing their cognitive capabilities.

We must make a distinction at the outset between social activity that, without design, may have the effect of facilitating development and that which is devised solely for such a purpose. In the former category are such experiences as parent–child communication, child–child play, teenagers' conversation about adolescent concerns, assertiveness training sessions, and senior citizen discussion groups. Whatever other benefits may accrue from those activities, there is reason to believe that they may contribute in varying degrees to the individual's achievement and use of knowledge.

Formal education falls in a no-man's-land so far as categorization is concerned. Unquestionably it is designed, but for what? In practice, schools are intended to provide individuals with the skills and habits appropriate to the occupational and social positions they will hold on leaving school. One of their functions is, in fact, a sorting out process, identifying, classifying, and preparing young people for their future places, including menial and repetitive jobs. In that sense schools play a conservative role, hardly one inclined to cultivate critical thinking and dissenting views.

Despite the cramped nature of its social role, there is evidence that traditional schooling does contribute to intellectual development, over and above the accumulation of information and acquisition of academic skills. Determining whether education has that influence is an enormously difficult task because the researcher must discount the effects of other influences. For example, life experience on a day-to-day basis seems to be creditable for making people "more intelligent." Then there is the impact of literacy that at a common sense level appears to be powerful enough to account for the development of mental processes. To control for those influences Scribner and Cole (1981) found the appropriate populations among the Vai people of Liberia: Groups of people essentially similar except that some only had the benefits of life experience, others of life experience and literacy, and still others of the latter two in addition to formal schooling. Using tests derived from native culture, they adduced evidence to show that formal education does make a significant difference. In particular, the cognitive superiority associated with schooling was exhibited in the domains of logical reasoning, and especially of verbal explanation. They attributed the advantages of the formally schooled subjects to such teacher practices as asking students to justify a solution or explain an answer.

This study and others give reason to believe that schooling in its current form promotes cognitive growth, but primarily as a by-product and rarely as a result of a clearly defined goal of enhancing children's thought processes. Probably the same may be said about educational and quasi-educational social agencies over the life span, including those for the aged — that they may have a salutary effect on stimulating and maintaining cognitive processes, although without that end being an explicit objective. Considering that even in the absence of such conscious commitment measurable gains are nonetheless achieved, it seems reasonable to expect more than that when facilitation of change becomes an operational goal.

Aspects of the Social Role

This section highlights four major functions of the social role in promoting cognitive growth. In one form or another these four are prominent features of subsequent chapters: mediation; fostering self-regulation and metacognition; assessment of short-range growth possibilities; and cultivating critical and creative thinking. We will discuss them in that order.

Mediation

The long prevailing belief that development precedes learning has been challenged by the following opposing view: learning stimulates development that, in turn, leads to more advanced learning, which leads to further development, and so forth, in a continuing spiral fashion. The latter view — that learning comes first — opens the door wider than ever to the possibility of influencing development through education. It encourages the design of educational experience for the express purpose of enhancing cognitive growth. In such newly designed programs the concept of mediation achieves prominence.

The term *mediation* in this context refers to the social role of assisting individuals to perceive and interpret their environment. One person, the mediator, helps another recognize significant physical or social features, either in contemporary or past experience, by filtering and organizing those features. Instead of the initial randomized appearance of stimuli in the environment, relationships among them of a causal, spatial, or temporal nature become apparent. In short, the mediator aids the individual in making sense of the universe.

To sharpen the meaning of the concept, one can picture fictional Martians landing in Times Square in New York City or in other equally distracting settings. To help them acquire meaning of their environment the mediator would direct their attention to the significant aspects of the environment, namely, people and theaters rather than pigeons. In like manner, parents, as mediators, begin to help children make sense of their experience.

As an illustration of the concept, we can imagine a child in a museum of art, confronted by a vast array of stimuli. What paintings or sculptures are to be looked at out of the hundreds? And in examining any one of them, what in particular should be noted? What relationships exist among them in temporal sequence, content, or style? What meaning is the artist conveying and how does it relate to the child's knowledge, that is, to what the child has already assimilated? These questions about significance, relationships, and meanings can be adapted to countless situations at virtually all periods in the life span. It may occur when a high school student is reading a difficult assignment, when a young adult is confronted with problems at work, or an older adult with decisions about retirement. Mediation in any of these situations occurs when another person helps the individual address these or similar questions, not by providing answers but by widening options, often by challenging the individual to look at the stimuli in new ways. A recent study of 5-year-old children who shared in decision making about the most efficient routes through a model grocery illustrates the benefits of mediation. Whether these children collaborated actively with peers or their mothers, later, in the posttest, they were more likely to engage in advance planning and to produce more efficient routes than those children who either worked alone or did little if any sharing in decision making (Gauvain & Rogoff, 1989).

From birth, humans experience the benefits of mediation. For some, the quantity and quality of mediation in childhood were inadequate. For them, special programs, like those devised by Reuven Feuerstein and described in part 2 (Feuerstein & Hoffman, chap. 6), compensate for the deficiency at least in part. As noted in the examples given earlier, this form of the social role is not restricted to childhood. Any type of instruction, formal or informal, in which people (teachers, counselors, therapists) interpose themselves between the environment and the individual, represents mediation. This includes courses to enhance creative thinking in university students, as described by Howard Gruber and Lucien Richard (chap. 7), or in older adults, as presented by Jacqui Smith and Paul Baltes (chap. 3). Further discussion on mediation is found in chapter 6 by Feuerstein (with Hoffman), who has been a pioneer in its use, and also the chapter of Carl Haywood and Penelope Brooks (chap. 8) for whom mediation contributes to the theoretical basis of their curriculum for children.

The increasing popularity of mediation accompanies growing awareness that the conditions necessary for free inquiry by scientists and scholars are not the same required by school age children, or for that matter by many or most people of all ages. It is not sufficient to provide children with a stimulating environment and expect them on their own to discover or to learn. A small percentage of children manage and a few even thrive, but examination of the background and family life of these children reveals that they get their guidance and instruction at home. Some specific aspects of the home environment, such as parent responsivity, were found to be more significant than socioeconomic status in determining developmental level in a longitudinal study of children in the first 3 years of life (Bradley et al., 1989). This finding simply underscores the importance of educating parents and teachers about the importance of adult responsivity and involvement. If children are left largely on their own, or even in the presence of an understanding but passive teacher, those who never had opportunity to acquire the prerequisites for learning will fail if they are given "freedom to learn" and no more than that. Even in the typical classroom where teachers are active in the traditional manner, children who lack the internalized cognitive processes essential to further learning are not likely to succeed.

Interest in mediation has also been stimulated by growth in the population of older adults. Aging adults are confronted with new problems requiring the use of cognitive processes that are rusty from long disuse or may never have been achieved. Older people must also cope with memory problems. For them, application of the concept of mediation holds promise for future advances in skill training, counseling, and other forms of care giving.

Self-Regulation and Metacognition

Starting at an early age children slowly begin to assume the social role of mediation; that is, they begin to mediate for themselves. They regulate their own thinking by interposing themselves between environmental stimuli and their own responses in self-critical ways. With passing years, they monitor and reflect on their own thought processes, a practice called *metacognition*. Some background on these processes may be helpful.

In his *Principles of Psychology,* William James (1890) anticipated by almost a century a principle of central importance to considerations about cognition and its development. At that time, under the influence of Darwin, many scholars were seeking to explain the mind in terms of evolutionary theory. For some, like Herbert Spencer, the function of human intelligence was that of adapting to the environment. To James, such an explanation was thoroughly unacceptable because it made the human species a prisoner of the environment. As he explained, mind was both a product of and a shaper of the environment. Humans are not passive reacters, simply adapting to circumstances; they change those circumstances (Cremins, 1961).

James' words have a modern ring to them because of current interest in self-regulation, and recognition that cognitive development is effectively promoted when individuals assume control over their thought processes. They learn to observe in planned fashion, differentiate the significant from the irrelevant, organize and communicate their thoughts systematically, and monitor their mental activity objectively. In James' terms, they take control over and change the circumstances of their environment.

The study of human development reveals a progression of increasing self-control from birth onward into adulthood. This process of change in infancy and childhood, and to a considerable extent in adolescence as well, is a product of the individual's own activity and adult interventions. In the cognitive domain it shows itself as the capacity to monitor and regulate one's own thinking, to engage in reflection and employ strategies involving introspection. Besides being able to use cognitive skills—to learn, memorize, recall, solve problems—they possess metacognitive skills. Up until now, adults served as mediators between them and the environment, protecting them from painful consequences of misguided thinking. Now children and teenagers increasingly serve as their own mediators as they use the skills of metacognition, which include the following: (a) *awareness*—for example, awareness that one is not comprehending the meaning of a text, leading to a search for the source of the problem; (b) *monitoring*—for example, establishing a clear-cut goal in one's reading or studying, checking on comprehension, using self-questioning and other forms of evaluation; (c) *regulating*—for example, employing strategies to overcome problems revealed through monitoring, so that when comprehension begins to falter while reading an assignment, one rereads, or engages in search strategies, or draws on prior knowledge to make more sense of the text (Haller, Child, & Walberg, 1988).

New developments in psychology and education involve both cognitive and metacognitive skills. Several literature reviews on studies concerning instruction in cognitive skills, for example, memory, demonstrated convincingly that cognitive instruction was insufficient. One review of 114 studies found that the children showed immediate improvements, yet in none were the gains sustained or the learning generalized to other tasks (Belmont & Butterfield, 1977). By contrast, in 6 studies in which self-regulating skills were part of the training, substantial transfer effects were produced. Here the subjects had been instructed in the need to define goals, design appropriate plans, and monitor both their implementation of the plans and the outcomes (Belmont, Butterfield, & Ferretti, 1982). A recent synthesized study of 20 studies on the effect of metacognitive instruction on reading comprehension involved a population of 1,553 students, divided in each case into experimental and control groups. The average effect of metacognitive instruction was substantial, in fact, one of the largest in educational research (Haller, Child, & Walberg, 1988).

So far, we have concentrated on that part of metacognition that represents individuals reflecting on cognitive aspects of their experience. Indisputably, the human need is as great to reflect on and control affect as cognition so that besides thinking about their thinking, individuals also think about their feelings. Studies of thinking and intelligence frequently ignore the relationship between cognition and emotion. Yet the link is strong, and study of the relationship between thought and affect is indispensable to give full meaning to them. Kagan (1984) examined that link and showed, for example, that the maturation of new cognitive functions elicits new emotional reactions. Other researchers have had results suggesting that learned helplessness does not manifest itself behaviorally until about the middle elementary school years when the child has developed the cognitive capacity for the emergence of a fairly stable self-concept (Fincham, Hokoda, & Sanders, 1989). This area of investigation, which links feeling and thinking, including the monitoring and regulation of feelings, is explored in Michael Lewis' chapter (5).

That self-control is a life-span issue was dramatically demonstrated by Langer and Rodin's landmark study of 91 nursing home residents, ranging in age from 65–91 (1976). This study showed the impact of self-control and regulation on affect and general psychosocial functioning. The "disengaged" group members were told that all their needs would be taken care of and decisions made for them, and that the potted plant that was now being presented to them would be watered and attended to by staff. The "activity" group members were given a wide scope for decision making, and told that the potted plant was to be entirely in their care. The variety of dependent variables included self-reports on happiness and social involvement, interviewer's rating of alertness, nurse's ratings on general improvement, records of time spent visiting other residents and staff, and even markings on white adhesive tape applied daily to one wheel of their wheel chair. Three weeks later the activity group showed significant improvements in happiness, alertness, and sense of well-being, which were associated with substantial increases in social activity. Meanwhile the comparison disengaged group showed declines in most of these variables. Eighteen months later, the activity group showed the same pattern of superiority, and about half as many of its members had died compared with the disengaged group.

Studies of practical intelligence, which span the adult years, are introducing a new area for mediation. This field has been opened so recently that few investigators have commented about the possibility of helping individuals develop cognitive skills that are useful to them no matter what their stage of adulthood may be (Wagner, 1986).

The contents of this book reflect a growing movement, in research and program development and evaluation, toward facilitating self-regulation in people of all ages, including the elderly. Cognitive and metacognitive skills, always accompanied by the possibility of mediation by another person, are intended not only to enhance mastery of basic knowledge and not restricted to the early years of life; they are meant to stimulate the natural human capacities to produce novel ideas and be creative in manifold ways, in coping with prosaic problems of daily life and confronting overarching social issues, and to do these throughout life.

Assessment of Growth Possibilities:
Zone of Proximal Development

A perennial question in education pertains to the individual's readiness to learn some subject or skill. Is this person ready to learn to read? Is this person ready to learn algebra? These questions imply that the students may not have reached the necessary developmental level to deal with the tasks involved in the given subjects. Such questions are usually answered by administering a test to ascertain the level of development the child has achieved.

A very different approach was proposed by Vygotsky (1978), who indicated that such questions could be answered only by assessing *two* developmental levels: the *actual* developmental level, meaning the already established mental functions of the individual; and the level of *potential* development, meaning those mental functions that are in process of maturing but are still, as Vygotsky said, in embryonic state. The level of potential development is assessed by use of a testing practice that violates traditional principles. The examiner determines the degree of mastery examinees exhibit when they are helped by the examiner who shows them how to handle the problems. The difference between the actual and the potential level of development is called the *zone of proximal development* (ZPD). That zone reveals the mental operations the children are still unable to use independently but can employ under guidance of a teacher or other capable person. In time, those functions will be available for use independently.

The ZPD can be seen in operation when an individual, with the help of a mediator (coach or instructor), is learning a performance skill, such as serving a tennis ball or backing an automobile into a parallel park position. The mediator assesses the quality of the performance: the velocity, accuracy of placement and consistency of the serve, the spatial judgment, wheel control, and visual-motor coordination of the student driver. Then, the mediator can appraise the learner's ZPD in that skill and estimate the instruction required for that learner to be able to perform the skill alone.

The zone of proximal development serves as a useful tool in planning programs to promote growth because it gives the planner an indication of growth possibilities. It indicates realistic capabilities and expectations. Once these are realized as a result of experience under the supervision of teacher or other, then a next assessment reveals the new ZPD, or the next higher level of potential development. Thus, learning with the guidance of a teacher in the ZPD leads to actual development, which may then be followed by assessment to establish the boundaries of the next ZPD, the next sequence of learning and development.

The ZPD is inseparable from mediation and metacognition. The mediator guides the individual through learning experiences that help bring mental functions from embryonic to mature development. During that process the individual, through observation and imitation of the mediator and through practical activity, acquires the metacognitive skills associated with self-mediation. Because of the ZPD's usefulness, it figures in a number of the chapters in this book and is the central focus in that by James Wertsch and Norris Minick (chap. 4).

Critical and Creative Thinking

Programs to promote cognitive growth have usually been initiated to compensate for inadequate preschool preparation and school instruction.

Often they have been born out of desperation over the failure of the regular curriculum to improve the academic lot of large numbers of students. As a consequence, attention has been directed toward achievement and use of basic knowledge, rather than on the higher mental functions like critical and creative thinking. This is not to say that such programs do not seek to foster independent thinking. They do, as chapters by Feuerstein (chap. 6), Haywood and Brooks (chap. 8), and De Coster, De Meyer and Parmentier (chap. 9) clearly reveal. Nevertheless, because of widespread preoccupation with reversing past inadequacies for those who have been educationally and usually economically disadvantaged, insufficient attention has been paid by psychologists, educators, and the community at large to shortcomings in regard to thinking and especially creativity in education for most people. Whatever the reason, the child has been seen "by nearly all researchers as an exclusively rational creature, a problem-solver—in fact, a scientist in knickers" (Gardner, 1982, p. xii).

The quality of mediation people experience is probably a major determinant of their critical and creative activity. The methods mediators employ to interpose themselves between the environment and individuals are likely adopted by the latter in their independent problem solving. Those methods could involve reliance on faith, tradition, or reasoning. Some mediators, like the university instructors described in the Gruber and Richard chapter (7), provide experiences that encourage creative thought. In different settings, Haywood and Brooks (chap. 8) draw on teachers' creative curricular ideas, and De Coster and colleagues (chap. 9) and Deana Kuhn (chap. 2) encourage independent thinking in children. In chapter 10 Jerome Kagan, in challenging psychology to take a rigorous look at why so little is still understood about cognition and cognitive development, is himself serving as mediator calling for more critical thinking.

Creativity is now being discovered in a new and unexpected quarter. The recent exploration of problem solving in every day life, and especially in the work place, has revealed that activities considered mundane by comparison with those found in the artist's studio or the composer's music room, also give rise to inventiveness on an ongoing basis. Ordinary people engaging in ordinary activities that require practical problem solving employ creative measures (Scribner, 1986).

IMPLEMENTATION AS A SOCIAL ROLE

The social role includes the implementation, evaluation, modification, and incorporation of programs to promote cognitive growth into the structure of an educational agency. Performing that role is no simple process, as some of our authors report, because it tends to arouse personal and institutional resistance. To Gruber and Richard (chap. 7), the manifestations of resistance in universities appeared in the guise of institutional and professorial self-satisfaction. De Coster and associates (chap. 9) observed it in teachers' reluctance to modify traditional classroom practices and parental noninvolvement with the school. Psychology, itself, is not immune to resistance to change. Kuhn's (chap. 2) charge that psychologists continue to study cognition in unreal settings and have little of use to offer in the way of programs to teach thinking raises the question whether, like teachers in the schools and professors in universities, psychologists are also content with traditional practice and unwilling to risk venturing into new ones. Kagan (chap. 10) argues that to promote knowledge about cognition psychology needs to overcome its own resistance to greater rigor.

Battle-scarred psychologists and educational researchers know that a beautifully reasoned program can come to a disastrous end at any stage between a pilot test and final incorporation because persons crucial to its success are not prepared to accept it. Given such painful experience, it is not surprising that innovators often experience the differences between "them and us" as personal ones. Yet, resistance to change is usually a reflection of prevailing social values and not just personal obstreperousness or professional conservatism. And those values frequently persist, as if on their own momentum, even when contemporary needs demand that they be replaced by more appropriate ones. At any rate, they may persist until there is palpable evidence that other social values now have precedence, as in the American reaction to the successful flight of Sputnik when mathematics and science education was elevated to a higher status and given substantially increased budgetary support.

The crucial role of social values in human development is evident in Kessen's assertion that what children become is a decision made by the community. In his own words, "the endpoint of development, to put it too baldly, is the achievement of that set of characteristics that the culture values" (Bronfenbrenner et al. 1986, p. 1223). And what the culture values is mightily influenced by material conditions in a given society. In that connection, Irvine and Berry (1988, p. 4) introduced the "law of cultural differentiation," which asserts that what is learned, and at what age it is learned in a given society, is determined by cultural factors. Cerebral structures adapt to ecological demands that prescribe what abilities are developed. According to this law, different patterns of ability are inevitable in societies with different cultural environments. Consequently, low-food-accumulating societies, whose populations must hunt and fish for food, tend to produce individuals who obtain higher scores on spatial ability and cognitive differentiation tests than those in high-food-accumulating societies, whose survival does not depend on such abilities. Extrapolating from inter-society comparisons to intra-society, the law of cultural differentiation suggests that cultural factors may also dictate what is learned by various subgroups within a nation, whether these are social class, racial, ethnic, or gender.

The proposition that resistance or support for change is socially determined is further illuminated by the "concept of practice" proposed by Scribner and Cole (1981). It means, in brief, that societies value the kinds of practices that are deemed necessary for their survival, if not prosperity. The practices are ingrained in the culture, people are motivated to learn them and the society to teach them, until they are replaced by others. A practice, as Scribner and Cole defined it, is "a recurrent, goal-directed sequence of activities using a particular technology and particular systems of knowledge" (p. 236). Skills (i.e., "coordinated sets of actions") are acquired in order to apply the knowledge.

The concept of practice implies that cognitive skills develop as a result of goal-oriented activity; and that such activity is not artificially imposed but arises out of the needs of the social system, so that a need for literacy, medicine, or shoe-repair must exist in order for individuals to be goal-directed to learn the cognitive and other skills associated with the practices. It follows from the concept of practice that cognitive activities like critical and creative thinking and problem solving must be regarded as essential to a society's welfare if their need is to be recognized and educational resources are to be made available.

The promotion of cognitive growth has become an area of special interest in the last 25 years in response to four social needs. First is the need for higher levels of cognitive functioning in larger proportions of the population, which has been made mandatory by scientific and technological advances, including those in information processing and communication. Second is the need for effective ways of improving education for that large sector of children and youth who fare poorly in school. Third is the need to improve education for all age groups, regardless of age, sex, race, or ethnicity. Fourth, in societies with rapidly increasing proportions of older adults, is the need for understanding and control over cognitive decline with age.

Needs do not become instant values and may, indeed, be given the "back-burner" treatment. With different needs competing for attention and resources, those that are deemed to be essential to economic survival and prosperity, like the first of the four listed earlier, are likely to win out. Even technologicaly advanced societies today do not require a labor force composed of critical and creative thinkers. Under the circumstances, it is not surprising that there is no mandate to provide resources for research and education to enable entire populations to reach high levels of intellectual functioning; and that major efforts have encountered bitter opposition, as in the case of Bruner (1983) and Ziegler (Ziegler & Valentine, 1979) in the United States, Edelstein (1985) in Iceland, and Machado, as reported by Walsh (1981), in Venezuela.

Still, despite its infant status, the movement to promote cognitive growth is active and having its influence felt in some quarters. It probably has contributed to a growing tendency to find accommodations between antagonistic theoretical positions, and the result may be a richer understanding of development. It is well known that Piaget and Vygotsky are leading representatives of approaches that give prime attention respectively to the individual and the social in human development. Bidell (1988) sought a theoretical bridge between the two, claiming that they share much common ground and are not as antithetical as they have been regarded by their respective supporters. He showed that their theories reflect a dialectical orientation; that is, neither takes a static view about human life, both recognize the normality and necessity of change (individual and social) and both focus on interrelationships, such as those between the individual and the social group or between aspects of the individual. Bidell believed that by understanding the two theories as supplements to each other psychology may be more successful in coping with obdurate problems. Energy formerly devoted to arguing over differences can be assigned to the utilization of the enriched combined approach.

The press to apply theory to practice may account for the fact that linkages are being sought, and not only between the previous two, but also with information-processing and behavioral approaches. This may all be for the good. For the social role in promoting cognitive growth over the life span requires understanding of the process and context of human development and how to influence them rather than theoretical purity.

THE CHIEF FEATURES OF THE BOOK

This book presents a sample of programs and programmatic ideas for promoting cognitive growth. The programs illustrate the major aspects of the social role that will, we believe, increasingly influence thinking about fostering cognitive growth and maintaining its effective use over the life span. The programs represent diversity in grade level and age because this book is not intended to be about young children, teenagers, or the aged, but rather about principles of facilitating growth at all ages.

The introductions to parts 1 and 2 give overviews of the chapters they contain. In the following paragraphs we discuss some of the major issues about promoting cognitive growth that constitute the chief features of the book.

Form and Content of Programs

Probably no question is more perplexing than, "What kind of program to stimulate thinking is most likely to work for X group?", the X possibly being normal preschoolers or teenagers or older adults, or retarded members of those age groups. Psychologists propose varied ways to answer the question, their answers being derived from their understanding of how mental functions develop. The primary difference among them relates to the content and context of instruction. Kuhn (chap. 2), for example, argues that thinking can be effectively taught only in real-life contexts. Using artifical content in artificial contexts (like unreal laboratory situations) has had little pay-off in telling us about thinking skills in daily life. If educational policy makers are to approve support for instruction on thinking, they need evidence that the methods employed have a significant effect on skills used in daily life. Kuhn believes this can be accomplished by using contexts and content that are familiar and meaningful to students.

Feuerstein's position (chap. 6) is decidedly different from Kuhn's. He presents in detail reasons why instruction to modify the intellectual performance of low-functioning students should not focus on real-life situations and should even be independent of curriculum content. In fairness to both positions we should add that they are not as diametrically opposed as it appears. Feuerstein's approach, which is now used mostly in school settings, calls for bridging between what is learned through use of content-free, noncurricular material on the one hand, and real-life situations and curriculum content on the other.

In the years during which they worked to improve instruction for preschool and primary grade children, De Coster and associates (chap. 9) were committed to operating in traditional school settings and, unlike Feuerstein, to using the framework of traditional curricula. However, they freely experimented with variations in curricula content to make it, in Kuhn's terminology, more real-life for children of their age and family background. What De Coster and colleagues especially concentrated on, as indicated in the next section, were changes in mode of instruction.

The belief that formal education should be more "real" to children, or to students of any age, does not negate a fundamental difference between school and nonschool experience. Wertsch and Minick (chap. 4) use the term *rational discourse* for the forms of speaking used in educational institutions. Using an excerpt of a teacher-led discussion designed to help students learn in their zone of proximal development, they show how school experience stimulates the development of rational discourse. The forms of speaking in formal education represent a mode of communication that helps students become more logical, consistent, and systematic in their thought processes, and probably account to a large degree for the cognitive development that education fosters even without programs designed for that purpose. Real life outside school or university usually does not provide comparable experience in rational discourse.

So far, we have noted agreement among authors that experience in learning to think must be related to the context (e.g., school subjects) in which the cognitive skills are to be used. That is true even if, as in Feuerstein's case, initially the experiences are deliberately isolated from school and nonschool content. Moving to a deeper level, there is the question, once the cognitive processes are learned, let us say in connection with arithmetic or social studies, whether they are automatically transferred to other school subjects or nonschool problems. Once that was a widely held assumption, but no longer. In the view of the authors, emphatically expressed by Kagan, such activities as problem solving are very much bound up with the knowledge domain to which they are applied. According to that view, the strategies employed in problem solving at school in history and chemistry, on the job in a bakery and an auto-repair shop, at home in child care and family budgeting probably differ within each set of two and between sets. The differences arise, it is believed, from the fact that strategies are modified as they interact with distinctly different bodies of knowledge.

Mode of Instruction

The question about how to teach harks back to our earlier discussion about mediation. What form should mediation take? What desired outcomes does the mediator have in mind? Is awareness of process of thinking, problem solving, or creating one of the objectives? Almost uniformly, the instructional methods presented in this book are nontraditional in the sense that they are based on the assumption that students must be actively involved in working purposefully toward goals with which they personally identify. Teachers have clear-cut objectives and expectations, and structured approaches to achieve them, but teachers assume that the goals can be realized only if students see those objectives as their own.

Gruber and Richard (chap. 7) report that in teaching an introductory psychology course students were told before they enrolled that unless they were willing to participate actively they should choose another section of the course. Student participation was considered so essential that De Coster and colleagues (chap. 9) decided that teachers should not be expected to adopt the new approach unless they knew what that entailed and freely chose to work at transforming their old ways of teaching into the new. For the same reason — accepting the centrality of active student involvement — Haywood and Brooks (chap. 8) invited teachers to participate with them in developing a curriculum for young children. Feuerstein (chap. 6) required that prior to use of his materials teachers undergo training to acquaint themselves with the content and also to screen themselves out if they found their orientation and values discrepant with the necessary ones.

The issue of the nature of teacher and student participation in class activity is far from resolved. De Coster and associates wrestled with it for more than 10 years, sometimes painfully it seems, and while their experience led them to a system involving a high degree of student activity based on student interest, they did not exclude the use for special purposes of such traditional methods as drill in such subjects as spelling. Drill, too, can be an experience of active student involvement, especially when it is recognized as a mechanism to help achieve desired objectives.

It is apparent that purposeful activity on the part of the learner is a paramount feature in promoting cognitive growth. The reason for its importance is complex. Any given activity has an affective component that may take the form of pleasure in carrying out the activity, gratification in having been permitted and encouraged to engage in it, satisfaction in ones performance, or any two or all three of them. In the programs described in this book emotional factors are notably important.

The affective side of experience probably plays a greater part in cognitive development than was generally recognized. Piaget, associated though he was with knowledge development, said there was no such thing as a purely cognitive or purely affective state because both are always involved (1962). More than their seeming inseparability is the question about the role of feelings in cognitive development. Lewis proposes that cognition and emotion feed on each other, so to speak, so that emotional development may precede the cognitive which precedes the emotional, and so forth. He suggests that emotional states may give rise to self-directed thought, a matter of key importance because of the latter's relationship to metacognition and, of course, to instruction and learning.

Whatever the mix of cognitive and affective variables, there remains the question about the extent to which the effects of inadequate or insufficient mediation (disadvantaged opportunity) can be reversed by a given mode of instruction. Although the issue is not directly addressed in this book, the tone in some chapters (e.g., Feuerstein and Hoffman, chap. 6, and Smith and Baltes, chap. 3) is more optimistic than in others (e.g., De Coster et al., chap. 9). That difference may be a result of the contrasting environments and populations with which they worked: De Coster and associates with regular classes of students, organized in traditional fashion in a large urban center with an ethnically heterogeneous population; Feuerstein with children designated as retarded in their functioning, in his specially designed program and in settings in which he and his associates have had control or influence in the selection and training of instructors; and Smith and Baltes with older adults in controlled laboratory-type conditions. The differences among them may reflect differences in institutional resistance to change they encountered rather than in accessibility to growth promoting experience.

As a concluding note to the chapter, it is fair to say that readers with a tendency toward either optimism or pessimism can find support for their inclination in this book. But however much such readers may differ about the prospects for advances in knowledge about promoting cognitive growth, they are likely to share in the excitement engendered by efforts to sharpen the issues, test new ideas in laboratory or field, and attempt to have them incorporated into established institutions.

REFERENCES

Belmont, J. M., & Butterfield, E. C. (1977). The instructional approach to developmental cognitive research. In R. V. Kail & J. W. Hagen (Eds.), *Perspectives on the development of memory and cognition* (pp. 437–482). Hillsdale, NJ: Lawrence Erlbaum Associates.

Belmont, J. M., Butterfield, E. C., & Ferretti, R. P. (1982). To secure transfer of training, instruct self-management skills. In D. K. Detterman & R. J. Sternberg (Eds.), *How and how much can intelligence be increased* (pp. 147–155). Norwood, NJ: Ablex Publishing.

Bidell, T. (1988). Vygotsky, Piaget and the dialectic of development. *Human Development, 31,* 329–348.

Bradley, R. H., Caldwell, B. M., Rock, S. L., Ramey, C. T., Barnard, K. E., Gray, C., Hammond, M. A., Mitchell, S., Siegel, L., Ramey, C. T., Gottfried, A. W., & Johnson, D. L. (1989). Home environment and cognitive development in the first 3 years of life: A collaborative study involving six sites and three ethnic groups in North America. *Development Psychology, 25,* 217–235.

Bronfenbrenner, U., Kessel, F., Kessen, W., & White, S. (1986). Toward a critical social history of developmental psychology. *American Psychologist, 41,* 1218–1230.

Bruner, J. (1983). *In search of mind.* New York: Harper & Row.

Cremins, L. (1961). *The transformation of the school.* New York: Knopf.

Curtis, S. R. (1977). *Genie: A linguistic study of a modern-day "Wild Child."* New York: Academic Press.

Datta, L. (1986). Benefits without gains: The paradox of the cognitive effects of early childhood progrrams and implications for policy. In M. Schwebel & C. A. Maher (Eds.), *Facilitating cognitive development* (pp. 103–126). New York: Haworth Press.

Edelstein, W. (1985). *The rise and fall of the social science curriculum project in Iceland, 1974–84: Reflections on reason and power in educational progress.* Berlin: Max Planck Institute for Human Development and Education.

Fincham, F. D., Hokoda, A., & Sanders, R. (1989). Learned helplessness, test anxiety, and academic achievement: A longitudinal analysis. *Child Development, 60,* 138–145.

Gardner, H. (1982). *Art, mind, and brain.* New York: Basic Books.

Gauvain, M., & Rogoff, B. (1989). Collaborative problem solving and children's planning skills. *Developmental Psychology, 25,* 139–151.

Haller, E. P., Child, D. A., & Walberg, H. J. (1988). Can comprehension be taught: A quantitative synthesis of "metacognitive" studies. *Educational Researcher,* 5–8.

Irvine, S. H., & Berry, J. W. (1988). The abilities of mankind: A revaluation. In S. H. Irvine & J. W. Berry (Eds.) *Human abilities in cultural context* (pp. 3–59). Cambridge: Cambridge University Press.

Itard, J. M. G. (1894/1932). *The wild boy of Aveyron.* New York: Lane.

James, W. (1890/1930). *Principles of psychology.* New York: Holt, Rinehart & Winston.

Kagan, J. (1984). *The nature of the child.* New York: Basic Books.

Langer, E. J. & Rodin, J. (1976). The effects of choice and enhanced responsibility for the aged. *Journal of Personality and Social Psychology, 34,* 191–198.

Piaget, J. (1962). The relation of affectivity to intelligence in the mental development of the child. *Bulletin of the Menninger Clinic, 26,* 129–137.

Piaget, J. (1970). *Science of education and the psychology of the child.* New York: Orion Press.

Rogoff, B., & Lave, J. (Eds.). (1984). *Everyday cognition: Its developmenttal and social context.* Cambridge, MA: Cambridge University Press.

Schwebel, M. (1983). *Research on cognitive development and its facilitation: A state of the art report.* Paris: UNESCO.

Scribner, S. (1986). Thinking in action: some characteristics of practical thought. In R. J. Sternberg & R. K. Wagner (Eds.), *Practical intelligence,* Cambridge: Cambridge University Press.

Scribner, S., & Cole, M. (1981). *The psychology of literacy.* Cambridge: Harvard University Press.

Sternberg, R. J., & Wagner, R. K. (Eds.). (1986). *Practical intelligence.* Cambridge: Cambridge University Press.

Vygotsky, L. S. (1978). *Mind in society: The development of higher psychological processes.* Cambridge: Harvard University Press.

Wagner, R. K. (1986). The search for intraterrestrial intelligence. In R. J. Sternberg & R. K. Wagner (Eds.) *Practical intelligence.* Cambridge: Cambridge University Press.

Walsh, J. (1981). A pleni potentiary for human intelligence. *Science, 214,* 640–641.

Zigler, E., & Valentine, J. (Eds.). (1979). *Project Head Start, A legacy of the war on poverty.* New York: Free Press.

PART 1

CONCEPTUAL ISSUES
IN PROMOTING
COGNITIVE GROWTH

Insofar as [men and women's] powers are expressed and amplified through the instruments of culture, the limits to which [they] can attain excellence of intellect must surely be as wide as are the culture's combined capabilities. We do not know in any deep sense as yet how we shall, in the future, better empower [people]. Insofar as the sciences of knowing can throw light on the growth of mind, the efficacy of the culture in fulfilling its responsibility to the individual can likely be increased to levels higher than ever before imagined.
—Bruner, Jerome S. (1966). In J. S. Bruner, R. R. Olver, & P. M. Greenfield (Eds.). *Studies in cognitive growth.* New York: Wiley.

Kuhn opens part I (chap. 2) by arguing that if students are to value experiences designed to help them master cognitive skills, for example those involved in thinking, they must be convinced that such skills will enable them to function more effectively in situations that they consider to be important in school and "real life." Research that is limited to meaningless words in artificial research circumstances can hardly provide evidence of the practical usefulness of whatever might emerge from such investigations. Furthermore, it is not enough for instruction on thinking to be firmly rooted in knowledge on the origins of a skill. It should also be based on understanding how individuals develop self-control over the skill. Instruction that leaves off with the cognitive skill and fails to include the metacognitive produces learning that is neither lasting nor transferrable. Kuhn's research is about the cognitive skills used by children and adults in modifying theories under the impact of new evidence, and the metacognitive skills of being aware of and controlling what they are doing.

Cognition is life-long. In contrast with the traditional view that cognitive capacities are fated to wane with age, there is growing evidence that those capacities most essential to adult life can be sustained and some even wax during later years. Smith and Baltes (chap. 3), carrying us beyond the children, adolescents and young adults in programs previously discussed, examine the effects of aging, both those caused by physiological changes as well as those instigated by social bias. Contrasting the performance of young and old on measures of fluid and crystallized intelligence reported in the growing literature on older people, and critically examining the different interpretations about those findings, they are led to propose the following: in some areas of practical intelligence (which is the crystallized type acquired through long-term learning, in contrast with creative problem solving of the fluid type) older people not only maintain their ability but may also be open to continued growth. One area of strength of older people is in the possession of "wisdom," a topic of current interest in the literature and the subject of their own reported research. Realization of potential, with the aged as with the young, depends on opportunity and social attitude. Very practical educational steps, involving metacognitive skills, can be taken to prevent, halt, and reverse intellectual decline.

The search for a link between sociohistorical forces and psychological processes has been slow in coming, partly because of the difficulty of studying the connection. That problem seems to have been removed once it was recognized that the mental functioning of the individual (intrapsychological) has its origin in social interaction (interpsychological). The transformation of interpsychological to intrapsychological is seen in its simplest form when the mother's words to her child become the child's monologue, and later the child's thoughts. Wertsch and Minick (chap. 4) show how, through the interactions of formal education, the teacher guides students to mastery of various forms of rational discourse, which is a sociocultural phenomenon that is obviously essential to modern society. Using classroom excerpts, the authors illustrate the teacher's use of the zone of proximal development, as she leads the children from their current independent problem-solving ability to problem solving at a higher level under her guidance. The teacher is the instrument for the sociocultural impact on the developing minds of the children as they become more adept in using rational discourse.

In the final chapter of part I, Lewis (chap. 5) explores the often-neglected interrelationship of human affect and cognition. He examines the term *feeling* and shows that it has at least two meanings: When people declare "I am feeling happy," they are reporting a feeling and also that they are thinking about the feeling. Lewis shows that to be able to do the latter, to be self aware, one must have experienced a particular level of cognitive development. The capacity to think about ones feelings, a counterpart to metacognition, is the basis for awareness of such emotional states as guilt or empathy and hence for self-regulation in intra- and interpersonal relations.

Chapter 2

EDUCATION FOR THINKING: WHAT CAN PSYCHOLOGY CONTRIBUTE?

Deanna Kuhn
Teachers College, Columbia University

In 1961, a report by the Educational Policies Commission of the National Education Association titled *The Central Purpose of American Education* proclaimed, "The purpose which runs through and strengthens all other educational purposes—the common thread of education—is the development of the ability to think" (p. 12). The flurry of attention that has been given to the teaching of thinking skills in the last two decades certainly reflects endorsement of this view. Yet national indicators of student performance suggest that the goal of education for thinking has been at best only dimly realized. A recent NAEP report indicated that students between 9 and 17 were largely competent in summarizing the major theme of a passage but showed little ability to analyze or evaluate, drawing on portions of the text as evidence to support their judgments. Similarly, numerous reports of mathematical achievement have indicated that students are competent in basic computational skills but unable to apply those skills in situations that require quantitative reasoning and problem solving.

To mount effective education for thinking, educators need two basic kinds of knowledge—knowledge of the specific thinking skills that are to be the goal of instruction and knowledge of the mechanisms in terms of which these skills are attained. It is reasonable to suppose that psychological research would provide both kinds of knowledge, and indeed the 1961 NEA report quoted at the outset emphasized the critical role of such research:

> Thus, in the general area of the development of the ability to think, there is a field of new research of the greatest importance. It is essential that those who have responsibility for management and policy determination in educa-

tion commit themselves to expansion of such research and to the application of the fruits of this research. This is the context in which the significant answers to such issues as educational technology, length of school year, and content of teacher education must be sought and given (p. 13).

Though the NEA report did stimulate a variety of research, in the 25 years since publication of this report, not a great deal of progress has been made in developing the sorts of research programs the report refers to — programs addressed specifically to identifying the nature of thinking skills and the mechanisms underlying their development. The argument can thus be made that it is lack of the necessary knowledge base that severely handicaps current efforts both to teach thinking skills and to evaluate the outcomes of such instruction. In this chapter, I suggest some reasons that the field of psychological research may have been poorly equipped to provide such a knowledge base. Also, I describe some current research that we believe may contribute to establishing the knowledge base that would assist educators in realizing their goal of education for thinking.

The most striking respect, I would suggest, in which psychology research has failed to fulfill the needs of educators concerned with teaching thinking has been in its lack of attention to thinking in real-life contexts. How can the educator justify concentration on a particular set of thinking skills as the object of instruction? Only by documenting that these are skills that will enable students to think more effectively in the real-life contexts significant to them. Psychology is hard-pressed to supply such evidence. Psychological research traditionally has restricted itself to investigations of thinking about artificial material in artificial contexts, without regard to the individual's own purposes and goals; thus we know little about the thinking skills that people use in their personal or work lives. By what reasoning processes, for example, (to anticipate the research I discuss here) do people justify the beliefs they hold about the world around them? Paradoxically, perhaps, our society invests millions of dollars and great technical expertise each year to ascertain with considerable accuracy *what* people think about all sorts of social and political topics. *Why* they think what they do—that is, the thinking that underlies the judgments they make—is something we know very little about.

A second respect in which psychological research—in particular research in developmental psychology—may not have served the interests of educators is in its more recent preoccupation with the developmental origins of skills. Let me use an example that figures prominently in the research I am going to discuss on skills in the coordination of theory and evidence. Investigators have traced acquisition of a covariation strategy to an early age: Quite young children will attribute an outcome to an antecedent that covaries with outcome over one that does not (Shultz & Mendelson; 1975;

Siegler, 1975), on the basis of which the researcher concludes that the child is using a "covariation strategy." But, at most, such evidence reveals the emergence of a covariation principle, or strategy, in its most rudimentary form. Although such labeling may be useful from the observer's perspective, it is unlikely to have psychological reality from the subject's perspective. In any case, considerable development must take place before the individual could be regarded as having what I will refer to as explicit, or metacognitive, knowledge of the strategy, in the sense of being able to draw on it in a fully conscious, explicit manner for the purpose of justifying an inference.

Educators have taken for granted that the development of explicit, consciously controlled intellectual skills is of primary importance. In particular, skills having to do with coordination of theory and evidence, such as the ability to draw on evidence to support one's judgments, are assumed to be central goals of the educational process. In stark contrast, many psychologists in recent years have tended to regard such skills as epiphenomena, irrelevant to the "real" mental processes that produce a judgment. As a result, we know much less about the development of explicit, consciously controlled cognitive skills than we do about the earliest origins of these skills in their implicit forms.

A firm base of knowledge about the natural course of development of these explicit thinking skills, I would claim, is the foundation on which education for thinking must be based. In what respects do thinking skills routinely become more sophisticated and effective? What is the nature of the obstacles that are met and conquered in this process? In the absence of this developmental knowledge base, programs to teach thinking can be based only on one person's idea versus another's of the set of skills worthy of attention.

A third, related respect in which research in psychology has not met educational needs is in its inability to provide a metric in terms of which efforts to foster thinking skills can be evaluated. The problem is well exemplified by recent attempts to devise new, broader conceptions and measures of intelligence by those who have been dissatisfied with traditional conceptions and measures. Once such new measures are devised, often the criterion that has been invoked to validate them is their correlation with standard intelligence measures! Similarly, those wishing to evaluate thinking skills programs tend to look to scores on traditional tests of aptitude or school achievement, which reflects the same kind of circularity. Quite likely, learning such skills doesn't affect school grades because the skills are not entailed in mastering the existing school curriculum. Such an outcome says nothing about whether the skills are important and worth teaching. Whether teaching a certain set of skills is worthwhile depends really only on whether one thinks they are skills worth having. And this of course becomes largely a matter of values. The only data that are relevant in this respect are data of the type I referred to first, connecting such skills to those that are significant to individuals in their life activities.

In the research I describe briefly here, we make an attempt to do the things I have just argued are necessary to connect psychological research to education for thinking. We have undertaken to examine the development of explicit cognitive skills in the coordination of theory and evidence, first examining such skills in relatively well-structured (though still familiar and meaningful) contexts and then gradually extending our framework and observations to thinking of a broader sort, the sort that clearly occurs and matters in everyday life.

CRITICAL THINKING
AS THE SKILLED COORDINATION
OF THEORY AND EVIDENCE

The research was cast initially in the framework of scientific thinking (Kuhn, Amsel, & O'Loughlin, 1988). Yet, the set of skills we investigate—skills in the coordination of theory and evidence—are skills central to thinking in a much broader range of domains than science. Skillful coordination of theory and evidence entails a complex interplay. Whereas existing theories provide the basis for interpretation of new information, new information ideally is attended to and utilized as a basis for evaluating and revising theories. Skillful coordination of theory and evidence also entails a high degree of metacognitive function, that is, reflection on one's own cognition. The skilled, critical thinker presumably can say the following: I know this is my theory. I can conceive of alternative theories that might explain the same phenomenon and I understand that they are different from my theory. I can contemplate new evidence, and I can evaluate how it bears on both my own and alternative theories, drawing on rules of inductive inference that I am aware of and able to apply. I can recognize and acknowledge discrepancies between theories and evidence, and, based on such discrepancies, I can contemplate revision of a theory.

Such skills are clearly fundamental to what we would like students to learn regarding scientific method. For several years Columbia University has offered its undergraduates a course titled "Theory and Practice of Science," which is offered to nonmajors to fulfill a science requirement. Dean Robert Pollack of Columbia was quoted recently in the *New York Times* (January 4, 1987, Education Life Supplement) as commenting with respect to the course that "science is not a series of conclusions but a way of thinking about the world. [It] is essentially a structure for asking questions, and every five-year-old is a natural scientist because every five-year-old is curious about the world" (p. 23). In the research described here, we aim to define more precisely just what this "way of thinking" consists of, and also to identify important ways in which 5-year-old scientific thinking may differ from more mature forms.

The focus of our research, I have indicated, is on attainment of metacognitive control of the skills involved in the coordination of theory and evidence, and not on the developmental origins of these skills. Certainly, from an early age children form theories and modify them in the face of evidence. My interest is in examining how children develop the ability to access and apply such skills explicitly and reflectively, that is, to know that this is what they are doing and to be in control of the process.

Such investigation, I believe, addresses what can be regarded as the neglected core of metacognition. Most studies of metacognition are studies of cognition about how to learn and remember or the cognition involved in choosing and monitoring strategies to solve problems. In contrast, the metacognition I am concerned with is cognition about what one knows and how one knows it (though not in any formal, epistemological sense). It entails thinking explicit about a theory one holds (rather than only thinking with it) and about its relation to evidence that might or might not support it and provide a basis for one's belief in it.

Both novice and expert representations, or theories, of phenomena have been the subject of considerable research attention in recent years. These theories are of course elaborated and revised, yielding a sequence of partially correct theories that some theorists, such as Glaser (1984), have suggested is the heart of cognitive development. Yet, very little attention has been paid to the *process* of theory revision, in either adults or children. Although children undoubtedly revise their theories as their experience increases, young children are notoriously weak in reflecting on their own thought, and it is unlikely that their theory revision is based on the kind of reflective cognitive processing I portrayed earlier. How, then, does the ability to coordinate theory and evidence that may be present among even very young children develop into the sophisticated form characteristic of mature scientific or critical thought?

In a series of studies described by Kuhn, Amsel, and O'Loughlin (1988), we focus first on subjects' ability to explicitly evaluate the bearing of evidence on a theory. We posed this problem:

Some scientists have been studying whether the kinds of foods children eat make any difference in whether or not they get lots of colds. The scientists decided to do their study at a boarding school, where children live. The children eat all their meals in the school dining room and they all eat the same food. They sit in the dining room at tables of six children each. The scientists wanted to see if what the children eat makes a difference in whether or not they get lots of colds. So for six months they asked the dining room workers to serve certain foods at certain tables. During that time, the school nurse kept careful records of children's colds.

Following this introduction, a series of types of foods is presented and the subject's theories elicited regarding their relation to colds. From them, four foods are selected for each subject, two which the subject believes are related to colds and two which the subject believes are not. At a second session, the subject is asked to evaluate evidence bearing on the relation of these four foods to colds.

Eight instances of evidence are presented one at a time and the subject's evaluation elicited after each presentation. Each instance is represented visually by sketches of the four foods and outcome, presented on a large board, and each is summarized verbally by the interviewer. Figure 2.1 shows the first four instances of evidence as they appeared on the board in the case of the variables fruit, cereal, potato, and cola. The two variables portrayed at the top of each instance, fruit and cereal, are the variables the subject believes to be related to colds and the two at the bottom, potato and cola, the variables the subject believes not to be related. As seen in the figure, two of the variables (the two on the left) covary perfectly with outcome, one the subject believes to be related to colds and one the subject believes not related. The other two variables (the two on the right) are independent of outcome, again one the subject believes related to colds and one not. The remaining four instances (not shown in the figure) maintain this same pattern of covariation and independence, with the two covarying variables covarying with each other as well as with outcome. The evidence is thus identical for the two variables on the left (fruit and potato), but the prior theories differ, enabling us to examine how theoretical belief affects the interpretation of identical evidence, and likewise for the two variables on the right (cereal and cola).

Evaluating Evidence

Before examining its interaction with theoretical belief, let us look at subjects' inductive reasoning skill overall. Are subjects able to interpret noncovariation as evidence against a causal theory, that is, as evidence for *exclusion*? Do they interpret the covariation evidence as supportive but not conclusive evidence for a causal theory, that is, as insufficient evidence for *inclusion,* because there are multiple covariates?

We found subjects' inference skills weak in both these respects. Subjects were sixth and ninth graders, average (nonacademic) adults, and, for comparison, five advanced PhD candidates in philosophy. All but the

Instances 5–8, not shown, maintain the same pattern of covariation and noncovariation.

FIG. 2.1

31

philosophers frequently failed to make exclusion inferences, though the evidence was present to support them and did make inclusion inferences, though the evidence was not present to support them. Only 2 of 20 adults and 4 of the 5 philosophers resisted succumbing to false inclusion of one of the two covarying variables — in other words, claiming that one of the two "makes a difference" in whether children get lots of colds or not, when of course their common covariation with outcome makes it impossible to conclude whether one, the other, or both of them plays a causal role. About half the adults and just a few younger subjects recognized the indeterminacy at some point, but they then succumbed to false inclusion as the covariation evidence mounted. Only about half the sixth graders and two-thirds of the ninth graders and adults concluded that the two noncovarying variables did not make a difference. No subject attempted a controlled comparison, by looking for two instances where all foods but one were identical.

Coordinating Theories and Evidence

I go on now to our central concern of how subjects coordinated new evidence with existing theories. As we anticipated, identical evidence was interpreted in significantly different ways as a function of the subject's prior theory. Now, with the Bayesian statistical model in mind, one might immediately object that it is perfectly rational, or correct, to treat identical evidence differently in the context of different theoretical beliefs. The Bayesian model, however, in which prior probabilities condition the evaluation of evidence, carries the assumption that such adjustments are made at a level of highly conscious, rational awareness. In the terminology I use shortly, the evidence must first be encoded and represented as an entity distinct from the theory and its evaluation then adjusted as a function of the theory. In sharp contrast, as I illustrate, the theoretical beliefs of many of our subjects appeared to color their evaluation of evidence in ways quite out of their conscious control. The process in terms of which prior theories influence evaluation of evidence, then, may operate quite differently in the thought of a child than it does in the thought of a professional scientist.

Laura, for example, a ninth grader, correctly interpreted noncovariation evidence as indicating exclusion for kind of potato, which she believed noncausal. In contrast, identical evidence for the variable she believed causal, kind of relish (catsup or mustard), she interpreted as follows, after all eight instances of noncovariation evidence had been presented:

> Yes [it makes a difference]. Mostly likely all the time you get a cold with the mustard. Like there you did, and there you did.

Laura ignored, of course, the equal number of times that mustard co-occurred with no colds.

These predicted influences of subjects' theoretical beliefs on their evaluation of evidence resulted in statistically significant differences in the kinds of interpretations made when evidence was identical but theoretical beliefs differed. Yet, our interest in this work was not so much in documenting such bias as it was in examining in a microgenetic way how a subject attempted to reconcile his or her theory with accumulating discrepant evidence. Let us turn first to the case in which evidence and theory were compatible, for this turned out to be equally revealing.

Peter, a sixth grader, first made a theory-based response for the cake variable, which he believed causal:

It makes a difference. Carrot cake is made with carrots, and chocolate cake is made with a lot of sugar. This [carrot cake] is made with some sugar too, but it's made with less sugar.

The interviewer then posed the evidence-focus probe, designed to direct the subject's attention to the presented evidence: "Do the *findings of the scientists* [verbal emphasis] show that the kind of *(blank)* makes a difference, doesn't make a difference, or can't you tell what the scientists' findings show?" In response, Peter merely elaborated his theory:

Less sugar means your blood pressure doesn't go up. It makes a difference.

After the second instance, Peter first reiterated the theory but then in response to the evidence-focus probe did finally refer to the evidence:

(Do the *findings of the scientists* show it makes a difference. . . . ?) Yes. Because these [children] are like *"ugghh"* with tissues [the children held to their noses] and table 1 has no tissues. [Children at table 1 ate carrot cake and those at table 2 ate chocolate cake.]

One might suppose that having recognized and interpreted the fact that the evidence reflected covariation, Peter would continue to refer to the presented evidence, at least in his responses to the evidence-focus probe (Do the *findings of the scientists* show . . . ?). Following presentation of instance 3, however, he first reiterated the theory and then, in response to the evidence-focus probe, simply repeated the theory again:

(Do the *findings of the scientists* show it makes a difference . . . ?) Yes, because it [chocolate cake] has a lot of sugar and a lot of bad stuff in it.

Over the next few instances, Peter again noted the covariation several times. But following instance 7, by which time substantial covariation evidence was available, he again substituted a reiteration of his theory for evaluation of the evidence.

> (Do the *findings of the scientists* show it makes a difference . . . ?) Yes. Because the sugar; [it's] not [in] carrot cake.

Peter's theory of the relation between kind of cake and colds was completely compatible with the covariation evidence he was asked to evaluate. Yet the sequence of his responses is curious. Especially because they are compatible, perhaps, he appears not to clearly distinguish theory and evidence, responding to a request to evaluate the evidence with a reiteration of his theory even *after* he has attended to and interpreted the evidence. Both theory and evidence point to the same conclusion, and one thus seems to be the same as the other for purposes of justifying the conclusion.

This quality was rare in older subjects, supporting the claim that younger subjects' problems in coordinating theory and evidence are attributable to a limited differentiation between the two. Before elaborating on this claim, however, consider what happens when theory and evidence are at odds with one another. Doesn't this discrepancy force the subject into a clearer distinction between the two? The answer, in a word, is no.

Instead, most subjects exhibited strategies that served to bring theory and evidence into alignment with one another. A major, and anticipated, strategy, of course, was biased evaluation of the evidence, to reduce its inconsistency with theory, though it was a strategy that was hard to maintain as the discrepant evidence mounted. Another strategy, however, that we had not anticipated, was the adjustment of theory to reduce its inconsistency with the evidence. Most noteworthy about this strategy is the possibility that it may have occurred without the subject's conscious awareness. For example, suppose the subject's original theory was that kind of cola was not related to colds and covariation evidence was presented for cola. Following several responses in which this noncausal theory was expressed without acknowledgement of the evidence, the subject would again offer a theory-based response but this time voice a new theory espousing a causal connection between kind of cola and outcome. Only with this new theory in place would the subject then acknowledge and interpret the covariation evidence. A ninth grader, Terry, for example, initially expressed the plausible view that gum has nothing to do with colds, but then, after several instances of evidence had been presented (but not acknowledged by Terry), advanced the following theory:

> Yes [the kind of gum makes a difference], cause one kind got a lot of sugar and everything, get you all hyper. (Which one is that?) The Juicy Fruit. If you

eat a lot of sugar, you get all hyper, and if it's cold out and you get all hyper, you can catch a cold. You get hot, and then something like a little cold breeze comes out and you get a cold automatically.

A similar pattern occurred in the case of an initial causal theory and noncovariation evidence. It appears as if such subjects are unwilling to acknowledge the implications of the evidence unless they have a compatible theory in place that can provide an explanation of this evidence.

Theory/Evidence Coordination as a Metacognitive Skill

The findings that have been described suggest the intrusion of theory into the evaluation of evidence, in ways that appear to be outside the conscious control of the subject. Stated differently, subjects show limited skill in the coordination of theory and evidence. When theory and evidence are compatible, we see a melding of the two into a single representation of "the way things are." The pieces of evidence are regarded not as independent of the theory and bearing on it, but more as *instances* of the theory that serve to illustrate it. The theory in turn is capable of explaining the evidence – of making sense of it. In responding to a request to evaluate the evidence, articulating the theory is thus as good as making reference to the evidence.

Discrepancy between theory and evidence, we found, does not lead the subject to any clearer differentiation between the two. When theory and evidence are at odds with one another, rather than acknowledging the discrepancy, subjects use a variety of devices to attempt to bring them into alignment: either adjusting the theory, usually prior to acknowledging the evidence, or "adjusting" the evidence, by ignoring it or attending to it in a selective, distorting manner. More notable even than the devices themselves is the fact that the subject needs the two to be in alignment. Why do subjects need to discard their own very plausible theories that kind of cola or gum have nothing to do with getting colds and formulate new, often implausible theories about the relation of these variables to colds, before they are willing to acknowledge evidence showing covariation between these variables and colds? Why are they unable simply to acknowledge that the evidence shows covariation without needing first to explain why this is the outcome one should expect? The answer, I would claim, is that doing so would leave theory and evidence not in alignment with one another and therefore needing to be recognized as distinct entities.

What are the skills in coordinating theories and evidence that these subjects lack? The ability to evaluate the bearing of evidence on a theory at a minimum requires that the evidence be encoded and represented separate from a representation of the theory. If new evidence is merely assimilated to a theory, as an instance of it, the possibility of constructing relations between the two, as separate entities, is lost. Or if the subject cannot represent the theory itself as an object of cognition, evidence cannot be evaluated in relation to it. Furthermore, and somewhat paradoxically, the ability to coordinate theory and evidence requires temporarily bracketing, or setting aside, one's acceptance of the theory, in order to assess what the evidence by itself would mean for the theory, were it the only basis for making a judgment. Subjects who vacillated between theory and evidence as the basis for justifying inferences we hypothesize are weak in all three of these abilities: thinking about a theory, differentiating theory and evidence, and bracketing belief in the theory as a means of evaluating the relation of evidence to it.

Ability to "bracket one's experience" or beliefs has been discussed by Scribner (1977) and others as a product of schooling. As a result, it has tended to be regarded as the discourse mode of those who follow academic paths—an ability to contemplate the purely hypothetical, divorced from practical thought and life. But it can be claimed, paradoxically perhaps, that this bracketing ability is essential to the very practical activities of drawing inferences from one's observations and modifying them as new evidence emerges. Only by bracketing one's belief in the theory and temporarily regarding it as an object of cognition can one assess the relation of the evidence to it, and thereby effect conscious control over the interaction of theory and evidence in one's thinking.

The complete fusion of theory and evidence of course represents the extreme, reflected primarily in the protocols of younger subjects. Younger subjects differed from older ones in their lesser likelihood of distinguishing firmly between theory and evidence, and also, given they did experience a conflict between the two, in their ability to resolve it. More notable than any developmental change, however, is the lack of it, as reflected in the presence of all of the characteristics that have been described in the protocols of average adults, and their marked difference from the protocols of the philosophers.

I only mention some other measures included in this work, but they do lend support to the arguments made. We probed subjects' representations of both the evidence and their own theories by asking them to recall each, following the evidence evaluation. Some subjects recalled their own original theories inaccurately, representing them as consistent with the evidence that had been presented. Or, in reconstructing the evidence on the board, they represented it as more consistent with their theories than it in fact had been. Both of these tendencies, of course, reflect additional mechanisms for maintaining theory and evidence in alignment with one another.

COORDINATING THEORY AND EVIDENCE
IN INFORMAL REASONING

In other research we have undertaken to identify the broader range of contexts in which the skills I have described appear. Specifically, we have examined the reasoning of adolescents and young, middle-aged, and older adults about real-world, content-rich topics—for example, what causes prisoners to return to a life of crime after they're released, or what causes children to fail in school. Topics chosen were those people are likely to have occasion to think and talk about and about which people are able and willing to make causal inferences without a large base of technical knowledge. They nevertheless involve phenomena the true causal structure of which is complex and uncertain. The interview was presented to subjects as eliciting their views on urban social problems. After eliciting their causal theories, we ask subjects questions such as: How do you know that this is so, that this is the cause of prisoners returning to a life of crime? If you were trying to convince someone that your view is right, what evidence would you give to try to show this? Suppose that someone disagreed with your view; what might they say to show you were wrong? What could you say to show they were wrong? In other words, we ask subjects to generate multiple, contrasting theories and coordinate evidence with them.

The same kinds of weaknesses as described earlier appear. Subjects often relate a story, or script, of (in the case of one topic) a prisoner being released from prison, returning to his community, and falling back into crime. Our request for supporting evidence often produces merely an elaboration of the script. For example, the teenage subject quoted here initially indicated "problems at home" as the cause of children failing in school.

(How do you know that this is what causes children to fail in school?) Well, it's like mostly when the mother and father are divorced they can have psychological problems, you know, and they can't actually function in school. (Just to be sure I understand, can you explain exactly how this shows that problems at home are the cause?) Well, the kid, like, concentrates on how he's going to keep his mother and father together. He can't really concentrate on schoolwork. (If you were trying to convince someone else that your view that this is the cause is right, what *evidence* would you give to try to show this?) Well, let's see, I would take some kids maybe if their mother and father got divorced and show how it affects them mentally, you know. It makes them less alert in class. (Can you be very specific, and tell me some particular facts you could mention to try to convince the person?) Sometimes they have editorials in newspapers or on TV, you know, and maybe it could be a friend of yours that it happens to. (Is there anything further you could say to help show that what you've said is correct?) Not at the moment. (Is there anything someone could say or do to *prove* that this is what causes children to fail in school?) Yes. It could be, you know, partly, they could be the persons that have problems at home, and can't really handle it.

This subject shows a very similar nondifferentiation of theory and evidence to that exhibited by the subjects quoted earlier. The two are fused into a script of "how it happens." One of our adolescent subjects put it explicitly herself. When we asked her for evidence to support her theory, she replied, "Do you mean can I give you an example?"

Closely related to this fusion of theory and evidence into a script with accompanying instances is the inability to generate alternative theories or counterevidence for a theory. More sophisticated reasoners, in contrast, generate counterarguments, recognize existence of alternative theories, and cite evidence that is clearly differentiated from the theory itself and bears on its correctness. We also ask subjects how sure they are that what they have described is the cause, and of course the less sophisticated reasoners tend to be as or more sure than more sophisticated ones.

The broad claim I am making is that skills of the sort we are assessing "matter" in life, that people are better off with them than without them. I won't undertake any detailed defense of that assertion here. My more specific claims are that the key elements in a subject like the one just quoted developing skills in differentiating and coordinating theory and evidence are (a) recognition of the possibility of alternative theories to his own, and (b) recognition of the possibility of evidence that doesn't fit his theory. The first achievement is likely to facilitate the second, as the presence of multiple, opposing theories makes it difficult to assimilate the same evidence to both of them. In the case of each of these achievements, awareness that things could be otherwise is the key element. A script becomes a theory when its possible falsehood and the existence of alternative theories is recognized. Instances become evidence when the possibility of their lack of concordance with a theory is recognized. ⌐

Before leaving these data, one of the most exciting things observed in this work should be mentioned, and that is a strong association between reasoning expertise and education level. No sex differences have appeared and only slight age group differences, with the adolescent and 60-year-olds performing at slightly lower levels than 20 and 40-year-olds. We examined two educational levels within each age group, those that had some college education and those that did not. On all the measures we have looked at — forms of evidence offered, ability to generate alternative theories to one's own, and ability to generate rebuttals or counterarguments — college subjects demonstrate a striking superiority to noncollege subjects. We of course need to exercise considerable caution in identifying the college experience itself as the exclusive cause of these differences. Yet, at a time when a number of major studies have struggled to identify cognitive outcomes of a college education and obtained only weak results, we find these striking education differences in reasoning patterns quite exciting and promising.

FOSTERING THE DEVELOPMENT
OF THINKING SKILLS

The issue of education effects brings us directly to the topic of how the development I've described might occur. One finds a paradox in the educational literature on fostering effective thinking. The distinction underlying it is one of teaching people about thinking versus engaging them in it. Most programmatic efforts to teach thinking by both psychologists and educators have centered around teaching explicit principles or rules of sound thinking. Yet there exists a long and distinguished theoretical literature in the field of education, reflecting the view that the only effective way to teach people to think is to engage them in thinking.

Exercising Thinking

Dewey's classic *How We Think* (1910) certainly reflects the view that one learns to think by engaging in thinking, as does the writing of other respected educational theorists of his time. Symonds, for example, in *Education and the Psychology of Thinking* (1936) wrote, "In order to learn to think one must practice thinking in the situation in which it is to be used and on material on which it is to be exercised. . . . In short, practice in thinking itself is necessary for the improvement of thinking. There is no substitute for the actual wrestling with real problems in the development of thinking" (pp. 235–236). This view remained prevalent several decades later. To quote once more from the 1961 NEA report, *The Central Purpose of American Education:*

> The rational powers of any person are developed gradually and continuously as and when he uses them successfully. There is no evidence that they can be developed in any other way. They do not emerge quickly or without effort. . . . Thus, the learner must be encouraged in his early efforts to grapple with problems that engage his rational abilities at their current level of development. (p. 17)

Given this unusual consistency in theoretical position over so many decades, it is quite striking to discover how little empirical research exists pertaining to it. Instead, from the earliest experiments in teaching thinking skills by Edward Glaser (1941) and Osborn (1939) in the late 1930s, to most of the current programs, emphasis has been on teaching students about good thinking. Such programs risk suffering the same fate as so many intervention efforts in education and psychology. The competencies that are the object of instruction may be displayed in the narrow contexts in which they are taught but largely fail to generalize to a wider range of contexts in which they are equally appropriate. These all-too-characteristic failures of generalization limit the practical utility of such efforts as well as their scientific interpretability. One remains unsure of what individuals have grasped in the original teaching situation and to what extent the process that transpired resembles the process by which such acquisitions occur under natural conditions. What is at issue, in other words, is the thorny problem of transfer that has been a central preoccupation of psychology from the earliest times (James, 1890) to the present (Brown & Campione, 1984).

Little formal evidence is available regarding the effects of the newer programs on the thinking skills of those who participate in them. Results of the early experimental programs, however, substantiate the concern just raised. Osborn (1939), for example, whose instructional program focused on analysis of propaganda, included in addition to mastery tests of the instructional material a subsequent test of pupils' resistance to propaganda (in the form of a persuasive communication on capital punishment). Both immediate and delayed attitude shifts following the communication were no less for experimental subjects than they were for controls (not exposed to the education program), leading Osborn (1939) to a conclusion in fact very similar to those already quoted:

> The failure of the type of approach used in this study does not mean that it is impossible to teach critical thinking. Rather, it suggests that new attacks be made on the problem. . . . Possibly critical thinking can be developed best when pupils are taught in such a manner, throughout their school experiences, that they must constantly use information in problem-solving situations and in such a manner that they are constantly forced to make tentative conclusions as a result. In other words, it is just possible that the way to teach critical thinking is to give pupils long-term practice in it. (p. 16)

These "new attacks" advocated by Osborn nearly 50 years ago have not materialized. There exists scarcely any controlled observation of students engaged in continuing "efforts to grapple with problems that engage [their] rational abilities at their current level of development" (to borrow the words of the NEA report quoted several times), despite consistent argument by educational theorists over a number of decades that it is through such exercise that thinking skills develop.

Microgenetic Study of the Development of Thinking

The research that would bear on an exercise-based view of the development of thinking skills would be essentially observational in character, focusing on the manner in which thinking strategies evolve in the course of their exercise. In the last decade we have in fact begun to see an awakening of interest in the development of microgenetic methods for observing change that occurs gradually over a period of time. I conclude with a brief description of some of my own studies in this respect — studies that again focus on the thinking skills involved in the coordination of theory and evidence. We have used a variety of specific methods and materials, but the object in each case is to get subjects over a period of months to exercise existing reasoning strategies, to generate their own feedback from doing so, and as a result to improve those strategies. In all of our studies, we have found that the method is successful in eliciting progressive change in most, though not all, subjects. In observing these subjects, we have been able to learn something about the change process.

In an initial study by Kuhn and Phelps (1982), we asked the subject in a series of weekly sessions to experiment with chemicals to determine which of a number of ingredients was responsible for a chemical reaction when they were combined — again a problem in causal attribution. In more recent work we have asked subjects to coordinate theories and evidence in the case of a set of sports balls that vary along four dimensions (Kuhn, Amsel, & O'Loughlin, 1988). A Ms. S from the sports company, the subject is told for example, believes that the size of the ball is what makes a difference in its playing quality, while a Ms. T believes that the texture (rough or smooth) is what makes a difference. The actual balls are used to present different sets of evidence to the subject, and the subject is asked to coordinate the evidence with the multiple theories: What do these results have to say about Ms. S's theory? What do they say about Ms. T's theory? Do the results help more to show that Ms. S is right or Ms. T is right? Having to coordinate the same evidence with multiple, diverging theories, we reasoned, might help subjects to establish firmer differentiation between theory and evidence and to reduce the biases favoring their own theoretical preferences that are pronounced in subjects' initial performances.

In a related study with L. Schauble, students are exposed to a computerized microworld, consisting of cars that travel along a race track at varying speeds. The cars vary along five dimensions (for example, color and presence or absence of a tail fin). Two of the variables have no effect, two have an interactive effect, and one has a curvilinear relation to outcome. Over a series of weekly sessions subjects are asked to explore this microworld by conducting test runs with cars of their choice. The subjects' own theories regarding the influence of the different dimensions are assessed initially, enabling us to observe how their theoretical preferences influence the experimentation and interpretation strategies they use and how both this influence and the strategies themselves change over time.

So far, these studies have been largely restricted to subjects in the preadolescent age range who are just beginning to develop the skills in question. We would like to extend them to other age groups across the life span. Like Smith and Baltes (chap. 3 in this volume), I am very interested in the range of modifiability of cognitive skills at different points in the life span. Without knowledge of this sort, we have little basis for identifying those segments of the life span during which education for thinking can be most effectively concentrated.

Results of our studies with preadolescents have been consistent. For the large majority of subjects, change appears to be a very gradual, uneven process. During an often extended interval of change, subjects use both more and less advanced strategies in conjunction with one another, both within a single session and from one session to another. Insight gained in one session often does not carry over to the next. The major challenge appears to be the abandonment of less adequate, invalid strategies, rather than the acquisition of new strategies — a reversal of the way in which we typically think about development.

If subjects are already competent in the more advanced strategies, as evidenced by at least occasional display of these strategies early in the series of sessions, then why does the change process (to consolidated, exclusive use of the most advanced strategies) take so long? According to our hypothesis, during the period of observation subjects are not only acquiring exercise in the use of these strategies; they are also gaining in metacognitive understanding of them — that is, why they are the most useful strategies to apply, what their range of application is, why their earlier strategies are inappropriate, and so forth, and this metacognitive development is a much more complex, laborious acquisition. In other words, to use the terminology I used earlier, subjects are acquiring explicit or metacognitive awareness and control over their thinking skills.

These findings offer some suggestion with respect to the problem of transfer in fostering thinking skills. Accounts of transfer within traditional learning paradigms have focused on stimulus similarity as the critical feature governing the transfer of learned behaviors: To the extent that a new stimulus situation is similar to the one in which the behavior was originally learned, the behavior is likely to be elicited by the new situation. A different way to conceptualize transfer is to focus on the behavior, rather than the setting or stimulus thought to elicit that behavior. Such a conceptualization suggests why exercise of a strategy may be the most effective way to promote its transfer. Heightened metacognitive awareness of the strategy itself as a tool is likely to increase the probability of the user's recognizing the applicability of the strategy in other contexts. Likewise, increased metacognitive awareness of strategies that operate within limited contexts may promote recognition of the commonalities among these individual context-embedded strategies, thereby increasing their generality and hence their power. In both cases, increased metacognitive control of a strategy acquired through exercise promotes transfer and increases generality. Paradoxically, then, exercise of strategies within very specific, content-delimited contexts may promote their generalization, whereas didactic teaching of the same strategies in more abstract, general form may fail to achieve this same end.

If these ideas are at all on the right track, they suggest that the educator's role is one of facilitator rather than teacher of thinking skills. This does not trivialize the educator's role; to the contrary, it enhances it. Research has indicated that once problems become familiar, individuals tend to apply well-ingrained, more or less automatic routines to them, with little if any intervening thought. Such problems provide no opportunity for metacognitive deployment of strategic skills. The educator must therefore attempt continually to pose problems that are novel enough to require conscious, selective deployment of strategies but familiar enough to permit application of strategies within the student's competence.

Toward the Realization of Effective Education for Thinking

The view of exercise as the mechanism by which thinking skills are developed is well captured in the cartoon shown in Fig. 2.2. A point of view is indeed often lacking to the extent that someone has never had occasion to exercise it. When individuals are provided an opportunity to support and refute their own and others' assertions by bringing evidence to bear on them, their thinking skills obtain exercise, and, with that exercise, the potential for development. Implicit in this view is the assumption that critical thinking is not something to be taught and mastered as a specialized form of thought, distinct from "noncritical" thinking. Rather, it is through exercise that thinking becomes critical thinking.

For researchers in psychology and education, I would argue, the task of observing this process should be a number one priority. Its achievement is of course dependent on that of the research tasks I discussed initially— identifying the strategies that people actually use in their own thinking and understanding something about their natural course of development across the life span. Researchers, I suggested, have been poorly equipped to address these tasks, due in large part to a long tradition of studying thinking disembedded from the contexts in which it occurs naturally. Similarly, I would suggest, researchers may have been ill-equipped and ill-disposed to engage in research of the latter sort, having to do with mechanisms of development. Influenced by the domination of stimulus–response theoretical models, treatment–outcome models have to a very strong extent governed the design of research in psychology and education. Observational

ZIBELLI

"If you'd argue with me,
it would help me decide."

FIG. 2.2

studies of behavior change initiated by subjects themselves over time are not readily assimilable to such models. On the positive side, though researchers may have eschewed real-world content in favor of artificial tasks and observational study of change over time in favor of treatment–outcome experiments, these choices may be due not so much to the intractability of such context or the infeasability of such research methods as they are to aspects of the historical evolution of modern psychology. There is thus some reason to be optimistic that fulfillment of the research mandate contained in the 1961 NEA report is not beyond our reach and that psychologists might play a major role in building a knowledge base that would contribute to the realization of effective education for thinking.

REFERENCES

Brown, A., & Campione, J. (1984). Three faces of transfer: Implications for early competence, individual differences, and instruction. In M. Lamb, A. Brown, & B. Rogoff (Eds.), *Advances in developmental psychology* (Vol. 3, pp. 143–192). Hillsdale, NJ: Lawrence Erlbaum Associates.
Dewey, J. (1910). *How we think.* New York: D. C. Heath.

Glaser, E. (1941). *An experiment in the development of critical thinking.* New York: Bureau of Publications, Teachers College, Columbia University.

Glaser, R. (1984). Education and thinking: The role of knowledge. *American Psychologist, 39,* 93–104.

James, W. (1890). *Principles of psychology* (Vol. 1). New York: Henry Holt.

Kuhn, D., Amsel, E., & O'Loughlin, M. (1988). *The development of scientific thinking skills.* Orlando, FL: Academic Press.

Kuhn, D., & Phelps, E. (1982). The development of problem-solving strategies. In H. Reese (Ed.), *Advances in child development and behavior* (Vol. 17, pp. 1–44). New York: Academic Press.

National Education Association, Educational Policies Commission. (1961). *The central purpose of American education.* Washington, DC: National Education Association.

Osborn, W. (1939). An experiment in teaching resistance to propaganda. *Journal of Experimental Education, 8,* 1–17.

Scribner, S. (1977). Modes of thinking and ways of speaking. In P. Johnson-Laird & P. Wason (Eds.), *Thinking* (pp. 483–500). Cambridge : Cambridge University Press.

Shultz, T., & Mendelson, R. (1975). The use of covariation as a principle of causal analysis. *Child Development, 46,* 394–399.

Siegler, R. (1975). Defining the locus of developmental differences in children's causal reasoning. *Journal of Experimental Child Psychology, 20,* 512–525.

Symonds, P. (1936). *Education and the psychology of thinking.* New York: McGraw-Hill.

Chapter 3

A LIFE-SPAN
PERSPECTIVE ON THINKING
AND PROBLEM-SOLVING

Jacqui Smith
Paul B. Baltes
*Max Planck Institute for Human Development and Education,
Berlin, FRG*

The adult years typically represent the majority of an individual's intellectual life. Given this, it is important to ask about the contexts and characteristics of cognitive and intellectual performance during this life phase. To what extent, for example, is performance during adulthood merely a function of the developmental level reached by the end of adolescence? What constraints are set on performance by physiological changes associated with aging? What tests are appropriate for assessing intellectual performance in adulthood: Are some tests biased toward representing the negative aspects of aging? Do the ecologies of adulthood and old age provide individuals with the opportunities to maintain, extend, and expand their intellectual horizons?

In this chapter we review several propositions related to a life-span approach to cognitive and intellectual functioning during adulthood and into old age (Baltes, 1987; Baltes, Dittmann-Kohli, & Dixon, 1984), and describe some research illustrating these propositions. There are already many comprehensive reviews of research on problem solving and thinking in the adult development and cognitive literatures (e.g., Denney, 1982; Kausler, 1982; Mines & Kitchener, 1986; Reese & Rodeheaver, 1985; Salthouse, 1982; Sternberg, 1982), thus our discussion is selective. Our particular focus is the proposal that in select domains, specifically domains associated with the "pragmatics" of intelligence, there is a potential for continued growth in functioning during the adult years (see also Baltes and Smith, in press; Dixon & Baltes, 1986; Smith, Dixon, & Baltes, in press).

We outline several areas of functioning in which individuals may have opportunities to show continued growth and refer to our own research on wisdom as an illustration.

THE DYNAMICS OF GROWTH AND DECLINE
IN INTELLECTUAL FUNCTIONING

In general, theoretical discussion and research concerning changes in intellectual and cognitive performance in adulthood, and especially normative changes in late adulthood, have highlighted two themes. First, as individuals age, some aspects of performance on memory, reasoning, problem solving, and intellectual tasks deteriorate (relative to pre- and early-adult levels). The precise reason for this deterioration is not known. Current theories point to physical and/or chemical changes in neurophysiological and metabolic functioning. By far, the majority of empirical work in developmental psychology has been directed toward providing supportive evidence for the phenomena of age-related decline (Salthouse, 1985).

The second theme highlighted in theoretical discussions of aging, however, offers a more positive outlook. Here the focus is on understanding the role of knowledge and experience in cognitive and intellectual functioning. Associated theory and research deal with descriptions of expert performance in various occupations and disciplines (Glaser, 1984; Hoyer, 1985; Simonton, 1988) and also with concepts of intelligence emphasizing the influence of situational contexts (Berg & Sternberg, 1985; Labouvie-Vief, 1985; Perlmutter, in press) and age-related appropriation of cultural and collective knowledge (Berger & Luckmann, 1967; Cattell, 1963; Horn & Cattell, 1967). According to this second theme, individuals during their adult life can maintain and update old (i.e., previously acquired) skills and areas of expertise. Moreover, individuals can potentially continue to learn, expand, and extend their knowledge in new domains and skills.

The life-span perspective (for an overview see Baltes, 1987), and research associated with it, integrates these two themes. One of the central beliefs associated with this perspective is the proposal that lifelong development always consists of the joint occurrence of instances of gain (growth) and of loss (decline). Figure 3.1 illustrates this belief in the context of intellectual functioning. Different categories of cognitive and intellectual activities are expected to show different developmental trajectories. Specifically, cognitive activities associated with the "pragmatics of intelligence," which primarily involve or require general background or domain-specific knowledge for successful performance, are contrasted with a category of activities where performance is more a reflection of the basic operations and processes, or "mechanics," of the system. It is predicted that depending on

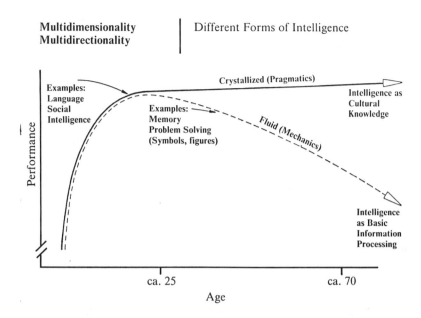

FIG. 3.1. One of the best known psychometric structural theories of intelligence is that of Cattell and Horn. The two main clusters of that theory, fluid and crystallized intelligence, are postulated to display different life-span developmental trajectories. (After Baltes, 1987.)

how representative a task is of one or other of these forms of intelligence, individuals will either show a growth or a decline in performance as they age. This dual-process model of life-span cognition builds on the earlier psychometric distinction between fluid and crystallized intelligence (Cattell, 1963) and research showing age-related decreases and increases in fluid and crystallized abilities respectively (Horn, 1982; Horn & Cattell, 1967).

SPECIFIC PROPOSITIONS CONCERNING THINKING AND PROBLEM-SOLVING IN ADULTHOOD

Six propositions concerning changes in thinking and problem-solving performance in adulthood and old age can be derived from the dual-process model outlined earlier and the general beliefs associated with the life-span perspective. These propositions are similar to those presented elsewhere (Baltes, Dittmann-Kohli, & Dixon, 1984; Dixon & Baltes, 1986 Staudinger, Cornelius, & Baltes, 1989) for intellectual functioning in general.

The first three propositions establish some general expectations about patterns of change that might be observed in performance on thinking and problem-solving tasks during adulthood and into old age. These patterns of change are normative: They do not describe disease-related patterns of aging. The last three propositions embed developmental change patterns into the context of adult life. Together these propositions encompass the key life-span concepts, *multidirectionality, multidimensionality, interindividual differences,* and *intraindividual plasticity.* It is important to note that the three patterns described in the first three propositions (stability, decline, and growth) could, in principle, characterize the performance of one individual observed on different tasks.

Proposal 1. The General Capacity (or Potential) to Think and Solve Problems Essentially Stays the Same Throughout Adulthood, at Least in "Average" Conditions.

We believe that for the majority of cognitive tasks and tests, performance deficits observed in adulthood reflect performance factors rather than changes in potential. For instance, the older the adult the more likely there will be a deficit of recent practice in test-taking and in working on the laboratory-type tasks traditionally used to assess thinking and problem-solving strategies (for example, reasoning, concept formation, and hypothesis-testing tasks). Observed age-related decline in performance could well reflect a lack of practice opportunity and/or motivation rather than an actual change in performance capacity (at least within the normal range).

The range of performance plasticity (or modifiability) is likely to remain relatively stable into old age, provided the individual is not hindered by illness. Even late into adulthood, individuals have the potential to learn new material and to improve their performance on familiar tasks, providing the intellectual activities do not overtax the cognitive system.

Such a statement may appear commonsense in the contemporary context of "mature-age" students, university for seniors and retirees, and newspaper reports of 70-year-olds graduating with a doctorate. Those individuals participating in later-life education are, however, often considered to be exceptional. Empirical work suggests that this is not the case. Numerous cognitive training studies (e.g., Baltes, Dittmann-Kohli, & Kliegl, 1986; Baltes & Willis, 1982; Schaie & Willis, 1986) point to the fact that older adults are able to substantially improve their performance after relatively short training and practice interventions (e.g., five 1-hour sessions). Schaie and Willis (1986), for example, demonstrated that longitudinal decline over a 14-year period in inductive reasoning and spatial orientation performance could be reliably reversed by training. Participants in their study were aged between 64 and 95 years. Training was also given to the 47% of the 229 participants in the Schaie and Willis sample who had shown stable performance levels over the 14 years. For this group as well, training produced significant improvement. This impressive finding adds support to the contention that performance factors and limited experiential opportunities are often highly relevant in explaining observed age differences and age-related declines, at least for the majority of cognitive tasks.

Proposal 2. There May Be Instances of Decline in Some Specific Functions

If aging decline in capacity to think and to solve problems exists, it will be manifested primarily in functioning at "maximum" and at very difficult levels of performance, on highly complex tasks and on tasks that overtax the cognitive system. That is, robust instances of decline are most likely to be observed under performance conditions or on tasks that reflect limits in the basic "mechanics" of the cognitive processing system. Examples of such conditions include problem solving and reasoning at speed, tasks involving a high working memory load, together with highly novel, unfamiliar, and/or complex tasks.

A research strategy known as *testing-the-limits* (Baltes, 1987; Baltes & Kindermann, 1985; Kliegl & Baltes, 1987) allows the separate assessment of plasticity (modifiability within a normal range) and limits of plasticity. This strategy involves the systematic exploration of performance changes in the context of a theory-guided training program. Performance under supportive conditions (e.g., following self-practice, various stages of instruction and training and in easy task conditions) is compared with performance in less supportive, or more demanding conditions (e.g., at very fast speeds).

To date, the testing-the-limits strategy has been used in a research project at the Berlin Max Planck Institute for Human Development and Education designed to assess age-correlated changes in limits of functioning on a memory task (Kliegl, Smith, & Baltes, 1986, 1989). Healthy young ($M = 24$ years) and older adults ($M = 72$ years) of above-average intelligence were trained to use the *Method of Loci* mnemonic to serially recall lists of words. The Method of Loci is a mnemonic technique said to have been invented by an ancient Greek poet, Simonides. The technique is based on the two simple concepts of places (loci) and images. It involves generating a highly familiar ordered sequence of places (loci) as a mental map. Items that are to be remembered are successively linked (e.g., via an imagined association) with the places on this mental map. At recall, one mentally revisits the ordered locations and retrieves the items imagined.

Both young and old adults in our training program quickly acquired this cognitive skill and used it to substantially improve their recall of word lists.

In supportive conditions (e.g., at self-paced and slow fixed-presentation rates), there was an overlap in the performance distributions for the young and older adults, even though on average the young recalled more words than the old adults. This overlap in performance distributions was eliminated in test conditions which placed heavy demands on the cognitive system: Whereas young adults could continue to use the Method of Loci mnemonic to serially recall word lists presented at 3-second and 1-second rates, older adults found it difficult to cope with 5-second presentation rates. In these and similar challenging conditions, and in experimental settings where it is possible to have some control over the processing strategies that individuals use, specific age-related losses can be observed.

Proposal 3. Some Individuals May Show Patterns of Growth in Problem-Solving and Thinking Skills

Growthlike changes (e.g., improvement) are possible especially in areas of functioning associated with a cumulative and experientially based build up and transformation of skills and knowledge systems (cf. proposals concerning crystallized intelligence, Cattell, 1963; Horn, 1982). Within the psychometric literature, tasks involving verbal comprehension, ideational fluency, general knowledge, social judgment and reasoning abilities, and experiential evaluation have been nominated as contexts in which adults may possibly show age-correlated performance increases. Although increases have been demonstrated in the confines of intelligence subtests (e.g., Horn, 1982; Horn & Cattell, 1967), investigations of various other problem-solving (e.g., concept formation and identification: Arenberg, 1982; Denney, 1982; Kausler, 1982) and cognitive activities (e.g., proverb interpretation, Bromley, 1957; and creativity measures, Dennis, 1966; Lehman, 1953) have been less successful in finding developmental patterns of growth into late adulthood.

There have been many critiques of these research endeavors (see Labouvie-Vief, 1985; Reese & Rodeheaver, 1985; Salthouse, 1985) but one is particularly relevant to our proposal; namely, that there are large interindividual variations at all age levels. Reports of group effects may well obscure the picture. Amongst older adults, there may be more who produce lower-level performances (for various reasons) compared to the young. It is likely, however, that there will also be *some* older adults who will produce top performances. We have referred to this as representing a weak life-span hypothesis (Baltes & Smith, in press). Examples supporting this proposal are in evidence. Lehman (1953), for instance, while suggesting that there is a general decline in creativity after middle-age, also provided many examples of individuals who produced highly creative works in later life. Similarly, Dennis (1966) reported that amongst people who have lived long lives many, especially those in the sciences and humanities, were highly productive after 60 years of age.

Other critiques of previous research point to the narrow set of cognitive tasks that have been investigated. Several other areas of cognitive activity have been nominated as appropriate contexts in which opportunities exist for continued growth. These areas include wisdom and social intelligence (Baltes & Smith, in press; Birren, 1969; Cantor & Kihlstrom, 1987; Dittmann-Kohli & Baltes, in press; Hall, 1922; Holliday & Chandler, 1986; Meacham, 1983; Smith, Dixon, & Baltes, in press), practical intelligence and everyday coping (Cornelius & Caspi, 1987; Sternberg & Wagner, 1986), and reasoning about social, philosophical, and moral dilemmas (Blanchard-Fields, 1986; Gilligan, 1982; Kuhn, Pennington, & Leadbeater, 1983; Labouvie-Vief, 1985; Mines & Kitchener, 1986).

Proposal 4. During Adulthood, There is Often a Shift in the Areas in Which Thinking and Problem-Solving Skills Are Practiced and Applied

Whereas the life goals and developmental tasks of most young adults are expected to be oriented toward cognitive efficacy in the academic areas, this is not the case for middle-aged and older adults. The structure of life goals tends to change such that the acquisition and maintenance of school-related cognitive skills becomes de-emphasized and is replaced by an accentuation of pragmatic skills, such as problem solving in social, family, personal, and professional activities (Erikson, 1959; Hagestad & Neugarten, 1985; Havighurst, 1972; Neugarten, Moore, & Lowe, 1968). Accompanying this shift there may also be changes in the criteria by which functioning is judged (Gilligan, 1982; Labouvie-Vief, 1985). In particular, older adults are likely to deal with problems that are characterized by high levels of uncertainty.

Proposal 5. Interindividual Differences Are Likely to Increase as a Function of Differences in Life Specializations and Trajectories

The general process of adult development and aging has a feature of individual specialization: individuals follow different trajectories in their social, family, personal, and professional lives and consequently have different life experiences. As a result, thinking and problem-solving skills may become increasingly specialized (domain-specific) and individualized. Support for this can be seen in research on life careers and professional socialization (e.g., Featherman, 1983; 1987; Kohn & Schooler, 1978), social planning and family management (Goodnow, 1986), specialized skills in specific leisure domains (e.g., card games, horse race handicapping, Ceci & Liker, 1986), and studies of the role of nonnormative life events in individualizing development (Brim & Ryff, 1980; Caspi & Elder, 1986).

Proposal 6. Aging Is Associated with Changes in Societally Supported Opportunities for High-Level Functioning and Growth

From a sociological viewpoint, aging in many countries is associated with a social-structural process of loss of development-enhancing expectations and social resources. These changes are not homogeneous: they occur differently for various areas of functioning and for different social groups (Baltes & Nesselroade, 1984; Dannefer, 1984; Riley, 1985).

THINKING, PROBLEM SOLVING AND CONCEPTIONS OF EXPERTISE

The concept of expertise and various theories about the nature and acquisition of expert knowledge provides a useful framework for considering the developmental changes in problem solving and thinking during adulthood and into old age outlined in the previous six propositions. Generally, the term *expertise* is associated with the long-term accumulation of an extensive, highly organized and integrated factual and procedural knowledge base and with high-level performance. In the course of adult activities (related to work, family, leisure, interpersonal contexts, and idiosyncratic interests) and by virtue of living longer, individuals have the opportunity to accumulate knowledge in a variety of domains. The extent to which these opportunities are realized will vary among individuals. Some individuals by virtue of their particular life ecology or their self-motivated concentration and specialization in one (or more) domain may develop areas of expertise and reach the status of an "expert" in a domain.

The research paradigm associated with the study of expertise and expert knowledge involves attempts to determine how differences in the organization of and access to a large knowledge base contribute to observed performance differences between experts and novices (Glaser, 1984). In relation to problem solving and thinking, a central finding has been that experts and novices differ primarily in an initial stage of the problem-solving process: namely, in their representation (or understanding) of the problem (e.g., Chi, Glaser, & Rees, 1982). As Glaser explained, "the knowledge of novices is organized around the literal objects explicitly given in a problem statement. Experts' knowledge, on the other hand, is organized around principles and abstractions that subsume these objects" (p. 98). In effect, an expert can call on intuition and general principles extracted from past experience whereas a novice must build a solution based on the information given.

The suggestion that experts often rely on intuitive judgments and representations is not new as the following statement from William James (1890) shows:

> Saturated with experience of a particular class of materials, an expert intuitively feels whether a newly-reported fact is probable or not, whether a proposed hypothesis is worthless or the reverse. He instinctively knows that, in a novel case, this and not that will be the promising course of action. The well-known story of the old judge advising the new one never to give reasons for his decisions, "the decision will probably be right, the reasons will surely be wrong," illustrates this. The doctor will feel that the patient is doomed, the dentist will have a premonition that the tooth will break, though neither can articulate a reason for this foreboding. The reason lies imbedded, but not yet laid bare, in all the countless previous cases dimly suggested by the actual one, all calling up the same conclusion which the adept thus finds himself swept on to, he knows not how or why. (p. 365)

The adept and implicit use of knowledge acquired through years of experience is, we suggest, a feature of adult functioning that, although studied in cognitive experimental settings, has received relatively little attention in developmental contexts. Traditional problem-solving tasks such as the Twenty Questions Game (Denney, 1982), the various concept formation tasks used by Arenberg (1982), anagrams and categorization tasks (see Kausler, 1982) seem to require very little of the type of knowledge described by James and studied by researchers interested in expertise and expert knowledge. In this regard, studies of thinking and problem-solving performance in contexts where adults can acquire expertise may well be a more appropriate measure of developmental change. Indeed, implicit theories about forms of advanced adult cognition (e.g., wisdom) often include intuition and experientially based reasoning and judgment as a focal dimension (Sternberg, 1985).

Everyday Problem Solving

One response to the search for age-appropriate tasks has been to investigate age differences in the solution of "everyday" problems (e.g., Camp, 1987;

Cornelius & Caspi, 1987; Denney, 1984). Some examples of the everyday problems that have been employed are given in Table 3.1.

Denney and Palmer (1981) compared performance on everyday problems to performance on a traditional problem-solving task, the Twenty Questions Game. They found that whereas performance (assessed by the number of constraint-seeking questions) on the traditional problem decreased from the mid-30s, performance on the everyday problems (assessed by the number of solutions offered involving self-action), peaked in the age range 40 to 59 years, and declined thereafter. Cornelius and Caspi (1987) matched subjects' responses to everyday problems against judges' evaluations of the immediate and long-term effectiveness of the solutions. On this dimension, older adults (aged 55–78 years) selected better solutions than young adults (aged 20–34 years). One difference between these studies is the response format: Denney and Palmer asked their subjects to generate solutions, whereas subjects in the Cornelius and Caspi study were required to select (i.e., recognize) an option describing what they would do. These variations in task requirements could explain the different age patterns that were found.

Although these (and other) attempts to investigate problem solving and thinking in the everyday and practical context of adult life have certainly revealed performance patterns that sharply contrast with those found on more formal tasks, the problems and the thought processes involved seem not to be as complex as those associated with the study of expertise. To cover the full spectrum of adult thinking, and to tap the dimensions of cognitive functioning linked with the long-term accumulation of knowledge, other domains of thinking and problem solving need to be explored. In the following section, we consider research in domains related to work, leisure, and life pragmatics.

TABLE 3.1
Examples of Everyday Problems

---

1. What would you do if you have a landlord who refused to make some expensive repairs you want done because he or she thinks they are too costly?
   a. Try to make the repairs yourself.
   b. Try to understand your landlord's view and decide whether they are necessary repairs.
   c. Try to get someone to settle the dispute between you and your landlord.
   d. Accept the situation and don't dwell on it.
2. Let's assume that you bought a vacuum cleaner from a door-to-door salesman. After two or three weeks of use, the vacuum cleaner will no longer work. What would you do?

---

1. Cornelius & Caspi, 1987
2. Denney & Palmer, 1981

Thinking at Work

The work environment offers many opportunities to apply the skills and knowledge acquired during adolescence and early adulthood, to specialize and extend these skills, and to acquire new skills. In some occupations these opportunities are institutionalized, for example, as part of the structural organization of a career ladder. In other occupations there is less structural support for continued development: Here, it is left to the individual to initiate their own structure. One consequence of the immense range of skills, career structures and career paths, and the variety of occupations undertaken in adult life in Western societies is (as suggested in our sixth proposal) an observed increase in interindividual differences. This is especially the case when adolescents are compared with middle-aged, midcareer adults. Theoretically, the range of differences could continue to expand into old age.

In the face of this variability, are there some experiential similarities and some career paths that appear to be associated with opportunities for continued growth in thinking and problem-solving skills? With regard to similarities, it is clear that long-term experience in working in a particular occupation leads to more efficient and, in some instances, more expert performance. Evidence in support of this can be cited from many occupations: office and warehouse workers in a dairy business (Scribner, 1986), academics and business managers (Wagner & Sternberg, 1986), medical doctors, clinical psychologists, and investment advisors (Goldberg, 1986), and parole officers and judges (Carroll, 1986). Although none of these cited studies were designed to be age comparative, most included comparisons of novice (young adults and students) and expert (highly experienced workers, presumably at least middle-aged) performance. All studies report that experts and experienced workers appear to rely on intuitive assessments of problems and tacit knowledge. Long-term experience, however, is not always correlated with expertise. Goldberg (1986) reviewed several studies revealing a relatively low agreement rate for patient diagnosis among highly experienced doctors and clinicians and similar disagreements in the forecasts of experienced investment advisors.

Apart from questions about the relationship between experience and expertise, developmental and social scientists are beginning to look at occupational experts as they age. Earlier studies mapped changes in productivity (e.g., Lehman, 1953), success and life satisfaction (e.g., Sears, 1977). Current studies are investigating possible changes in thinking and problem-solving orientations during individuals' working lives (Kohn & Schooler, 1978) and the relationships between these changes and particular careers (Featherman, 1987). Featherman and his coworker Peterson, for example, study expert engineers who have specialized in different tasks: as expert engineering problem solvers and as expert engineering planners and designers. Preliminary evidence suggests that these different specialities foster different styles of thinking. One style, which they have termed *reflective planning* is possibly linked, they suggest, with more successful aging because it is a style that could be transferred from job-related to more general problems of career and life (especially retirement) management.

Thinking at Leisure

Two studies serve to illustrate the complex level of thinking and problem-solving performance demonstrated by adults who have invested time and effort into a task typically associated with leisure interests. The first study deals with chess players (Charness, 1981), the second with horse race handicappers (Ceci & Liker, 1986).

Charness devised several memory and problem-solving tasks to evaluate whether aging influenced the processing strategies of competition chess players. His subjects ranged from 16 to 64 years of age, and at each age level individuals were selected from various skill levels. On average, these people played chess for 6 hours a week. The problem-solving tasks involved thinking aloud about selecting a move in a specific game with and without time pressures. Charness found that the more skilled the player, the longer it took them to choose a move. Older skilled players, however, took a shorter time and selected better moves. Furthermore, older skilled chess players were not disadvantaged by a time pressure. Clearly, these older adults, functioning in a domain in which they were highly experienced, were not inferior to young adults with similar levels of chess skill.

Ceci and Liker (1986) demonstrated that performance on the Wechsler Adult Intelligence Scale (WAIS) was unrelated to the highly sophisticated and complex reasoning shown by men who were expert in race handicapping. The men were regular race attenders with track experiences ranging from 7 to 23 years. They all maintained other occupations. Nonexpert handicappers, classified by their success in predicting race winners, had similar amounts of track experience. Unfortunately, Ceci and Liker did not note their subjects' age: It is reasonable to assume, however, that they were middle-aged. Experts, regardless of their IQ levels, were found to consistently use a reasoning model involving multiple interactions between at least seven variables on a simulation task that required two-horse comparisons. Ceci and Liker pointed out that in real-life situations, where races are between 8 to 10, horses many additional variables would be successfully added to this model. Surprisingly, subjects' scores on the arithmetic subtest of the WAIS were found to be unrelated to the reasoning feats demonstrated on the simulation task.

The race handicappers, like the chess players studied by Charness, had developed highly complex thinking and problem-solving skills in the course of their adult lives. Unlike professional domains where there are often structured educational entrances to the realms of expertise, skill in leisure activities and in social domains is most likely self-instructed.

Wisdom: Expert Knowledge in the Domain, Fundamental Life Pragmatics

Our own research on sophisticated thinking and problem solving in adulthood has been carried out in the context of the study of "wisdom." In everyday language, wisdom is associated with experientially based intellectual functioning in adulthood and with specific insight into difficult life matters. People distinguish "wisdom" from intelligence in general (Sternberg, 1985). They acknowledge the attribution "wise person" (Clayton & Birren, 1980; Holliday & Chandler, 1986; Sowarka, 1989) and they perceive a gain in wisdom as one of the developmental goals of late adulthood (Heckhausen, Dixon, & Baltes, 1989). Dittmann-Kohli and Baltes (in press, see also Baltes, Dittmann-Kohli, & Dixon, 1984; Dixon & Baltes, 1986) summarized these everyday conceptions by describing wisdom as "sound or good judgement about difficult and uncertain life decisions."

How can wisdom be defined and empirically investigated? Theoretically, we have chosen to characterize wisdom as expert knowledge and functioning in the domain, fundamental pragmatics of life (Baltes & Smith, in press; Smith & Baltes, in press). This domain encompasses knowledge about life matters: for example, knowledge about the variations and conditions of life-span development (one's own development and that of others), human nature and conduct, life tasks and goals, social and intergenerational relations, and life's uncertainties. Adults spend a considerable amount of time thinking in this domain—as they manage their day-to-day lives, plan for and decide on their own future and the future of others, and evaluate their past. Life management, life review, and life planning are, we suggest, three areas in which it might be possible to observe instances of cognitive growth in later adulthood.

We do not expect all adults to become experts (i.e., wise) in the domain, fundamental life pragmatics. Whereas most individuals will acquire some knowledge in the domain and will evolve subgroup and personal aspects, only a few will reach expertlike levels of functioning. Individual differences are likely to be a function of ontogenetic differences in the mechanics of intelligence, sociocultural learning opportunities, personality and motivational dispositions, and idiosyncratic life biographies.

Several factors might facilitate the acquisition of expertise in the domain, fundamental life pragmatics. These may include (a) extensive and well-organized experiences with a wide range of human conditions, and (b) the ability to function effectively in human affairs. It is possible, for example, that individuals who come from walks of life where participation in societal domains of wisdom are optimized (e.g., educational, human services, judicial, and welfare services), would be likely candidates for reaching a high level of expert knowledge about fundamental life pragmatics. Furthermore, we expect that because of the amount of practice and the range of experiences involved, living longer (i.e., into old age) may be a necessary (but not sufficient) condition for the acquisition of wisdom.

We have derived a family of five criteria from cognitive psychology and life-span theory to specify the nature of wisdom-related knowledge and its manifestation in terms of expert judgment and advice about life matters. The five-criterion set is summarized in Table 3.2 The first two criteria, rich factual and procedural knowledge about life, are consistent with general models of expertise. The remaining criteria, life-span contextualism, relativistic thinking associated with an awareness of variations in values and priorities, and the recognition and management of uncertainty, define several of the critical meta-level dimensions around which knowledge about fundamental life pragmatics is organized. Taken together, this family of criteria distinguish "wise" from "less-than-expert" judgment and discourse about life problems and life conduct.

The criterion, *life-span contextualism* connotes an understanding that an individual or a life event cannot be considered in isolation, but rather in

TABLE 3.2
Wisdom: A Working Framework

Theoretical Definition

An expert knowledge system in the domain, fundamental life pragmatics (e.g., life planning, life management, life review)

Functional consequence: Exceptional insight into human development and life matters, exceptionally good judgment, advice and commentary about difficult life problems

Family of Five Criteria

1. Rich factual knowledge: General and specific knowledge about the conditions of life and its variations
2. Rich procedural knowledge: General and specific knowledge about strategies of judgment and advice concerning matters of life
3. Life-span contextualism: Knowledge about the contexts of life and their temporal (developmental) relationships
4. Relativism: Knowledge about differences in values, goals, and priorities
5. Uncertainty: Knowledge about the relative indeterminacy and unpredictability of life and ways to manage

relation to a system of social ecologies (family, work, peers, etc.) which have a developmental timeline. These ecologies can reflect three life-span contexts, age-related, culture-related and idiosyncratic. Priorities within and between these ecologies can change as a function of the life-span contexts. Moreover, the influence of these contexts is not always coordinated but can involve tension and conflict. High-level life-span contextualism thus involves knowledge about the possible set of contexts and ecologies relevant to life problems, knowledge of ontogenetic relationships and priorities, knowledge about tensions between contexts (short-term and long-term), and knowledge about time-linked changes in the relative importance of contexts.

We have defined the criterion, *relativism,* in terms of the knowledge that all judgments are a function of, and are relative to, a given cultural and personal value system. High-level performance (i.e., good judgment and advice) will include some acknowledgement of this together with strategies for dealing with it. For example, in our analyses of responses to life problems (presented later), we would look for subjects' attempts to maintain a certain personal detachment from the problems, and to differentiate possible values and goals underlying alternative problem definitions and solutions.

Finally, the criterion uncertainty connotes an awareness that no analysis of a life problem can be complete and definitive: The future is not fully predictable and not all aspects of the past or present can be known. Nevertheless, there are strategies for managing and dealing with uncertainty. An expert, we suggest, would focus both on the recognition of uncertainty and on its management.

Wisdom-related Tasks

At present, we are exploring ways of capturing wisdom-related knowledge and performance in the laboratory in two areas of life pragmatics, life planning (Smith & Baltes, in press; Smith, Dixon, & Baltes, in press), and life review (Staudinger, 1988). In each area, we have begun to devise models of associated thought processes. Life review, for example, involves the construction of life scenarios (based on remembered life events and idealized event scripts) and the interpretation and evaluation of the constructed life course. Life planning involves several processes: the generation and evaluation of future scenarios, the selection of life goals, planning (organizing) to achieve these goals, and monitoring progress. Decisions about the future and interpretations of the past are based on incomplete and uncertain information. Scenarios that individuals generate in the context of life planning and life review and in discourse of life matters are based on their knowledge of themselves, human development, and society; that is, on knowledge about the fundamental pragmatics of life.

We have developed tasks that simulate discourse about life planning and life review and designed measures based on the five wisdom criteria (in Table 3.2) to analyze responses to these tasks. The tasks call for subjects to "think aloud" about a life dilemma ascribed to a fictitious person. Table 3.3 gives examples of the problem texts we use. Each text provides some limited information about the future plans or the life history of a fictitious person. Subjects are invited to discuss and offer advice about what the person might do when facing such a dilemma. They are instructed in the method of "thinking aloud" to facilitate the reporting of their knowledge and thoughts. In addition, after spontaneously offered responses are collected, a set of prompting questions are used to probe further into the knowledge systems available to subjects. The transcribed protocols are scored by trained raters for evidence of the five wisdom criteria. In addition, the responses are content-analyzed (Sörensen, 1988) to provide a description of the themes subjects address and the focus of their contextualistic and relativistic statements and their comments regarding uncertainty.

To illustrate the meaning of the wisdom criteria, Table 3.4 gives an example of how such evidence may be detectable in a protocol collected for

TABLE 3.3
Examples of Life Planning and Life Review Tasks

Subjects are asked to "think aloud" about the following:

Life Planning   Joyce, a widow aged 60 years, recently completed a degree in business management and opened her own business. She has been looking forward to this new challenge. She has just heard that her son has been left with two small children to care for. Joyce is considering the following options: She could plan to give up her business and move to live with her son, or she could plan to arrange for financial assistance for her son to cover child-care costs. What should Joyce do and consider in planning for her future? What extra information would you like to have available?

Life Review   Martha, an elderly woman, had once decided to have a family and not to have a career. Her children left home some years ago. One day Martha meets a woman friend whom she has not seen for a long time. The friend had decided to have a career and no family. She has retired some years ago. This meeting causes Martha to think back over her life. What might her life review look like? Which aspects of her life might she remember? How might she explain her life? How might she evaluate her life retrospectively?

Note. Tasks vary in type of problem (e.g., normative versus nonnormative), age, and gender of target character. Furthermore, prompting questions are given at the completion of the spontaneous protocol (see Smith & Baltes, in press).

TABLE 3.4
Use of the Wisdom Criteria to Evaluate Verbal Protocols

Example: Life Planning Problem about Joyce

Criterion	Instantiation in Verbal Protocol
Rich Knowledge	- Discusses problem-specific *and* general themes: e.g., underlying emotions, vulnerabilities, social relationships and setting
Procedural Knowledge	- Strategies of decision making, planning and advice giving - Heuristics of cost–benefit analysis - Timing of decision, sequence of comments - Follow-up strategies
Life-Span Contextualism	- Social ecologies, relations with son, family, children, friends - Age-related, historical and idiosyncratic contexts - Tensions and conflicts - Short/long-term priorities
Relativism	- Distance from personal preferences - Consider various goals, values, motives - Cultural relativism
Uncertainty	- No perfect solution - Outlines the unknown: what would happen if . . . - Ways to deal with the unexpected (e.g., illness, wife returns) - Back-up solutions

the life-planning problem about "Joyce." An expertlike answer indicative of wisdom would reflect solid evidence for the entire family of criteria. In general, we argue that, in a given protocol, each of the criteria needs to be identifiable to qualify as a truly wise response.

To date, we have collected 240 responses to life-planning problems and 63 responses to our life review dilemmas. These responses came from young (25–35 years), middle-aged (45–55 years), and older adults (over 60 years) from various professions (50% were teachers). By and large, the results have been consistent with our expectations. As we predicted, only few responses (5%) have been judged to be wise by panels of trained "expert" raters. Furthermore, the dominant finding is an absence of marked age differences. On average, young and middle-aged adults were rated the same or only marginally better than older adults. Older adults, however, produced as many of the top (5%) performances as young adults. There is also evidence that performances were best when the fictitious character's age matched that of the subject, suggesting a certain degree of age-specific knowledge in matters of wisdom.

We are presently investigating top performances in greater depth. For example, we are investigating the performance of individuals from criterion groups who by virtue of their professional life or idiosyncratic life experiences might have had the opportunity to develop expert knowledge of life matters. We also intend to interview people in public life who have been nominated as "wise."

Our research on wisdom is still in its infancy but it has shown some promise. Certainly, it does appear that unlike many other areas of cognitive and intellectual functioning, knowledge and discourse about life matters may well be an area where performances remain stable for the majority of adults and perhaps increase for a select few. Furthermore, knowledge about fundamental life pragmatics is central in systems of intergenerational information transfer. Even in these times of technological and communication advances, many people would agree that there remains something useful in personal experiences and in hearing about the experiences of others first-hand. Older adults, in this context, are valuable resources as teachers and deposits of information about the past. In many instances, although they may not necessarily provide the solutions for the new problems facing the young generation, their ideas and evaluations may anticipate (and perhaps stimulate others to find) solutions.

CONCLUSION

In this chapter, we have presented an overview of life-span propositions and research dealing with thinking and problem solving in adulthood and into old age. Our focus has been the proposal that the likelihood of fairly stable levels of functioning is for most adults quite high. Moreover, we have suggested that, at least in some areas, there exists the potential for continued growth. Physical deterioration and the normal mechanisms of aging will obviously set some limits or constraints on performance. The extent to which these constraints are visible in performance will depend on the nature of the cognitive task, the task context and social environment, and the individual. Essentially, in some select domains, in optimal performance conditions, and where individuals have knowledge relevant to high performance, it should be possible to observe some older adults performing at least as well, if not better than younger adults.

The degree to which this potential can be realized, however, depends to a large extent on the social structure and the educational and occupational opportunities available to adults in all age groups to maintain, restore, and apply old skills and to acquire new ones. The social environment carries expectations and stereotypes about age-related competencies in relation to problem-solving and decision-making skills. These expectations tend to favor young over older adults. Older workers, for example, find few chances to move *up* the career ladder: these opportunities are typically reserved for the young. Only one concept, "wisdom," tends to be linked to a positive scenario about cognitive functioning in late adulthood. Educational policy might well be directed toward extending the opportunities for continued growth in adulthood, toward encouraging "mental exercise" as a part of successful and healthy aging, and toward changing the stereotypes about age-related intellectual decline.

ACKNOWLEDGMENTS

The Berlin work on thinking and problem solving is conducted under the auspices of a research project on "Wisdom and Life-Span Cognition" codirected by Paul B. Baltes and Jacqui Smith. We appreciate helpful discussions of the ideas contained in this chapter with our colleagues Freya Dittmann-Kohli, Jutta Heckhausen, Reinhold Kliegl, Ulman Lindenberger, Doris Sowarka, and Ursula M. Staudinger.

REFERENCES

Arenberg, D. (1982). Changes with age in problem solving. In F. I. M. Craik & S. Trehub (Eds.), *Advances in the study of communication and affect: Vol. 8. Aging and cognitive processes* (pp. 221–235). New York: Plenum.

Baltes, M. M., & Kindermann, T. (1985). Die Bedeutung der Plastizität für die klinische Beurteilung des Leistungsverhaltens im Alter [The significance of plasticity in the clinical assessment of aging]. In D. Bente, H. Coper, & S. Kanowski (Eds.), *Hirnorganische Psychosyndrome im Alter: Vol. 2. Methoden zur Objektivierung pharmakotherapeutischer Wirkungen* (pp. 171–184). Berlin: Springer-Verlag.

Baltes, P. B. (1987). Theoretical propositions of life-span developmental psychology: On the dynamics between growth and decline. *Developmental Psychology, 23,* 611–626.

Baltes, P. B., Dittmann-Kohli, F., & Dixon, R. A. (1984). New perspectives on the development of intelligence in adulthood: Toward a dual-process conception and a model of selective optimization with compensation. In P. B. Baltes & O. G. Brim, Jr. (Eds.), *Life-span development and behavior* (Vol. 6., pp. 33–76). New York: Academic Press.

Baltes, P. B., Dittmann-Kohli, F., & Kliegl, R. (1986). Reserve capacity of the elderly in aging-sensitive tests of fluid intelligence: Replication and extension. *Psychology and Aging, 1,* 172–177.

Baltes, P. B., & Nesselroade, J. R. (1984). Paradigm lost and paradigm regained: Critique of Dannefer's portrayal of life-span developmental psychology. *American Sociological Review, 49,* 841–847.

Baltes, P. B., & Smith, J. (in press). Toward a psychology of wisdom and its ontogenesis. In R. J. Sternberg (Ed.), *Wisdom: Its nature, origins, and development.* New York: Cambridge University Press.

Baltes, P. B., & Willis, S. L. (1982). Plasticity and enhancement of intellectual functioning in old age. In F. I. M. Craik & E. E. Trehub (Eds.), *Aging and cognitive processes* (pp. 353–389). New York: Plenum.

Berg, C. A., & Sternberg, R. J. (1985). A triarchic theory of intellectual development. *Developmental Review, 5,* 334–370.

Berger, P. L., & Luckmann, T. (1967). *The social construction of reality.* New York: Doubleday Anchor.

Birren, J. E. (1969). Age and decision strategies. In A. T. Welford & J. E. Birren (Eds.), *Decision making and age: Interdisciplinary topics in gerontology* (Vol. 4, pp. 23–36). Basel, Switzerland: Karger.

Blanchard-Fields, F. (1986). Reasoning on social dilemmas varying in emotional saliency: An adult developmental perspective. *Psychology and Aging, 1,* 325–333.

Brim, O. G., Jr., & Ryff, C. D. (1980). On the properties of life events. In P. B. Baltes & O. G. Brim, Jr. (Eds.), *Life-span development and behavior* (Vol. 3, pp. 368–388). New York: Academic Press.

Bromley, D. B. (1957). Some effects of age on the quality of intellectual output. *Journal of Gerontology, 12,* 318–323.

Camp, L. J. (1987, November). *Research in real-world problem solving: A pilgrim's progress.* Paper presented at the Annual Conference of the Gerontological Society of America, Washington DC.

Cantor, N., & Kihlstrom, J. F. (1987). *Personality and social intelligence.* Englewood Cliffs, NJ: Prentice-Hall.

Carroll, J. S. (1986). Causal theories of crime and their effect upon expert parole decisions. In H. R. Arkes & K. R. Hammond (Eds.), *Judgment and decision making: An interdisciplinary reader* (pp. 243–254). Cambridge: Cambridge University Press

Caspi, A., & Elder, G. H., Jr. (1986). Life satisfaction in old age: Linking social psychology and history. *Journal of Psychology and Aging, 1,* 18–26.

Cattell, R. B. (1963). Theory of fluid and crystallized intelligence: A critical experiment. *Journal of Educational Psychology, 54,* 1–22.

Ceci, S. J., & Liker, J. K. (1986). A day at the races: A study of IQ, expertise, and cognitive complexity. *Journal of Experimental Psychology: General, 115,* 255–266.

Charness, N. (1981). Aging and skilled problem solving. *Journal of Experimental Psychology: General, 110,* 21–38.

Chi, M. T. H., Glaser, R., & Rees, E. (1982). Expertise in problem solving. In R. J. Sternberg (Ed.), *Advances in the psychology of human intelligence* (Vol. 7, pp. 7–76). Hillsdale, NJ: Lawrence Erlbaum Associates.

Clayton, V., & Birren, J. (1980). The development of wisdom across the life span: A reexamination of an ancient topic. In P. B. Baltes & O. G. Brim, Jr. (Eds.), *Life-span development and behavior* (Vol. 3, pp. 103–135). New York: Academic Press.

Cornelius, S. W., & Caspi, A. (1987). Everyday problem solving in adulthood and old age. *Psychology and Aging, 2,* 144–153.

Dannefer, D. (1984). Adult development and social theory: A paradigmatic reappraisal. *American Sociological Review, 49,* 100–116.

Denney, N. W. (1982). Aging and cognitive changes. In B. B. Wolman (Ed.), *Handbook of developmental psychology* (pp. 807–827). Englewood Cliffs, NJ: Prentice-Hall.

Denney, N. W. (1984). A model of cognitive development across the life span. *Developmental Review, 4,* 171–191.

Denney, N. W., & Palmer, A. M. (1981). Adult age differences on traditional and practical problem-solving measures. *Journal of Gerontology, 36,* 323–328.

Dennis, W. (1966). Creative productivity between ages of 20 and 80 years. *Journal of Gerontology, 21,* 1–8.

Dittmann-Kohli, F., & Baltes, P. B. (in press). Toward a neofunctionalist conception of adult intellectual development: Wisdom as a prototypical case of intellectual growth. In C. Alexander & E. Langer (Eds.), *Beyond formal operations: Alternative endpoints to human development.* New York: Oxford University Press.

Dixon, R. A., & Baltes, P. B. (1986). Toward life-span research on the functions and pragmatics of intelligence. In R. J. Sternberg & R. K. Wagner (Eds.), *Practical intelligence: Nature and origins of competence in the everyday word* (pp. 203–235). Cambridge: Cambridge University Press.

Erikson, E. (1959). Identity and the life cycle. *Psychological Issues Monograph I.* New York: International Universities Press.

Featherman, D. L. (1983). The life-span perspective in social science research. In P. B. Baltes & O. G. Brim, Jr. (Eds.), *Life-span development and behavior* (Vol. 5, pp. 1–59). New York: Academic Press.

Featherman, D. L. (1987, July). *Work, adaptive competence, and successful aging: A theory of adult cognitive development.* Paper presented at the IX Biennial Meeting of the International Society for the Study of Behavioural Development, Tokyo, Japan.

Gilligan, C. (1982). *In a different voice: Psychological theory and women's development.* Cambridge, MA: Harvard University Press.

Glaser, R. (1984). Education and thinking: The role of knowledge. *American Psychologist, 34,* 93–104.

Goldberg, L. R. (1986). Simple models or simple processes? Some research on clinical judgments. In H. R. Arkes & K. R. Hammond (Eds.), *Judgment and decision making: An interdisciplinary reader* (pp. 335–353). Cambridge: Cambridge University Press.

Goodnow, J. J. (1986). Some lifelong everyday forms of intelligent behavior: Organizing and reorganizing. In R. J. Sternberg & R. K. Wagner (Eds.), *Practical intelligence: Nature and origins of competence in the everyday world* (pp. 143–162). Cambridge: Cambridge University Press.

Hagestad, G., & Neugarten, B. L. (1985). Age and the life course. In R. H. Binstock & E. Shanas (Eds.), *Handbook of aging and the social sciences* (pp. 35–81). New York: Van Nostrand Reinhold.

Hall, G. S. (1922). *Senescence: The last half of life.* New York: Appleton.

Havighurst, R. J. (1972). *Developmental tasks and education* (3rd. ed.). New York: D. McKay. (Original work published 1948)

Heckhausen, J., Dixon, R. A., & Baltes, P. B. (1989). Gains and losses in development throughout adulthood as perceived by different adult age groups. *Developmental Psychology, 25,* 109–121.

Holliday, S. G., & Chandler, M. J. (1986). Wisdom: Explorations in adult competence. In J. A. Meacham (Ed.), *Contributions to human development* (Vol. 17). Basel, Switzerland: Karger.

Horn, J. L. (1982). The aging of human abilities. In B. B. Wolman (Ed.), *Handbook of developmental psychology* (pp. 847–870). Englewood Cliffs, NJ: Prentice-Hall.

Horn, J. L., & Cattell, R. G. (1967). Age differences in fluid and crystallized intelligence. *Acta Psychologia, 26,* 107–129.

Hoyer, W. J. (1985). Aging and the development of expert cognition. In T. M. Schlechter & M. P. Toglia (Eds.), *New directions in cognitive science* (pp. 69–87). Norwood, NJ: Ablex.

James, W. (1890). *The principles of psychology* (2 Vols.). New York: Dover.

Kausler, D. H. (1982). *Experimental psychology and human aging.* New York: Wiley.

Kliegl, R., & Baltes, P. B. (1987). Theory-guided analysis of aging mechanisms through testing-the-limits and research on expertise. In C. Schooler & K. W. Schaie (Eds.), *Social structure and individual aging processes* (pp. 95–119). Norwood, NJ: Ablex.

Kliegl, R., Smith, J., & Baltes, P. B. (1986). Testing-the-limits, expertise and memory in old age. In F. Klix & H. Hagendorf (Eds.), *Human memory and cognitive capabilities: Mechanisms and performances* (pp. 395–407). Amsterdam: North Holland.

Kliegl, R., Smith, J., & Baltes, P. B. (1989). Testing-the-limits and the study of age differences in cognitive plasticity of a mnemonic skill. *Developmental Psychology, 25,* 247–256.

Kohn, M. L., & Schooler, C. (1978). The reciprocal effects of the substantive complexity of work and intellectual flexibility: A longitudinal assessment. *American Journal of Sociology, 84,* 24–52.

Kuhn, D., Pennington, N., & Leadbeater, B. (1983). Adult thinking in developmental perspective. In P. B. Baltes & O. G. Brim, Jr. (Eds.), *Life-span development and behavior*

(Vol. 5, pp. 158-195). New York: Academic Press.

Labouvie-Vief, G. (1985). Intelligence and cognition. In J. E. Birren & K. W. Schaie (Eds.), *Handbook of the psychology of aging* (2nd ed., pp. 500-530). New York: Van Nostrand Reinhold.

Lehman, H. C. (1953). *Age and achievement.* Princeton, NJ: Princeton University Press.

Meacham, J. A. (1983). Wisdom and the context of knowledge: Knowing that one doesn't know. In D. Kuhn & J. A. Meacham (Eds.), *On the development of developmental psychology: Contributions to human development* (Vol. 8, pp. 111-134). Basel: Karger.

Mines, R. A., & Kitchener, K. S. (1986). *Adult cognitive development.* New York: Praeger.

Neugarten, B. L., Moore, J. W., & Lowe, J. C. (1968). Age norms, age constraints, and adult socialization. In B. L. Neugarten (Ed.), *Middle age and aging* (pp. 22-28). Chicago: University of Chicago Press.

Perlmutter, M. (in press). Cognitive development in life-span perspective: From description of differences to explanation of changes. In E. M. Hetherington, R. M. Lerner, & M. Perlmutter (Eds.), *Child development in life-span perspective.* Hillsdale, NJ: Lawrence Erlbaum Associates.

Reese, H. W., & Rodeheaver, D. (1985). Problem solving and complex decision making. In J. E. Birren & K. W. Schaie (Eds.), *Handbook of the psychology of aging* (2nd ed., pp. 474-499). New York: Van Nostrand Reinhold.

Riley, M. W. (1985). Age strata in social systems. In R. H. Binstock & E. Shanas (Eds.), *Handbook of aging and the social sciences* (Vol. 3, pp. 369-411). New York: Van Nostrand Reinhold.

Salthouse, T. A. (1982). *Adult cognition: An experimental psychology of human aging.* New York: Springer.

Salthouse, T. A. (1985). *A theory of cognitive aging.* Amsterdam: North Holland.

Schaie, K. W., & Willis, S. L. (1986). Can decline in adult intellectual functioning be reversed? *Developmental Psychology, 22,* 223-232.

Scribner, S. (1986). Thinking in action: Some characteristics of practical thought. In R. J. Sternberg & R. K. Wagner (Eds.), *Practical intelligence: Nature and origins of competence in the everyday world* (pp. 13-30). Cambridge: Cambridge University Press.

Sears, R. R. (1977). Sources of life satisfactions of the Terman Gifted Men. *American Psychologist, 32,* 119-128.

Simonton, D. K. (1988). *Scientific genius: A psychology of science.* Cambridge: Cambridge University Press.

Smith, J., & Baltes, P. B. (in press). A study of wisdom-related knowledge: Age/cohort differences in responses to life planning problems. *Developmental Psychology.*

Smith, J., Dixon, R. A., & Baltes, P. B. (in press). Expertise in life planning: A new approach to investigating aspects of wisdom. In M. L. Commons, J. D. Sinnott, F. A. Richards, & C. Armon (Eds.), *Beyond formal operations: Vol. 2 Comparisons and applications of adolescent and adult developmental models.* New York: Praeger.

Sörensen, S. (1988). *Age differences in wisdom-related expertise: Content analysis of verbal protocols for knowledge about life pragmatics.* Diplomarbeit (Masters Thesis), Free University Berlin, FRG.

Sowarka, D. (1989). Weisheit und weise Personen: Common-Sense-Konzepte älterer Menschen. *Zeitschrift für Entwicklungspsychologie und Pädagogische Psychologie, 21,* 87-109.

Staudinger, U. M. (1988). *Life review and its contribution to the development of knowledge about the pragmatics of life.* Published doctoral dissertation, Free University of Berlin & Max Planck Institute for Human Development and Education, Berlin, FRG. [Verlag Klett-Cotta, Stuttgart, 1989]

Staudinger, U. M., Cornelius, S., & Baltes, P. B. (1989). The aging of intelligence: Potential and Limits. In M. W. Riley & J. Riley (Eds.), *Annals of the Academy of Political and Social Sciences, 503,* 43-58.

Sternberg, J. J. (1982). Reasoning, problem solving, and intelligence. In R. J. Sternberg (Ed.), *Handbook of human intelligence.* Cambridge: Cambridge University Press.

Sternberg, R. J. (1985). Implicit theories of intelligence, creativity, and wisdom. *Journal of Personality and Social Psychology, 49,* 607–627.

Sternberg, R. J., & Wagner, R. K. (Eds.). (1986). *Practical intelligence: Nature and origins of competence in the everyday world.* Cambridge: Cambridge University Press.

Wagner, R. K., & Sternberg, R. J. (1986). Practical intelligence in real-world pursuits: The role of tacit knowledge. *Journal of Personality and Social Psychology, 49,* 436–458.

Chapter 4

NEGOTIATING SENSE IN THE ZONE OF PROXIMAL DEVELOPMENT

James V. Wertsch
Norris Minick
Frances L. Hiatt School of Psychology
Clark University

The goal of a sociocultural account of mind is to provide an analysis of mental functioning that reflects historical, cultural, and institutional situatedness.[1] Instead of focusing on cultural universals or making a historical assumption, such an approach seeks to explicate the cultural, institutional, and historical situatedness of thinking, memory, and other mental processes. For example, it might seek to identify differences in the mental processes of the Vai in Liberia and middle-class Americans (Cole & Scribner, 1974), or it may wish to compare the thinking processes of nonliterate and literate people in Soviet Central Asia (Luria, 1976). This is not to say that all sociocultural analyses of mind must be comparative. They may also focus on mental functioning in a single sociocultural setting, so long as some link between this setting and psychological processes is explicated.

During the past century, many studies of the emergence of modern technological societies have focused on *rationality* as a critical feature that connects human consciousness and institutional organization. The notion of rationality was originally outlined by Weber as a tool for analyzing capitalist economic activity, bourgeois private law, and bureaucratic authority. Since its introduction, it has frequently been integrated with Marx's

---

[1]When referring to the Vygotskian School, Soviet authors have tended to use the terms *sociohistorical* or *cultural-historical*. We have chosen to use *sociocultural* here because it is the most concise term that reflects both the social theoretical and the cultural aspects of what we believe the Vygotskian approach is capable of addressing.

ideas on exchange value and commodity fetishism, which were developed at about the same time. For example. Lukacs (1971) did this in his account of "reification."

Over the past two decades Habermas (1970, 1984) extended and refined several of Weber's ideas on rationality and rationalization. In this connection Habermas argued that Weber viewed the concept of rationalization as a key to understanding the impact of scientific-technological progress on the institutional organization of societies engaged in modernization. Rationalization, under this definition, means first of all "the extension of the areas of society subject to the criteria of rational decision" (1970, p. 81). Rational decision is grounded in "purposive-rational" action with its fixed, unquestioned goals, technical rules, context-free language, and problem-solving orientation. By nature of its very structure, purposive-rational, "instrumental," or "strategic" action constitutes the exercise of control. This control, or mastery is first exercised over natural processes, but it is often extended to control over other humans or groups of humans, thus becoming a means for social and political domination.

Although social theorists from Weber to Habermas have argued that rationality has come to be a criterial feature of modern human consciousness, little has been done to specify its concrete psychological manifestations. There are several reasons for this. On the part of social theories, there has been the implicit assumption that once sociohistorical forces are mapped out, their psychological correlates would be obvious. On the part of psychological theories there has been a tendency to develop approaches that remain isolated from the issues raised by social theorists. Indeed, there is often a tendency for psychological theories to be grounded in units of analysis and other constructs that make it difficult to identify ways in which psychological processes are related to the sociocultural setting in which they occur. At least in some cases this stems from the fact that modern psychological theories themselves tend to be grounded in the acceptance of instrumental rationality, that is, have a strong scientific-technological orientation. In any event, the upshot of this state of affairs in social science is that while rationality is widely recognized in social theory as a central feature of modern life and is presumably a major objective of formal education, there has been little success in specifying how it is manifested in psychological processes.

We believe that it is possible to forge a principled link between the sociocultural phenomenon of rationality and psychological processes by employing the approach to mind outlined by Vygotsky (1987; Wertsch, 1985). It is more than coincidence that the term *instrumental* appears in Vygotsky's writings (e.g., see his proposal for an "instrumental method"; Vygotsky, 1981) and in the writings of social theorists concerned with instrumental rationality. The fact that part (though by no means all[2]) of Vygotsky's theoretical framework focuses on what was later to be called instrumental rationality is attributable to the fact that he wanted to help develop the kind of rational cognition needed in Soviet efforts to build a modern technological society (cf. Wertsch & Youniss, 1987).

Following Vygotsky's general tenet of genetic analysis, we assume that tracing the ontogenesis of mental functioning in sociocultural context is one of the best ways to understand the phenomenon. Following Vygotskian theoretical tenets further, we argue that the origins of mental functioning are to be found in human social life. As Luria (1981) noted, these first two tenets of Vygotsky's approach reflect a basic assumption that at first glance seems paradoxical. In reviewing the basic tenets of Vygotsky's approach he wrote:

> In order to explain the highly complex forms of human consciousness one must go beyond the human organism. One must seek the origins of conscious activity and "categorical" behavior not in the recesses of the human brain or in the depths of the spirit, but in the external conditions of life. Above all, this means that one must seek these origins in the external processes of social life, in the social and historical forms of human existence. (p. 25)

Vygotsky linked his claims about genetic analysis and the social origins of individual functioning with a third theme concerned with semiotic mediation (i.e., the claim that mental functioning is inherently shaped by the sign systems, or semiotic means that mediate it). As we argued elsewhere (Wertsch, 1985), his claims about semiotic mediation are analytically prior to the other two major themes. This is because development, as well as the form that social and psychological processes take, are shaped by sign systems — in particular human language.

There are several ways to operationalize these basic tenets, that is, to explicate the "social and historical forms of human existence," but following Vygotsky's insights about semiotic mediation we focus on one in particular here. This concerns metaphors of "languages" or "voices" that have appeared recently in several analyses of contemporary human consciousness (e.g., Bellah, Madsen, Sullivan, Swidler, & Tipton, 1985; Gilligan, 1982). According to this metaphor children are socialized into various sociocultural settings by learning to speak in specific languages or voices. Building on another tradition in the social sciences, Ochs and Schieffelin (1984) made a similar point in their statement that "the process

---

[2]In addition to focusing on the instrumental rationality required to build the modern technological society under construction at the time, Vygotsky specifically dealt with other, "nonrational" aspects of mental life such as aesthetics (1934, chap. 7, 1971).

of becoming a competent member of society is realized to a large extent through language, by acquiring knowledge of its functions, social distribution, and interpretations in and across socially defined situations, i.e., through exchanges of language in particular social situations" (p. 277). In the view of all these authors, a close tie between ways of speaking and ways of thinking is assumed — something that is compatible with Vygotsky's claim that certain fundamental aspects of thinking are shaped through the internalization of speech.

While the notion of language or voice has served as a central metaphor for researchers like Bellah and his associates and for Gilligan, the specific languages or voices involved have not been explicated in great detail. Bellah and his associates (1985) did note that when they use the term *language,* they did not mean what the linguist studies. That is, they were not studying a system of sign types removed from their concrete instantiation in real communicative contexts, but "modes of moral discourse that include distinct vocabularies and characteristic patterns of moral reasoning" (p. 334).

We believe that with further explication this metaphor of the languages — or what we term "modes of discourse" — used by contemporary Americans can be a useful tool in understanding the socialization of psychological processes. Specifically, it provides the foundation for the claim that the appearance of rationality as a fundamental aspect of contemporary American consciousness can be studied by examining the ontogenesis of a particular mode of discourse, namely one grounded in categories of rationality.

Our particular interest is with some of the forms of speaking found in formal educational settings. They fall under the heading of what Scribner and Cole (1981) termed *literacy practice,* and they are what we call *rational discourse.* In order to pursue these claims, several ideas must be clarified. First, it is incumbent on us to specify the nature of rational discourse. Second, we must specify the processes whereby a mode of discourse is mastered. And finally, we must provide an account of the contextual factors that govern the use of various discourse modes. These are the topics of the three remaining sections of this chapter.

RATIONAL DISCOURSE

The fundamental property of rational discourse in school is the fact that it is concerned with what we shall term *text-based realities.* A variety of kinds of texts and realities may be involved, but in all cases a reality or "problem-space" (Karmiloff-Smith, 1979) is created, maintained, and operated on through semiotic (usually linguistic) means. As an example, consider the operations involved in dealing with syllogisms. In syllogistic reasoning tasks the premises (which constitute a text of their own) are to be used to create a reality. For example, premises such as, (a) "All men are mortal," and (b) "Socrates is a man," may be used to create a problem space or reality. Such a reality can then be operated on to derive a conclusion. The reality outlined in the premises may not be familiar to a subject or may even be known to be counterfactual. For example, instead of (a) one might encounter (a'), "It is not the case that all men are mortal." Such a premise would of course create a different reality. Regardless of whether or not information stated in the premises conforms to what we know to be true in other contexts or from other sources, in order to carry out a syllogistic reasoning task appropriately, one must create, maintain, and manipulate the reality explicitly stated in these premises. Within this reality certain conclusions necessarily follow from the premises.

Investigators such as Luria (1976), Scribner (1977), and Wason and Johnson-Laird (1972) showed that one of the primary difficulties encountered by subjects carrying out syllogistic reasoning tasks is the tendency to go beyond the information provided in the premises by incorporating information from other sources in deriving a conclusion. This finding reflects a general property of text-based realities: they have strict boundaries within which one must operate. When dealing with text-based realities in the rational discourse of school settings, one ground rule requires that one must stay within the bounds of the reality created by the linguistic means. Indeed a primary goal of teachers' efforts to socialize children into the rational discourse of the classroom is to get them to operate within the "space" of text-based realities, which are bound off from other areas of experience such as those having to do with everyday experience at home, on the playground, and so forth.

A second, related property of the text-based realities involves *decontextualization*. This means that linguistic segments (phonemes, words, sentences, etc.) are lifted out of the communicative contexts in which they are otherwise used and viewed as abstract objects of analysis. In this practice, language becomes an object of reflection while simultaneously continuing to be an instrument of communication.

When reflecting on language, it is possible to focus either on form or on meaning. For example, a focus on form might involve identifying all the words in a list that begin with *b*. This can be done without processing, or even knowing the meanings of the words involved. Conversely, one can focus on meaning, for example, by talking about synonyms or antonyms. In the case of syllogisms one also focuses on the meaning of the premises and the conclusion that necessarily follows within the bounds of a text-based reality.

The particular text-based reality we focus on here has to do with sense relations that exist among various vocabulary items or "lexemes" in natural language.[3] As Lyons (1977) noted, " 'sense' is a term used by a number of philosophers for what others would describe simply as their meaning, or perhaps more narrowly as their cognitive or descriptive meaning" (p. 197). In Lyons' (1977) usage, sense is associated with decontextualized sign types rather than the sign tokens that "instantiate" these sign types in real, spatiotemporally located speech events. For example, the definition that goes with an entry in a standard dictionary is its sense, and this sense is viewed as remaining constant across the concrete contexts of speech events, that is, across token instantiations of the sign type. Thus, in the analysis of sense relations one is concerned with sign type–sign type relations (Wertsch, 1985) that exist independently of any particular speech event. As a concrete example consider the equivalence relation "opthalmologist = eye doctor." This is a relationship that holds independently of any particular speech context in which either of the terms might be used. The focus here is on the fact that "opthalmologist" means "eye doctor" regardless of when and where either of the terms is instantiated in communication.

There is little need for the explication of sense relations in the conduct of everyday communication. Instead of using language to speak about linguistic objects, that is, to create abstract, decontextualized definitions, the focus is typically on communicating about other objects. This by no means entails the claim that there is a lack of clarity in such communication. It does, however, reflect a focus on a different kind of object. In contrast, in the rational discourse of formal schooling there is a great deal of attention paid to decontextualized semiotic relations such as those involved in the analysis of sense. In this setting sense relations are one of the primary foci of text-based realities, and students are presented with the "semiotic challenge" (Wertsch, 1985) of entering into these realities, staying within their boundaries, and operating on their objects to arrive at certain answers to the questions posed by teachers and instructional materials.

An early example of the research concerned with the text-based realities created in rational school discourse can be found in the studies done by Luria and Vygotsky in Central Asia in the early 1930s (Luria, 1976). In this research subjects who had no schooling, subjects who had some basic literacy schooling, and subjects who had several years of formal schooling were compared. One of the tasks used in this study required subjects to categorize sets of objects (often pictures of objects). For example, subjects

---

[3]The term *sense* here is based on the normal practice found in the writings of Anglo-American semantic theorists such as Lyons (1977). Unfortunately, it conflicts with the translation practice used for Vygotsky's term *smysl*, which also appears as "sense" in English but is highly context specific. What is appears as "meaning" in English translations of his writings is termed "sense" in this chapter.

were shown drawings of a bird, a rifle, a dagger, and a bullet and asked to state, "Which one does not belong?" or "Which three go together?" Luria reported that subjects who had no schooling refused or were unable to categorize objects in ways generally recognized as "correct" by subjects who had even a few months of schooling. Instead of using "theoretical" reasoning, the nonliterate subjects tended to rely on "practical" or "situational" reasoning.

As an example of this, consider the following excerpt from a transcript of experimenter–subject interaction. In this case the task was to specify which three of a set of four drawings (a hammer, a saw, a hatchet, and a log) go together. The subject was a 39-year-old nonliterate peasant from a rural area.

Subject: They're all alike. I think all of them have to be here. See, if you're going to saw, you need a saw, and if you have to split something you need a hatchet. So they're *all* needed here.

Experimenter: Which of these things could you call by one word?

Subject: How's that? If you call all three of them a "hammer," that won't be right either.

(Rejects use of general term.)

Experimenter: But one fellow picked three things—the hammer, saw, and hatchet—and said that they were alike.

Subject: A saw, a hammer, and hatchet all have to work together. But the log has to be there too!

(Reverts to situational thinking.)

Experimenter: Why do you think he picked these three things and not the log?

Subject: Probably he's got a lot of firewood, but if we'll be left without firewood, we won't be able to do anything.

(Explains selection in strictly situational terms.)

Experimenter: True, but a hammer, a saw, and a hatchet are all tools.

Subject: Yes, but even if we have tools, we still need wood—otherwise, we can't build anything.

(Persists in situational thinking despite disclosure of categorical terms.) (after pp. 55–56)

In this interchange, Luria and the subject were able to communicate at one level, but they clearly failed to achieve "intersubjectivity" (Rommetviet, 1979; Wertsch, 1985) at another level; they used the same words, but they did not agree on their meanings in an essential way. The problem is that

Luria wanted to have the subject speak and think about the terms involved from the perspective of the decontextualized sense relations into which they enter. From this perspective, "hammer," "saw," and "hatchet" go together because they are all hyponyms of "tool." Without this perspective, there is little reason to group these three objects together. The subject approached the task from the perspective of the objects to which terms like "hammer" and "saw" could be used to refer; instead of staying within the bounds of the text-based reality defined by abstract sense relations, he insisted on dealing with the task from the perspective of activity with real, concrete, non-linguistic objects.

At issue here is not a difference between Russian and another language such as Uzbek. Any language clearly has the "semiotic potential" (Wertsch, 1985) to be used to form sense relations (i.e., decontextualized definitions), as well as to refer to nonlinguistic objects. Instead, the difference is one of the language function or use that is deemed appropriate or is "privileged" (Wertsch, 1987) in the context. In one case the focus is on operating within the boundaries of text-based realities generated by decontextualized sense relations; in the other the focus is on the way in which objects identified by language can be grouped on the basis of concrete activity with them. In recent years several authors (e.g., Lucy, 1985; Tulviste, 1981) have formulated a more general theoretical framework for what we are saying here by expanding on Hymes' (1966) comments about the functional relativity of language. In this view speech communities often differ as much in terms of the language functions (e.g., narrative, ritual, rational discourse) they employ in socioculturally defined situations as they do in terms of structural differences in the languages involved (i.e., Uzbek, English, Russian). Among other things, a functional relativity argument purports that in the end there is no absolute criterion by which one could argue that one method for responding to Luria's questions is more intelligent than another; rather, it is a matter of preferring one use of language over others.

Thus we have seen that rational discourse in school can largely be explicated in terms of text-based realities. The problem space of a text-based reality is created, maintained, and manipulated through the semiotic means employed in discourse. Furthermore, a text-based reality is characterized by boundedness and decontextualization. This decontextualization, which may focus either on the form or the meaning of an expression, involves making words and other signs into objects of reflection instead of means of communication. The example we explicated from Luria's research illustrates the fact that it is possible for two interlocutors to take linguistic expressions to have distinct functions, thereby creating a sort of miscommunication. We argued that an account of this miscommunication cannot be grounded in the assumption that one function is simply an incorrect or less developed version of the other. Instead, the two functions must be understood as being equally developed, yet qualitatively distinct.

HOW A MODE OF DISCOURSE IS MASTERED

As already noted, a general theme that runs throughout Vygotsky's writings purports that higher mental functioning in the individual has its origins in social, or "interpsychological" processes. As part of his analysis of the dynamics of the transition from interpsychological to intrapsychological functioning, Vygotsky introduced the notion of the "zone of proximal development." He defined this zone as the distance between a child's *"actual developmental level as determined by independent problem solving"* and the higher level of *"potential development as determined through problem solving under adult guidance or in collaboration with more capable peers"* (1978, p. 86). Vygotsky's analysis of the zone of proximal development was motivated by two general concerns: providing a more dynamic account of mental testing and accounting for the processes that occur in good instructional practices. In the latter connection (the one of primary concern here), Vygotsky noted that "instruction *creates* the zone of proximal development" (1956, p. 450). Furthermore, *"Instruction is good only when it proceeds ahead of development.* Then it *awakens and rouses to life an entire set of functions which are in the stage of maturing, which lie in the zone of proximal development.* It is in this way that instruction plays an extremely important role in development" (1934, p. 222).

Several authors (e.g., Bruner, 1984; Griffin & Cole, 1984; McNamee, in press; Rogoff, Malkin, & Gilbride, 1984; Saxe, Gearhart, & Guberman, 1984; Wertsch, 1979, 1980) have recently examined the processes whereby a variety of skills come to be mastered through participating in interpsychological functioning in the zone of proximal development. As Wertsch (1984) noted, the key to doing these kinds of analyses is to identify differences in the ways adults and children define the task situation and then to examine the semiotic mechanisms (e.g., nonverbal pointing, verbal referring expressions) that allow them to communicate (i.e., to attain intersubjectivity) in spite of these differences. The ultimate goal of this communication is to socialize the tutee into the tutor's situation definition. A fundamental aspect of the dynamics in this process requires that adult tutors have the "semiotic flexibility" to communicate with the children on the basis of the latter's situation definition while simultaneously keeping a culturally accepted situation definition in the back of their mind as the goal of socialization.

In the case of the rational discourse of text-based realities grounded in sense relations, there would appear to be two basic options for carrying out socialization. First, one could use "metalinguistic" (Silverstein, 1985) means (i.e., language about language) to instruct children explicitly on the nature of sense relations. To some extent teachers do rely on metalinguistic discourse in elementary school instruction to deal with form (e.g., the use of terms like *vowel, consonant,* and *capital letter*) and meaning (e.g., the use of terms like *synonym* and *antonym*). However, in the kind of categorization task used by Luria (and often employed in school), metalinguistic terms (e.g., "hyponym," "superordinate term") are seldom used by elementary school teachers. Instead, teachers seem to rely more heavily on a second mode of instruction. The goal of this instruction remains one of socializing children into employing text-based realities grounded in sense relations such as synonymy and antonymy, but the means are not metalinguistic in the sense previously noted. Instead, the means employed are those typically used in other cases of instruction in the zone of proximal development where no metalinguistic terms are employed. The process involves (a) transforming a task into a form of interpsychological functioning between adult and child that the latter can understand; (b) encouraging the child to accept a new situation definition; and (c) transferring strategic responsibility to the child.

On behalf of tutors this calls for some mechanism for engaging tutees in a task setting before the tutees really understand it (i.e., before they approach it on the basis of the tutor's situation definition). Thus an inherent tension is involved in this interaction. On the one hand, tutors must be able to communicate with the tutee in terms the latter can understand; on the other, tutors are constantly striving to induce the tutee to redefine the situation in different (i.e., more culturally appropriate) terms. This involves a switch in the way the tutee is to speak and think about objects (e.g., pictures in workbooks) and behaviors (e.g., circling or marking out various pictures with a pencil) in the task setting. Hence from tutors' perspective a form of negotiation is involved in which they are constantly trying to "lure" tutees into defining the situation in a new way while not frustrating or losing communicative contact with them. This requires semiotic flexibility. Tutees have problems dealing with text-based realities grounded in sense relations because they typically view linguistic terms as means for talking about nonlinguistic objects and events rather than as decontextualized expressions that themselves serve as objects of reflection. As a result, tutees are likely to encounter difficulties in understanding tutors' comments if these comments presuppose that terms are viewed as objects of reflection.

In order to illustrate how tutors can negotiate communication with tutees in the zone of proximal development when dealing with sense relations, we briefly analyze a segment of classroom interaction. This segment involves an experienced teacher interacting with a group of six students in her first-grade classroom. The school involved is in the Chicago suburbs, and it had been in session for slightly over 2 months at the time the data were gathered. In no sense should the use of this excerpt of interaction be taken to involve a positive or negative evaluation of the quality of teaching involved. Such an evaluation would require much more extensive information about the context, goals, and so forth. The segment of interaction we examine is intended to serve only as an example of points in our argument. This segment went as follows:

1. T: OK. Let's turn over . . . This is fun. There's one picture in every row that does *not* belong. (episode 1 begins) Which one doesn't belong in the first one? John, what doesn't belong?

2. C: Key.

3. T: Key. Put an X on the key. Why doesn't the key belong Mikey?

4. C: Umm . . . They can't open doors.

5. T: Oh . . . That's not a good answer. Why doesn't the key belong with the ham and a tomato and a banana, Mikey?

6. C: Because the key isn't a fruit.

7. T: Well, a ham isn't a fruit. What are all those things? Things you can . . .

8. C: Eat.

9. T: Eat. Things you can eat. You can eat a ham. You can eat a tomato. You can eat a banana. Can you eat a key?

10. C: No.

11. T: No. So cross it off. (episode 2 begins) OK, now do the next one. Let's take a look. Which one are we going to put an X on, Jessica?

12. C: The plant.

13. T: The plant. Why? Annie.

14. C: Because it's not clothes.

15. T: It's not clothes. Good. All the rest are clothes. (epidose 3 begins) OK, how about the next one. What are you going to put an X on, Fuad?

16. C: Umm. Apple.

17. T: Why?

18. C: It's not a tool.

19. T: It's not a tool. (epidose 4 begins) Patrick, which one are you going to *eliminate* in the last one?

20. C: Umm . . . The goose.

21. T: Why.

22. C: Because it's not something you can sit on or sleep on.

23. T: Very good. It's not furniture, right? We can call that furniture.

As in the categorization tasks used by Luria, this workbook exercise concerned text-based realities grounded in sense relations (specifically relations of hyponomy, i.e., relations among terms that can be arranged hierarchically on the basis of semantic features, terms such as "food" and "ham"). Hence the teacher's situation definition was based on the assumption that sense relations of superordination and subordination were the appropriate criteria to employ. However, as the interaction reveals, the children were not completely at home in defining the situation in this way. Instead, they tended to approach the task from the perspective of the concrete objects depicted and how one could interact with them. Thus, as in Luria's study, one party in the interaction viewed the task in terms of sense relations, and the other tended to view it in terms of concrete objects.

Unlike Luria, however, the teacher did not simply document children's problems with sense relations or insist on the need to use them to formulate an appropriate response to the task. Instead, she helped them continue to participate in the task by switching back and forth between two basic situation definitions: one within the bounds of a text-based reality grounded in sense relations and the other outside of these bounds. By following this switching procedure, she was able to communicate with the children on the basis of their situation definition, thereby avoiding undue frustration on their part. At the same time, however, she continued to urge them to make a "situation redefinition" (Wertsch, 1984) that would allow them to approach the task in the "correct" way (i.e., in accordance with the dictates of rational discourse). A closer look at the transcript reveals the subtlety and sophistication involved in what at first appears to be a mundane classroom interchange.

In the first episode (utterances 1 through part of 11), the pupil involved experienced some difficulty in operating within the confines of a text-based reality grounded in sense relations. On the one hand, the child made the correct choice (utterance 2). However, Mikey's answer was based on the way in which the object being depicted functions in the world of concrete actions. The criterion he chose for why the other objects do not belong with the key ("They can't open doors.") would in fact function effectively to differentiate the two categories. The teacher, however, clearly did not agree that this is an appropriate criterion. Instead, she turned to another student for another answer. This student used a superordinate term ("fruit"), but all the objects other than the key are not hyponyms of it. At this point, the teacher seemed to sense that there was enough difficulty with this item that she should "retreat" a bit to avoid frustrating the children. She did this by switching the kind of answer that she would accept. Instead of searching for a superordinate term (i.e., instead of continuing to insist that they all function within the text-based reality grounded in sense relations), she switched to a new criterion for grouping objects. This criterion is one concerned with how actual objects can be operated on in the real world (what can be eaten). In this way she actually retreated to a situation definition similar to the one Mikey used earlier in providing his answer. When explicating the switching procedure used here, it is essential to recognize that it does not involve some kind of simple renaming; rather, it is a matter of making a qualitative shift in situation definitions that either are or are not grounded in text-based realities.

In the next episode (last part of utterance 11 through first part of utterance 15), Jessica provided an answer within the boundaries of a text-based reality grounded in sense relations. The shirt, pants, and shoes in the pictures can be distinguished from the plant on the basis of the fact that they are all hyponyms of "clothes." In the third episode (last part of 15 through first part of 19) Fuad followed the pattern of the previous episode by functioning within the bounds of a text-based reality grounded in sense relations. Thus when considering a set of items composed of a hammer, a saw, a pair of pliers, and a hat, he identified the hat as not being a "tool." In the fourth and final episode (last part of 19 through 23), Patrick experienced some initial difficulty in providing an answer based on the criteria the teacher wanted to privilege. He did make the correct categorization of objects, but as a criterion he talked about what can be sat or slept upon. At this point the teacher encouraged him but reformulated his response in such a way that the criterion for categorization was sense relations rather than activities with the concrete objects depicted. That is, she reformulated his response in terms of the situation definition she deemed appropriate.

In all of these cases shifts in situation definition involved operating within or outside a text-based reality grounded in sense relations. In some cases (e.g., episode 1) a retreat from the teacher's preferred situation definition was involved, and in other cases (e.g., episode 4) the situation redefinition involved a reformulation of the student's answer. Whatever the "direction" of the situation redefinition, however, the shift was usually quite subtle. It occurred "simply" by changing the way that objects were represented in speech, but such a change actually involved changing what the relevant objects were.

CONTEXTUAL FACTORS

In formulating his outline of a sociocultural approach to mind Vygotsky clearly recognized rationality as an essential aspect of modern human consciousness. Specifically, he dealt with this claim in his treatment of "scientific concepts."[4] As Minick (1987) noted, Vygotsky's understanding of scientific concepts changed over the last decade of his life. In his earlier formulations, he focused on the psychological and semiotic nature of scientific concepts, whereas near the end of his life he moved to talking about them in terms of the forms of discourse used in a specific social institutional setting, namely formal schooling. This does not mean that he no longer thought of scientific concepts as having a psychological moment—the tie between social communication and individual psychological

---

[4]Although the term *nauchnyi* has usually been translated as "scientific" when associated with concepts in Vygotsky's writings, it has also been translated as "academic" in Luria's (1976) writings. This reflects the slight difference between "nauchnyi" in Russian and "scientific" in English and reinforces our claim that Vygotsky's concern with scientific concepts reflected a concern with the discourse of formal schooling.

processes was always at the center of his analysis. Instead, it means that he recognized that scientitic concepts were as much a phenomenon of an institutional semiotic process (i.e., rational discourse in formal schooling), as they were a phenomenon of psychological functioning.

An issue that must be addressed in any complete account of the role of rational discourse in a sociocultural approach to mind is the relationship between it and other forms of speaking and thinking. In this connection Vygotsky proposed that the mastery of rational discourse in the form of scientific concepts results in the subsequent reorganization of other (presumably nonrational) aspects of mental functioning in accordance with the decontextualized logic of text-based realities. In this view, formal schooling would produce people who are rational in all aspects of their speech and thinking. However, a spate of recent studies in psychology do not support Vygotsky's hypothesis on this issue. Authors such as Tversky and Kahneman (1974) and Wason and Johnson-Laird (1972) noted that even people with clear expertise in rational thinking often do not follow its dictates when dealing with certain types of mental problems. For example, instead of staying within the bounds of a text-based reality in solving syllogistic reasoning problems, Wason and Johnson-Laird (1972) showed that highly educated subjects often import information from everyday experience into their thinking.

Such findings suggest that the mastery of rational discourse should not be thought of as causing or reflecting some kind of general, all-encompassing rational approach to life. Instead, its analogue may be mastering a second language, dialect, or code.[5] Instead of heralding a new age in which all other discourse forms are overridden or precluded, the mastery of rational discourse seems to exist alongside them and is used only (and not always even then) in situationally appropriate ways. In this sense, it is like a code involved in the phenomenon of code switching outlined by sociolinguists such as Gumperz (1982). Such an impression is supported by Habermas' (1970) comment that rationalization "generates subcultures that train the individual to be able to 'switch over' at any moment from an interaction context to purposive-rational action" (p. 98).

For the child this means that mastering rational discourse involves more than using decontextualized language within the confines of a text-based reality. It also means knowing how to recognize and create contexts in which the use of rational discourse is appropriate. This is an essential part of what Ochs and Schieffelin (1984) included in their claim about the role of language in becoming a competent member of a society, and it is part of

---

[5]The use of the term *code* in Bernstein's (1971) writings on restricted and elaborated codes is quite relevant here.

4. NEGOTIATING SENSE 85

what a complete analysis of the role of rational discourse in a sociocultural account of mind must address. Although we have not dealt concretely with it here, it is interesting to note in passing that part of the teacher's implicit message to the children in the excerpt of interaction analyzed earlier was the fact that it was appropriate, if not mandatory, to define the situation they were in as one requiring the use of text-based realities grounded in sense relations. It might have been possible to make this message explicit through the use of some kind of metalinguistic terminology (e.g., "Think of a superordinate term."), but it seems that teachers as well as students are usually so unaware of the nature of the implicit message being conveyed here that such means are seldom used. How this is done and how procedures might be improved in doing it remain issues for future research.

The excerpt of concrete interaction we analyzed in the previous section was interpreted in terms of the zone of proximal development. However, our goal was not simply to provide another account of the dynamics involved in this zone. Instead, our hope was to begin to locate interaction in the zone of proximal development in sociohistorical context. Specifically, we are interested in how the institutional setting of formal schooling shapes discourse patterns. In this connection, we have focused on rational discourse as a language or voice that children are encouraged to master in the literacy practice of formal schooling. This is not to say that this is the only area of competence that emerges on the interpsychological plane and is then taken over by children on the intrapsychological plane.[6] It is to say, however, that rational discourse is a dominant, privileged mode of thinking and speaking in formal schooling and therefore needs to be examined from the perspective of the dynamics Vygotsky outlined in connection with the zone of proximal development and elsewhere. In this connection, it is essential to understand the special problems presented by attempts to induce children to define a situation in terms of text-based realities grounded in sense relations.

Finally, it is important to understand the way in which rational discourse fits into the larger picture of the overall organization of children's discourse in modern society. Does the pattern of privileging certain forms of discourse in the institutional setting of formal schooling reflect patterns found in other institutional settings? How does this pattern of privileging match or fail to match patterns generally found in various cultural and subcultural groups? Has this pattern changed over history? These complex questions just begin to hint at the kinds of issues that will eventually need to be addressed in any kind of complete sociocultural approach to mind.

---

[6]It is interesting, however, to note that most of Vygotsky's comments on the zone of proximal development were made in connection with the emergence of scientific concepts.

ACKNOWLEDGMENTS

The research reported in this chapter was assisted by the Spencer Foundation. The data presented, the statements made, and the views expressed are solely the responsbility of the authors.

REFERENCES

Bellah, R. N., Madsen, R., Sullivan, W. M., Swidler, A., & Tipton, S. M. (1985). *Habits of the heart: Individualism and commitment in American life*. New York: Harper & Row.

Bernstein, B. (1971). *Class, codes, and control*. London: Routledge & Kegan Paul.

Bruner, J. S. (1984). Vygotsky's zone of proximal development: The hidden agenda. In B. Rogoff & J. V. Wertsch (Eds.), *Children's learning in the "zone of proximal development"* (pp. 93–98). San Francisco, CA: Jossey-Bass.

Cole, M., & Scribner, S. (1974). *Culture and thought: A psychological introduction*. New York: Wiley.

Gilligan, C. (1982). *In a different voice: Psychological theory and women's development*. Cambridge, MA: Harvard University Press.

Griffin, P., & Cole, M. (1984). Current activity for the future. The zo-ped. In B. Rogoff & J. V. Wertsch (Eds.), *Children's learning in the "zone of proximal development"* (pp. 45–64). San Francisco, CA: Jossey-Bass.

Gumperz, J. (1982). *Discourse strategies*. Cambridge: Cambridge University Press.

Habermas, J. (1970). *Toward a rational society: Student protest, science, and politics*. Boston: Beacon Press.

Habermas, J. (1984). *The theory of communicative action. Volume 1. Reason and rationalization of society*. Boston: Beacon Press.

Hymes, D. (1966). Two types of linguistic relativity (with examples from Amerindian ethnography). In W. Bright (Ed.), *Janua linguarum, Series Maior* (No. 20, pp. 114–167). The Hague: Mouton.

Karmiloff-Smith, A. (1979). *Language as a formal problem-space for children*. Paper presented at the MPG/NIAS Conference on "Beyond description in child language," Nijmegen, Holland.

Lucy, J. A. (1985). Whorf's view of the linguistic mediation of thought. In E. Mertz & R. J. Parmentier (Eds.), *Semiotic mediation: Sociocultural and psychological perspectives*. Orlando: Academic Press.

Lukacs, G. (1971). *History and class consciousness: Studies in Marxist dialectics*. Cambridge, MA: MIT Press.

Luria, A. R. (1976). *Cognitive development: Its cultural and social foundations*. Cambridge, MA: Harvard University Press.

Luria, A. R. (1981). *Language and cognition*. New York: Wiley Intersciences.

Lyons, J. (1977). *Semantics* (vol. 1). Cambridge: Cambridge University Press.

McNamee, G. (in press). The social origins of narrative skills. In M. Hickmann (Ed.), *Social and functional approaches to language and thought*. New York: Academic Press.

Minick, N. (1987). Introduction. *The collected works of L.S. Vygotsky. Vol. 1. Problems of general psychology. Including the volume Thinking and speech*. New York: Plenum.

Ochs, E., & Scheiffelin, B. B. (1984) Language acquisition and socialization: Three developmental stories and their implications. In R. A. Shweder & R. A. Levine (Eds.), *Culture theory: Essays on mind, self, emotion* (pp. 276–322). Cambridge: Cambridge University Press.

Rogoff, B., Malkin, C., & Gilbride, K. (1984). Interaction with babies as guidance in development. In B. Rogoff & J. V. Wertsch (Eds.), *Children's learning in the "zone of proximal development"* (pp. 31–44). San Francisco, CA: Jossey-Bass.

Rommetviet, R. (1979). On the architecture of intersubjectivity. In R. Rommetveit & R. Blakar (Eds.), *Studies of language, thought, and verbal communication* (pp. 93–108). London: Academic Press.

Saxe, G. B., Gearhart, M., & Guberman, S. R. (1984). The social organization of early number development. In B. Rogoff & J. V. Wertsch (Eds.), *Children's learning in the "zone of proximal development"* (pp. 19–30). San Francisco, CA: Jossey-Bass.

Scribner, S. (1977) Modes of thinking and ways of speaking. In P. N. Johnson-Laird & P. C. Wason (Eds.), *Thinking: Readings in cognitive science* (pp. 483–500). New York: Cambridge University Press.

Scribner, S., & Cole, M. (1981). *The psychological consequences of literacy.* Cambridge, MA: Harvard University Press.

Silverstein, M. (1985). The functional stratification of language in ontogenesis. In J. V. Wertsch (Ed.), *Culture, communication, and cognition: Vygotskian perspectives* (pp. 205–235). New York: Cambridge University Press.

Tulviste, P. (1981). O lingvistecheskoi i deyatel'nostnoi otnocitel'nosti [On linguistic and activity relativity]. *Trudy po psikhologii: Problemy poznaniya i deyatel'nosti.* [Works in psychology: Problems of cognition and activity]. Tartu: Uchenye Zapiski Tartuskogo Gosudarstvennogo Universiteta.

Tversky, A., & Kahneman, D. (1974). Judgment under uncertainty: Heuristics and biases. *Science, 185,* 1124–1131.

Vygotsky, L. S. (1934). *Myshlenie i rech': Psikhologicheskie issledovaniya* [Thinking and speech: Psychological investigations]. Moscow and Leningrad: Gosudarstvennoe Sotsial'no-Ekonomicheskoe Izdatel'stvo.

Vygotsky, L. S. (1956). *Izbrannye psikhologicheskie issledovaniya* [Selected psychological investigations]. Moscow: Izdatel'stvo Akademii Pedagogicheskikh Nauk SSSR.

Vygotsky, L. S. (1971). *The psychology of art.* (Scripta Technica, Trans.) Cambridge, MA: MIT Press.

Vygotsky, L. S. (1978). *Mind in society: The development of higher psychological processes.* (M. Cole, V. John-Steiner, S. Scribner, & E. Soubermans, Eds.). Cambridge, MA: Harvard University Press.

Vygotsky, L. S. (1981). The instrumental method in psychology. In J. V. Wertsch (Ed.), *The concept of activity in Soviet psychology* (pp. 134–143). Armonk, NY: M. E. Sharpe.

Vygotsky, L. S. (1987). *The collected works of L.S. Vygotsky. Vol. 1. Problems of general psychology. Including the volume Thinking and speech.* New York: Plenum.

Wason, P. C., & Johnson-Laird, P. N. (1972). *The psychology of reasoning.* London: Batsford.

Wertsch, J. V. (1978) Adult-child interaction and the roots of metacognition. *Quarterly newsletter of the Institute for Comparative Human Development, 2*(1), 15–18.

Wertsch, J. V. (1979). From social interaction to higher psychological processes: A clarification and application of Vygotsky's theory. *Human development, 22* (1), 1–22.

Wertsch, J. V. (1980). The significance of dialogue in Vygotsky's account of social, egocentric, and inner speech. *Contemporary Educational Psychology, 5,* 150–162.

Wertsch, J. V. (1984). The zone of proximal development: Some conceptual issues. In B. Rogoff & J. V. Wertsch (Eds.), *Children's learning in the "zone of proximal development"* (pp. 7–18). San Francisco, CA: Jossey-Bass.

Wertsch, J. V. (1985). *Vygotsky and the social formation of mind.* Cambridge, MA: Harvard University Press.
Wertsch, J. V. (1987). The fragmentation of discourse in the nuclear arms debate. *Current research on peace and violence,* 2-3.
Wertsch, J. V., & Youniss, J. (1987). Contextualizing the investigator: The case of developmental psychology. *Human Development, 30,* 18-31.

Chapter 5

THINKING AND FEELING – THE ELEPHANT'S TAIL

Michael Lewis
Institute for the Study of Child Development
University of Medicine and Dentistry of New Jersey
Robert Wood Johnson Medical School

THE PROBLEM OF THINKING ABOUT FEELING

The focus of this chapter derives from our broad interest in the relationship between thinking and feeling. The Western mind, at least since pre-socratic times, has been comfortable in separating thinking and feeling and in giving each a reality of their own. Perhaps they are separate, however it is reasonable to consider the proposition that these two actions constitute in reality a single action viewed from two perspectives. Consider two examples. In the first, the infant exhibits an action (a set of behaviors including facial expression and autonomic and central nervous system changes) when a novel event follows a familiar one. We use the term *surprise* to capture this set of behaviors. Surprise is used by the observer (and by the child when old enough) to reference a cognitive as well as an affective action, yet all we observe is a set of co-occurring behaviors. The second example utilizes Jaynes' (1977) notion that the pre-Greeks considered the action of their right hemisphere to be the gods' communication to them, whereas we now consider this same hemispheric action to be our own thinking. What we (as those who experience the actions directly, or observe them indirectly in others) choose to call "thinking" or "feeling" may be no closer to reality than what Jaynes' primitives called their action. Such concerns give rise to the possibility that in examining the actions we call "thinking" and "feeling" we are behaving as the blind men in their examination of the elephant. Recall that their blindness led them to conclude that each limb and tail of the elephant was a separate and accurate description of what they experienced. The error of reification of these terms, even when we substitute for them the terms "cognition" and "emotion," is an error that must concern us, especially because our common language is all that we have when we set about to study these problems. As becomes evident, these terms cause trouble enough. Although we are aware of this problem of reification, we do not avoid it. Rather we seek to articulate our meanings more carefully and thus sharpen the argument.

Here, our specific interest in this broad question assumes a more limited developmental perspective, focusing on the relation between cognitive and emotional actions and their development. Elsewhere (Lewis, 1987; Lewis & Michalson, 1983; Lewis & Rosenblum, 1978), I have attempted to disassemble emotional life into five components including emotional stimuli, receptors, expressions, states, and experiences in order to clarify what we mean when we use the term *emotion*. Moreover, I have tried to show how each emotional component has cognitive features. This approach continues focusing on self-conscious emotions, a class of emotions that can only exist as a consequence of a particular cognitive development, itself a possible consequence of still earlier emotional behavior.

In order to pursue this inquiry it will be necessary for us first to consider what we mean when we use the term *feeling*. As we demonstrate, feeling has at least two meanings referring both to emotional actions and to thinking actions. We pursue our interest in thinking by next focusing on the thinking aspect of feeling in order to argue that thinking about one's feeling (like thinking about one's thinking) requires a consideration of self-awareness. This feature of the self system can be shown to evolve around the last half of the second year of life (Lewis & Brooks-Gunn, 1979a).

Once self-awareness occurs it gives rise to an entirely new set of feelings that we have called *self-conscious emotions*. Thus, our developmental model links thinking and feeling into a fuguelike structure; feelings give rise to thinking about feelings, which in turn give rise to new feelings. Data supporting this model exist and are presented to demonstrate its utility. The comments to follow, then, are divided into four parts: Feeling as Thinking; Self Awareness—Thinking About Feeling; Feeling-Thinking-Feeling—A Fugue; Thinking and Feeling—A Multi-Directional View.

FEELING AS THINKING

The term *feeling* is most often used when talking about emotional behavior. We use this term to denote the difference between emotional and cognitive life. Although "feeling" has implicit meaning—that is, the English speaker knows what is meant when one says "feeling" as opposed to "thinking"—unfortunately, the term has other implications and thus creates considerable confusion. "Feelings" appears to denote two meanings, the nature of which lies at the very heart of any discussion of the relationship of thinking and feeling. For example, when we say, "I am feeling happy" we mean first, that "I am in a state of happiness" and second, that "I am aware that I am in this state" (see James, 1884).

Feeling Without Thinking

Some have argued for a restricted meaning of feeling and have suggested that feeling refers only to the first definition, namely, that "I am in a state of happiness." This restricted meaning implies that feeling is something real, much like an internal state, which, given the proper observational techniques, could be measured and described. Indeed, such a view of feeling as an internal emotional state has preoccupied theorists since the earliest writings on emotion (see Cannon, 1927). Several different locations for this state have been proposed and it is not possible in this discussion to elaborate extensively on them (see Lewis & Michalson, 1983, chap. 3 for a more complete discussion). Some have located this state in the soma (for example, see James, 1895), some in the autonomic nervous system (Wegner, Jones, & Jones, 1956), some in the central nervous system (Cannon, 1929; Olds & Forbes, 1981) some in the endocrine hormonal system (Watson, 1934), and some in all three (Izard, 1977). Following Darwin (1872), who observed external manifestations of these presumed internal emotional states in the facial, vocal, and postural behavior of men and beasts, more recent theorists have looked specifically at facial expressions as a direct measure of these states (see Ekman, Freisen, & Ellsworth, 1972; Izard, 1977; Tomkins, 1962). Such a view of the term feeling as an internal emotional state, that is, physically real and measurable, allows for the conceptualization of feelings or internal emotional states independent of cognition (see for example, Zajonc, 1980). In theories such as the one proposed by Zajonc (1984) and others, eliciting stimulus events acts in some manner so as to produce an emotional state or feeling. Although some types of cognition may be necessary to link these eliciting stimulus events to feeling, cognition is not involved in the feeling (or state) itself. One needs the cognitions necessary for perceptual discriminations or the cognitions associated with the meaning of an emotional elicitor but one does not need cognition for the feeling itself. For example, cognition is needed to discriminate a doctor's white coat from another color and is also needed for the association between the white coat and past pain, but cognition is not needed for the emotional response of fear. In other words, once the elicitor does its job, cognition gives rise to feeling but is not the feeling state. This view of the term feeling appears perfectly reasonable, although the measurement of feeling of these internal emotional states has been somewhat elusive. Even facial expression, which has been argued to have a one-to-one correspondence with feeling (see for example, Eibl-Eibesfedt, 1970, and Ekman's 1973(a) work on universal facial expression), the correspondence between facial expression and feeling is known to be perturbated by socialization factors (Ekman, 1972; Lewis & Michalson, 1984).

Feeling and Thinking

The second meaning of the term feeling has more to do with thinking. Here feeling has to do with the conceptualization that while emotional states may exist independently of cognition, our awareness of them in and of itself is a very important factor in emotional life. Such awareness is itself cognition, a cognition about a feeling state. Analogous to knowing about knowing, it is knowing about feeling, a counterpart to metacognition. Thus, it might be the case that I am in a state of happiness yet I do not feel happy; that is to say, I do not have awareness of my happiness. Although it is presumed that there is self-awareness of happiness most of the time, there are many emotional states occurring at many different times of which we are not aware. Three classes of such happenings follow as examples of potentially different processes at work in associating or disassociating the thinking or awareness aspect of feeling from the state aspect of feeling.

Unnoticed Feeling

While driving my car at 60 miles per hour, the front left tire has a blowout. For the next 15 seconds I struggle with the steering wheel to try to bring the car safely to a halt on the side of the road. Once having succeeded in bringing the car to a stop, I observe that I am fearful. I further observe that my fearfulness started at the point that I noticed my hands were shaking and that I was reflecting on the last 15 seconds of events.

The question here to be asked is: Was I, from the point of the blowout until I noticed that I was fearful, feeling fear? It seems reasonable to assume that had we the proper measurement system (for example, the measurement of facial expression or various body behaviors) and if we knew what the correct constellation of fear behaviors was, we might have determined that I was in a fearful state during that time period. However, because I was attending to stimuli other than those emanating from my "emotional centers"—perceptions of the road, the direction of the car, etc.—I was not aware of these states and therefore not feeling the emotion of fear. In this situation, the entire array of proprioceptive feedback from the wheels and visual information around me was so intense, and the situation so grave, as to force or require me to focus on those external events rather than myself.

The degree to which I was focused on other events, was the degree to which I was unaware of my state.

Disassociated Feeling

John recently received the news that a very dear relative, an aunt, just died and John reports at first experiencing great sadness at her loss. During the last few weeks, he found himself rather agitated and had some trouble eating and sleeping. When John was asked how he felt he replied that he was feeling rather tired lately. If you asked him whether he was depressed, he would say to you that he did not feel depressed.

In this example, John reports that he feels, that is, he is aware of a particular emotional state. In this case, the emotional state that he is aware of and the state he reports is that of fatigue. Here, rather than distraction, another mechanism may be at work that can disassociate the feeling as self-awareness from the feeling as state. In this example, John engages in an active attempt to pay attention to and focus on one feature or aspect of his feeling rather than another. What might be the mechanism(s) that might cause him to focus on one aspect of his feelings (his emotional state) as opposed to another, or in some cases, might cause him to state that he is feeling fine rather than feeling sad or depressed?

Two possible causes for such a disassociation of awareness from emotional state might account for these findings. In the first, the notion of an active and perhaps unconscious mechanism called intrapsychic censorship (see Freud, 1949) might seek to prevent one's conscious self-awareness from engaging the "true" emotional state of sadness. Such a proposition takes the form: "I am unaware that I am aware of a feeling or internal state." For some intrapsychic reason, one aspect of myself prevents another aspect of myself from being aware of a particular emotional state. Such a system requires both a cognitive self-awareness and a cognitive unconscious endowed with the same or similar cognitive structures that occupy my conscious self. In this system, these unconscious cognitive structures, called unconscious self-awareness, act on one's self-conscious self-awareness as it pertains to "feeling" or emotional state. Although such a model has been articulated by others, I am not sure how one would go about empirically putting such a conception to the test.

Nevertheless, the notion of unconscious mental processes has great appeal and has been widely used as an explanatory device, because it accounts for a wide range of phenomena. Consider the following:

Unconscious or Unlearned Feeling

John is informed by a therapist that in her view, his awareness of being tired is an incomplete self-awareness; in fact, he is sad or depressed at the aunt's death. The therapist's understanding in some fashion acts to alter John's self-awareness and he suddenly discovers that the other's observation is correct. John realizes that he is more than just tired, he is depressed.

Whether or not this change in awareness represents (a) bringing into consciousness that which his unconscious was already aware, or (b) simply John's succumbing to the suggestions of another remains an important distinction. If it were the former, we would have evidence of an unconscious awareness that is different from conscious awareness, whereas, in the latter, it would simply be a change in his conscious awareness.

The second mechanism that has been invoked to explain why John focused on fatigue rather than sadness has to do less with a conflicting topology of self-features, or the mechanisms of repression or suppression, and more with simple learning processes. Lewis and Michalson (1984b) suggested that during socialization children are given specific verbal labels and are sometimes responded to in a unique fashion when they exhibit certain emotional behaviors. Ideally, parental responses to emotional states and their associated behaviors should result in children learning to think about and having *self-awareness* about their emotional states. However, when parents teach children their unique and inappropriate label for an emotion, children may come to have an awareness not in agreement with their internal states. For example, John as a child may have exhibited the same sad behaviors (both externally and internally) to a situation of loss; however, his social environment informed him that those behaviors in those situations meant he was tired, not sad. In other words, using simple learning processes we can argue that past experience may be capable of shaping people's self-awareness about an emotion, even producing an awareness that is idiosyncratic vis-à-vis the emotional state that actually exists. This type of learning is likely to account not only for differences termed pathological, but perhaps also for familial, group, and cultural differences in emotional experience.

In a study reported by Lewis and Michalson (1983a), we observed the response of 111 mothers to their 1-year-old children's distress. This distress was caused by the child's having been left alone in a playroom. When the mothers returned to the playroom only a portion of them provided an emotional term to describe their child's behavior (26%). Of the mothers who produced an emotional description, 7 remarked to their children that they "were sad or tired", 7 remarked that their children "were angry or mad", 7 said that they were "scared or frightened." There were 7 others who asked "Did you miss me?" Observation of the children's responses revealed that in all cases mothers faced an upset child on their return to the room and there were few differences in the children's behavior. Perhaps these differences were noticed by the mothers and their labeling behavior was based directly on their ability to discriminate different types of distress. Alternatively, mothers' attributions may have been responsible for the labels they applied to their children's similar behavior. The findings revealed that mothers with higher verbal Wechsler Adult Intelligence Scale (WAIS) scores more frequently labeled their children "scared/upset" compared to mothers with lower verbal WAIS scores who more frequently used "angry/mad" and "tired/sad." Such findings lend at least some support to the belief that the labeling and responsiveness to internal states may play a role in children's and adults' self-awareness of these states. If a parent labels correctly, vis à vis how others in the culture label the state (given the same behaviors in the same situation), then the child's self-awareness will match that of others so taught.[1] Mismatches result from idiosyncratic labeling.

Development of Feeling

It would be a serious error in such a discussion not to mention still another possible disassociation between emotional state and thinking of self-awareness. This occurs when there is self-awareness without an accompanying emotional state; that is, when there is an awareness about a feeling state when the state itself does not exist. For example, it has been stated that people are able to experience orgasmic behavior even though their spinal cord injury has resulted in the inability of internal state information (i.e., bodily sensations) to reach the centers of awareness. Such an example alerts us to the possibility that thinking as feeling may not have any correspondence to feeling the states themselves.

Susan, a 7-month-old, sits in a chair watching a stranger move toward her. When the stranger reaches over to touch her hand, Susan pulls it away and begins to cry.

This example pertains to a situation in which an organism is too young to have cognitions necessary for self-awareness. Thus, Susan, who is a 7-month-old infant, can be said to have a feeling state of fear as a person unknown to her approaches. Susan's behavior, her crying, pushing away and fearful face, suggests she is in a state of fear and from this, we can state that she is feeling fear. If, however, we ask whether she is aware of being fearful, we would have to conclude that she is not. From a variety of studies we have reason to believe that self-awareness does not emerge until the second half of the second year. As such, we may say that, although she is in a state of fear, she is not aware of being fearful. Thus, from a

---

[1]By labeling we mean the verbal labeling and all other verbal and nonverbal adult behavior that may be associated with the children's behavior.

developmental perspective, it is reasonable to talk about Susan as having a disassociation between the emotional state and its awareness.

These examples allow us to consider the disassociation between emotional states and experiences (see Lewis & Michalson, 1984b). Furthermore, and perhaps more importantly, they indicate the need to distinguish between the two aspects of feeling. It should now be clear that the term feeling has at least two different meanings, and therefore is not a useful term for our theoretical and empirical inquiries. Moreover, these examples illustrate the need to consider—from the point of view of individual difference, situational constraint, and development—the nature of the association between states (or feelings) and self-awareness (or thinking about feelings). In the comments to follow, we focus on the development of thinking about feelings as a critical cognitive milestone vital in understanding emotional life.

SELF-AWARENESS—THINKING ABOUT FEELING

As increased focus on the self and the self systems becomes evident, it is clear that the terms *self, self-development,* and *self-schema* are insufficient to carry the meaning assigned to them by various investigators. Since self-development is a major feature of object relation theory and child development, conflicts in terms of what is meant by the self schema are bound to occur. Although we have attempted to address some of this difficulty in earlier discussions, it is important that we consider these features once again (see Lewis & Brooks-Gunn, 1979a, 1979b). In some sense, the use of self or self-schema imply various features of the self system. Without careful articulation of these different features, we are bound to find ourselves enmeshed again in semantic confusion.

The self system is made up of many features and aspects, only some of which have been explored and discussed. We would hold that these different features of the self system emerge at different times and provide the basis for different emotional and social behavior. Likewise, differences in emotional and social behavior are likely to affect the development of different features of the self system. In any event, throughout our discussion, we hold that the self is fundamentally a cognitive system, although to some significant degree, there are important emotional features intertwined as well.

At least three features of the self system have been discussed by others and although we mention all three, it is really the last that is most relevant for our remarks at the moment. The self system has been considered as (a) self–other differentiation, (b) self-permanence, and (c) self-referential behavior, that is, thinking about the self or self-awareness. These features appear to be different and to have different temporal aspects in terms of their development.

Self–Other Differentiation

To a large extent this differentiation is supported by perceptual and proprioceptive information. Quite early in life, such information allows the organism to act in a fashion so that an observer recording the infant's behavior can rightly conclude that the infant does not mistake itself for another, or another for itself. The exact nature of the support for this self–other concept or schema is unclear. However, it is likely to be the case that many organisms, beside human infants, possess such self–other discrimination ability. For example, observe the white rat running down a corridor. Notice as it arrives at a wall that it makes no attempt to run into that wall, but alters its body position and travels along the wall. Such behavior informs the observer that a distinction between self and other is made by the animal. Such ability does not need to invoke any concept having to do with a self system of awareness. The self–other differentiation is likely to occur early in the child's life and is likely to be supported by the physical properties of the environment (see Gibson, 1960). On the other hand, such ability may be related to basic reflexive and unlearned response systems located in the organism, or it may result from some combination of the two. Self/other differentiation as a feature of the self system emerges early and is what many mean when discussing the child–mother interactive patterns (see Stern, 1985). Although such discrimination ability is needed for subsequent development, we need not impart any extraordinary attribution to the child's self system. Rather, we should be prepared to consider it similar to that behavior exhibited by the white rat when it goes around a solid object. Self-awareness is not necessary for such action.

Self-Permanence

Another feature of the self system and one that has been discussed by a number of investigators (see Bertenthal & Fischer, 1978; Lewis & Brooks-Gunn, 1979b) is self-permanence. This feature of the self system requires a higher level of cognitive capacity than the first, one in which the organism is able to maintain constancy vis à vis itself in terms of changes in physical features or interactions in its environment. Self-permanence, like object permanence, is a very early feature of a knowledge system, in which, according to Piaget (1954), the child has gained some knowledge of object (or self). This early ability is the knowledge of existence versus nonexistence. Although Piaget clearly demonstrated that object permanence as a process begins at 8 months and is not completed until 18 months, many investigators have assumed that children possess object permanence as early as 8 months of age. Whereas it may be true that children at this early age can find an object that is hidden, it is equally true that this age marks the beginning, rather than the culmination, of object permanence. Many have argued that self-permanence has a direct parallel to object permanence, thus one should expect that this feature of the self system would have the same developmental course: starting at 8 months and ending somewhat earlier than object permanence, but nonetheless not being completed until well after the end of the first year of life.

Self-permanence, like object permanence, allows the organism to engage in more complicated cognitive and emotional acts, because the organism acquires an increased sense of orderliness both within and outside its own particular system. Self-permanence is essential for the development of many other aspects of the self system. For example, one feature of the self system that is acquired as the child acquires self-permanence is gender identity (Lewis & Weinraub, 1979). Thus, self-permanence should be considered to represent the beginning of the process of identity, and in that sense, related to the final feature of the self system considered here, namely, self-referential or self-awareness ability.

Self-Awareness

We make no distinction between self-awareness and self-referential behavior. They refer to a particular feature of the self system that does not emerge until the middle of the second year of life, namely thinking about the self. From an adult perspective, the feature of the self system that I refer to is best addressed by using an example from R. D. Laing's book *Knots* (1970). Laing, as well as others (see Dennett, 1979), argued for the importance and uniqueness of the human capacity for reflexive behavior. Such behavior can be observed in verb usage, for example, the difference when one makes reference to washing oneself as opposed to washing anything other than self. In French the sentence structure would be *se laver* for washing oneself as opposed to *faire la vaisalle* for washing the dishes. Such reflexive behavior is seen as well in the social knots as described by Laing. Consider the example: "I know my wife knows that I know that she bought a new tie." Such an example of reflexive behavior implies that not only do I have knowledge of myself, but I have knowledge of someone else's self having knowledge of myself. Such complex recursive behavior is what must be considered when we discuss self-referential behavior or self-awareness, especially from a developmental perspective. As we have tried to demonstrate, this feature of the self system, that is, thinking about the self, does not emerge until the second half of the second year of life (Lewis, Sullivan, Weiss, & Stanger, 1987). Moreover, we have been able to demonstrate that the emergence of self-awareness is dependent on a certain level of general mental maturity. Thus, mentally retarded children older than 18 months, but having a 15- to 18-month mental age, are able to show self-referential behavior, whereas retarded children of older ages not having a mental age of 15 to 18 months are unable to do so.

Not all children show self-referential behavior at 15 to 18 months. It appears that there is a period as to when this self system is likely to be established. Our data suggest that individual differences in the acquisition of self-referential behavior or self-awareness can occur anywhere from 15 to 24 months, or perhaps even older in cases of more serious deviation. The early relationship the child has with its primary caregivers seems to affect the unfolding of this feature, such that children who have less secure bases are more likely to show self-awareness at earlier ages than children who have more secure relationships (Lewis, Brooks-Gunn, & Jaskir, 1985). This would follow from our belief that both too little caregiving and overprotective caregiving are likely to result in individuation at different points from that in which the caregiving is appropriate (see also Mahler, Pine, & Gerbman, 1975). Although more work on the causes of individual differences in the development of this self system is necessary, it does appear as if this feature of the self begins to emerge by 15 to 18 months.

There has been some concern about how to measure self-referential behavior. We, among others, have argued for the use of nonverbal techniques to get at this behavior; in particular, we have utilized the mirror-rouge situation (Lewis & Brooks-Gunn, 1979a, 1979b). We have suggested that the child's ability to understand that the image in the mirror located "there" refers to an object located "here" in space (here being where the self is) seems to be a good measure of self-referential behavior. Until recently, there have been little data that could be used as confirmation that this is the case. In the work to be reported, not only will we show that this cognitive milestone of the self system can be measured by self-recognition in the mirror situation, but that self-recognition is tied to other important features of emotional development that could not occur until self-awareness emerges. Thus, by demonstrating the connection between self-recognition and emotional states that require self-awareness, we are able to confirm our belief in self-recognition as an important cognitive milestone.

FEELING-THINKING-FEELING – A FUGUE

The model that we wish to argue for is presented in Fig. 5.1. Notice the features of the model. We suggest that the primary emotions emerge in the

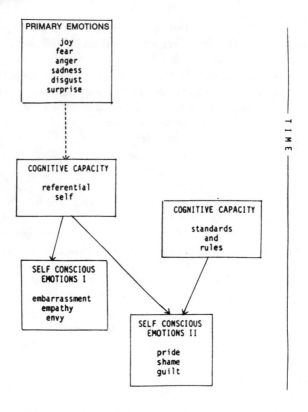

FIG. 5.1

first stage. Here we refer to the emotional states of interest, disgust, fear, anger, joy, and sadness (see Izard, 1977; Plutchik, 1980a, 1980b). These states and their development have been explored by any number of investigators and, depending on the situation used to elicit them, have been found by 8 months of life. The causes for these emotional states are specified in a variety of theories; their developmental emergence is reviewed by Lewis and Michalson (1983). This model does not focus on these primary states which are assumed to exist at this time. The next two features of the model follow from these earlier emotional states. Although the primary emotions precede the emergence of these other features, it is unclear whether, in a developmental sense, they give rise to the next phase. It may be that the early emotional states give rise to the acquisition of cognitive ability in general and of the self system in particular. On the other hand, one might assume that they are unrelated and each controlled by different mechanisms. Finally, it is possible that some combination of these two basic models occurs; for example, although the two paths are controlled by different mechanisms, these mechanisms are interrelated and each requires the presence of the other in order for them to be activated. We have used the metaphor of a fugue to imply such a developmental interconnected model (Lewis, Sullivan, & Michalson, 1984).

Whatever the cause, starting at about 15 to 18 months, a particularly important feature of the child's self system emerges. This we have called self-referential or self-aware behavior. It is characterized by self-recognition in the mirror situation as well as the emergence of self-referential pronoun use, in particular, the use of terms *me* and *mine*. We believe that the emergence of this cognitive milestone, which, as we have said, is comparable to metacognition, provides the basis for the occurrence of two separate and important features of emotional development.

First, self-awareness allows for the development of awareness of the primary emotions. Prior to this development, the child might have an emotional state of fear. However, it is not until self-awareness emerges that the child is aware of its emotional state. Thus, this milestone allows for self-awareness to occur for all those emotional states that exist and are exhibited by the child prior to the occurrence of this milestone.

Second, and as significant, this milestone allows for the generation of a set of new emotional states that can occur only as a consequence of self-awareness. These emotional states constitute what has been called by others "secondary emotions," or what we have preferred to call "self aware emotions" (Plutchik, 1980a; Stipek, 1983). Consider, for example, the variety of emotional states that are unlikely to occur unless the development of self-awareness has occurred, in particular, the emotions of embarrassment, shame/guilt, empathy and efficacy (sometimes referred to as mastery motive or competence).

Self-Exposure Emotions

Embarrassed behavior has been discussed recently by several investigators, but in general, all agree that embarrassment is likely to occur at least as a consequence of conspicuous behavior (Buss, 1980). For example, one may become embarrassed by simply being noticed as one walks down an aisle, or by another's compliment, or perhaps, even by some mild infraction of a standard. In all these cases, self-awareness needs to be invoked in order to understand the emotional state. In each of these occasions, subjects paying attention to themselves because others are paying attention to them is the source of embarrassment. Elsewhere we have argued that only on development of self-awareness is it possible for an organism to be self-conscious or to have an emotional state of embarrassment (Lewis et al., 1989). Indeed, investigators studying self-awareness have found a strong relationship between self-awareness and embarrassment when children look at themselves in mirrors (Amsterdam, 1972; Lewis & Brooks-Gunn, 1979b; Lewis et al., 1987).

Empathy also requires a self-awareness, because in empathic responses the child places itself in the role of the other. In other words, the child must ask itself, "How would I feel, or what would I think or do if I were in the other's place?" Such action, by definition, implies self-awareness as well as other features of a self system. In regard to empathy, it is interesting to note that some have spoken of empathic behavior at much earlier ages than one would wish to believe self-awareness occurs. Here we must rely on the distinction between empathic reflexive behavior and true empathic behavior (Hoffman, 1978). In the former, empathic reflexive behavior may be elicited by classes of events that are biologically tied to behaviors or emotional states in the perceiver. True empathic behavior, however, requires a self-aware organism and is not reflexive in nature.

Self-Standard Emotions

Shame or guilt on the other hand requires self-awareness because these emotions are experienced when the subject reflects on its own actions, thoughts, and feelings and finds them to be inadequate vis-à-vis a standard either externally or internally imposed. Self-awareness is required because the organism must reflect on itself in order to have these emotional states. Likewise, for emotions such as competence, pride, and self-satisfaction, it is necessary to have self-awareness because the subject needs to evaluate its thoughts, emotions, and actions in terms of a standard. In this case, subjects find that their behavior equals or exceeds that of the standard and therefore experiences these positive emotions.

Notice that in some of the self-aware (or self-conscious) emotions, not only is self-awareness necessary, but so is the child's growing understanding of standards, either those externally enforced or those internal standards that are already created. Standards undergo change as a function of the child, the nature of the caregiving experience, and the individual's cognitive capacity, thus one should expect changes in what produces these emotional states as a function of development. Nevertheless, as soon as self-awareness and some standards emerge, potential for these emotions will be exhibited. We suspect that this happens somewhere toward the end of the second year or the beginning of the third year of life.

As we examine this model more carefully, (see Fig. 5.1) it may be the case that the first emotions to emerge prior to any standard are those emotions requiring only self-awareness (or exposure). In our analysis, described in some detail in a description of our empirical findings (Lewis et al., 1987), we have argued that embarrassment may be the likely candidates. It appears that elicitation of embarrassment requires only the occurrence of conspicuous behavior, for example, focusing attention on children by complimenting them or by asking them to perform. Conspicuous behavior is the exposure of the self that can only occur with self-awareness. Embarrassed states appear to occur independent of any standard. Likewise, empathic behavior and envy do not have standards associated with them. It might be useful then to distinguish between two classes of self-aware emotions; those that do and those that do not require standards. The former set, because it requires more elaborate cognition, should occur later. Such a distinction between self-aware emotions, although useful, will not be pursued further here.

EMPIRICAL EVIDENCE SUPPORTING
SUCH A MODEL

The Creation Myth

Although there is considerable empirical support for our view that a certain level of cognitive ability is necessary for the emergence of self-conscious emotions, other support is available as well. We first consider a quotation from the first five books of the Western Bible, which speaks of creation and God's work. Of particular importance for our discussion is the creation of humankind and of the state in which we find ourselves. It is a state in which we are forced out of Eden and, therefore, need to work for our survival, required to bear children in pain, frightened by snakes, learn to discriminate good from evil, and to be conscious of ourselves and the nakedness of our bodies.

> And the Lord God planted a garden of Eden . . . and caused to grow out of the ground every tree . . . and the tree of life in the midst of the garden, and the tree of knowledge of good and evil . . . God commanded the man, saying of every tree of the garden thou mayest freely eat. But of the tree of the knowledge of good and evil, thou shalt not eat of it, for on the day that thou eatest thereof thou shalt surely die.

> And the serpent (to encourage evil said) Ye will surely not die, for God doth know that, on the day ye eat thereof, your eyes will be opened, and ye will be as God, knowing good and evil . . .

> She took of its fruit, and did eat, and gave also unto her husband with her and he did eat. **And the eyes of both of them were opened, and they felt that they were naked.**

Careful reading of this account reveals that becoming knowledgeable — knowing right from wrong — results in God's punishment. Even more particular, becoming knowledgeable results in self-conspicuousness and this in turn results in embarrassment and knowing right from wrong.

From a developmental point of view, simple emotions, interest, love, and so forth, occur before knowledge. However, only after one acquires knowledge are self-consciousness, embarrassment over being naked, and moral behavior possible. In effect, this account of creation suggests that certain levels of cognition are necessary for the emergence of certain other skills, in particular self-consciousness and embarrassment.

Our biblical quotation supports our view that the development of emotional life is highly dependent on a critical cognitive milestone, the development of self-consciousness. In turn, this cognition even gives rise to embarrassment and other self-conscious emotions such as shame and guilt.

Empirical Test

From a more empirical perspective, there is some evidence to suggest that conspicuous behavior, at least as seen in mirrors, is likely to occur at that point in which the child shows self-recognition in the mirror (see for example, Lewis & Brooks-Gunn, 1979 for a review of those studies). However, it seems possible to test such a relationship directly. Recently, in a series of studies Lewis and colleagues (1987) looked at children's emotional states of wariness and embarrassment. In these studies, two situations were found that were good candidates for the production of each of these emotions. For example, wariness or fear in children as young as 6 months of age has been shown to occur during the approach of a stranger. Finding situations that reflect embarrassment is somewhat more difficult. Nevertheless, utilizing the concept of conspicuousness, Lewis and colleagues generated four situations likely to be candidates for the production of embarrassment. These were: (a) children observing themselves in the mirror (without any rouge marked on their noses) in the presence of a female experimenter and the child's mother; (b) the female experimenter repeatedly complimenting the children on their clothing, hairstyle, behavior, and so forth; (c) the female experimenter asking the child to dance while the experimenter played a musical instrument; and (d) on a separate occasion, the mother of the child trying to get the child to dance. The results of these studies supported the hypotheses. First, fear is much more likely to occur in the stranger approach situation than in the other situations, whereas embarrassment is much more likely to occur in the mirror, compliment and dance situations than in the stranger approach situations. More important from the point of view of our interest is the finding of a direct and highly significant relationship between self-referential behavior and embarrassment, but no relationship between self-referential behavior and wariness.

Table 5.1 presents these data. Notice that 80;pc of the children who showed embarrassment also touched their noses in the rouge condition, whereas 20;pc of those children who showed embarrassment did not touch their noses. Moreover, the data on wariness (or fear) indicate that the elicitation of this emotion was equally likely to occur for those infants who touched or did not touch their nose in the rouge self-recognition situation. Such data are directly related to the model as presented. Recall that we hypothesized that wariness/fear, a primary emotional state that is displayed early, does not need self-awareness for its existence. Embarrassment, a later developing emotion, cannot occur until self-awareness has emerged. The results are reported in detail in Lewis and colleagues (1987) and support both our specific predictions and our overall model, which suggests that cognitive and emotional development are intertwined. Of note also is the fact that changes in emotional behavior — in particular, the development of embarrassment and its link to self-recognition behavior — provides powerful congruent support for the belief that nose directed behavior in the mirror rouge context is evidence of the advent or consolidation of self-awareness.

THINKING AND FEELING –
A MULTIDIRECTIONAL VIEW

We have chosen to look at cognitive development as it relates to emotional development in order to understand some of the many aspects of thinking. Our general model of development requires an organismic approach (this in common with Werner, 1957) in which we cannot imagine the development of one thread in a complex cloth as being independent of another (Lewis, 1984; Lewis, Sullivan & Michalson, 1985). Our metaphor of fugue is intended to focus attention on our belief that the thinking and feeling actions of the human organism in the opening years of life, if not forever, are intimately connected, and that the study of one can be nothing more than another view of the other. For us, cognitive development, itself a function of preceding emotional development, acts to enrich and enhance the emotional life of the child.

TABLE 5.1
Percentage of Embarrassed and Wary Subjects Who Exhibit Self Recognition

Self Recognition	Study 1		Study 2	
	Embarrassed	Wary	Embarrassed	Wary
Yes	80	34	79	59
No	20	61	21	41

In the example given, we argue for the need to consider two features of emotional life, both often confused because the single term — feeling — has been used to signify each. We prefer to talk about emotional states and emotional experiences to delineate these different aspects. Cognitive development, in particular the development of that aspect of the self system we call self-awareness or thinking about ourselves, plays a vital role in emotional life, whereas emotional life itself may be the basis for the developing of thinking about ourselves.[2] Primary emotional states may give rise to self-directed thought. Not until children have the capacity to consider themselves, including their earlier emotional states, can they be said to have more advanced emotions such as embarrassment, guilt, shame, pride, achievement, and empathy, to mention just some. Moreover, and perhaps equally important, not until children have awareness of themselves can it be said that they are able to form mature relationships; as Sullivan (1953) informed us, relationships consist of a negotiation between two selves (see also Hinde, 1979; Lewis, 1987).

The rapid development that takes place in the first 2 years of life can be viewed from a variety of perspectives. We have chosen to emphasize the interdependency of thinking and feeling. To do so is to reify these two actions as separate realities, an error we have warned of. Nevertheless, until we are able to discover new ways of conceptualizing, the most we can accomplish is to embed these actions in each other and to demonstrate that feelings require thinking as thinking requires feeling.

THE ROLE OF THINKING AND FEELING
IN EDUCATION

Emotional behavior is an essential dimension when considering both what and how infants and young children learn. Learning in general and early learning in particular cannot be separated from its social context because it requires a strong socioemotional component. For example, the teacher--learner relationship is significant only to the degree that it is embedded within the common social–emotional experience of both. Even more formal learning situations require that the learner be embedded within the social and emotional context of the teacher. One can think, for example, of apprenticeship or tutorial systems as a case in point.

The importance of the teacher–learner interpersonal relationship appears to have been lost as the system of public and free universal schooling

---

[2]Although we have focused our argument on the role of thinking in feeling, we have paid less attention to the role of feeling in thinking. This lack does not reflex any bias, rather only the limited focus on this chapter and volume.

evolved. The present model of teacher–learner, one that can be viewed as chiefly an exchange of information, may be derived from the requirement that public education teach many children at the same point in time. Public education and the model it produces, has built into it a separation of the learning experience of the child from the fabric of the underlying affective motivational system and as such may be a unique model of education rather than the prototypic one.

Moreover, the interrelationship of learning within a social–emotional context may be developmentally bound. That is, the younger the children, the more incapable they may be of separating action (and responses) into their various domains. It would appear reasonable to assume that the younger the child, the greater the need is to embed any learning experience within a social and emotional context. In fact, for the very young, they may be inseparable. Here, one can think of the attachment relationship as both a learning and affective situation.

Individual differences in learning ability may not always be a function of some underlying cognitive deficit, per se. Differences in learning may have to do with the emotional context in which learning takes place. For example, a powerful social class difference may be the degree to which the child is either peer or adult-oriented. If poor children have less adult and more peer orientation (see for example Brown, 1971), then learning differences with an adult teacher could be caused by learning context rather than cognitive differences. In a word, if I am more used to listening to adults than is another, then I am likely to do better in school than those others, because an adult is the teacher.

Our notion that learning or cognition and emotion take place together in a fugue, suggests a more united framework of viewing their impact on education. Looking at interpersonal interactions with difficult to teach children, Lewis (1977) examined a young child named Sarah. Sarah was a 4-year-old who was unable to engage her nursery school teacher in language interaction. Examination of the interaction of Sarah and her teacher reveals that Sarah had not been taught the interactive turn-taking that normally takes place between mother and child. In fact, Sarah, a battered child, had just the wrong experiences to either (a) establish a strong emotional bond to an adult or (b) learn the social/emotional rules of turn-taking and question/asking and answering.

With the help of the nursery school teacher, a curriculum was designed for Sarah that involved (a) spending long periods of time with her at quiet play in order to establish an important emotional attachment with her; and (b) the direct teaching of turn-taking ability. This curriculum did not focus on teaching the child specific cognitive skills or in giving her specific information about the world. Rather, it was designed around the social and emotional needs of the child as these impact on her learning experience. The results of the work with Sarah confirm the importance of emotional life in children's learning, and children's learning in affecting their emotional lives.

Our results in working with such children lead us to believe that learning in general and, at least, the pragmatic features of language acquisition in particular, involve the social and emotional environment of the child. Moreover, there is a strong interconnection between competencies (social, emotional, cognitive) and that this interconnectedness may change as a function of ontogeny—the younger the child, the greater the interrelatedness (see also Lewis & Cherry, 1977). The implication for education and curriculum development is broad. It is necessary for us to understand and consider these dimensions and their relatedness in the life of the child. Only through an understanding of the complex nature of feelings, and thinking about feelings as they impact on learning, can we create the optimal learning environment for children.

ACKNOWLEDGMENTS

This research was supported in part by a Grant from the W. T. Grant Foundation. Reprint request should be sent to Michael Lewis, Institute for the Study of Child Development, UMDNJ-Robert Wood Johnson Medical School, One Robert Wood Johnson Place, CN19, New Brunswick, NJ 08903-0019.

REFERENCES

Amsterdam, B. K. (1972). Mirror self image reactions before age two. *Developmental Psychology, 5,* 297–305.

Bertenthal, F. I. & Fischer, K. W. (1978). The development of self-recognition in the infant. *Developmental Psychology, 11,* 44–50.

Brown, C. (1971). *Manchild in the promised land.* New York: Signet.

Buss, A. H. (1980). *Self-consciousness and social anxiety.* San Francisco, CA: W. H. Freeman.

Cannon, W. B. (1927). The James-Lange theory of emotion: A critical examination and an alternative theory. *American Journal of Psychology, 39,* 106–124.

Cannon, W. B. (1929). *Bodily changes in pain, hunger, fear, and rage.* New York: Appleton.

Darwin, C. (1965/1872). *The expression of emotion in animals and man.* Chicago: University of Chicago Press. (Original work published 1872)

Dennett, D. C. (1979). *Brainstorms.* Cambridge, MA: MIT Press.

Eibl-Eibesfeldt, I. (1970). *Ethology: The biology of behavior.* New York: Holt, Rinehart & Winston.

Ekman, P. (1972). Universal and cultural differences in facial expression of emotion. In J. R. Cole (Ed.), *Nebraska symposium on motivation* (pp. 237–274). Lincoln: University of Nebraska Press.

Ekman, P. (1973a). Cross-cultural studies of facial expression. In P. Ekman (Ed.), *Darwin and facial expression* (pp. 185–202). New York: Academic Press.

Ekman, P. (Ed.). (1973b). *Darwin and facial expression: A century of research in review.* New York: Academic Press.

Ekman, P., Friesen, W. V., & Ellsworth, P. (1972). *Emotion in the human face: Guidelines for research and an integration of findings.* New York: Pergamon Press.

Freud, S. (1949). *Repression.* In S. Freud, (Ed.), *Collected Papers* (Vol. 3). London: Hogarth. (Original work published 1915)

Gibson, J. J. (1960). The concept of the stimulus in psychology. *American Psychologist, 15,* 694–703.

Hinde, R. A. (1979). *Towards understanding relationships.* London: Academic Press.

Hoffman, M. L. (1978). Toward a theory of empathic arousal and development. In M. Lewis & L. A. Rosenblum (Eds.), *The development of affect* (pp. 227–256). New York: Plenum.

Izard, C. E. (1977). *Human emotions.* New York: Plenum.

James. W. (1884). What is emotion? *Mind, 19,* 188–205.

Jaynes, J. (1977). *The origin of consciousness in the breakdown of the bicameral mind.* Boston: Houghton Mifflin.

Laing, R. D. (1970). *Knots.* New York: Pantheon.

Lewis, M. (1984). Social influences in development. In M. Lewis (Ed.), *Beyond the dyad: The genesis of behavior* (Vol. 4, pp. 1–12). New York: Plenum.

Lewis, M. (1985). Social, emotional and cognitive development: Complex models involving the self. In E. McDonald & D. Gallagher (Eds.), *Facilitating social-emotional development in multiply handicapped children* (pp. 53–69). Philadelphia: Home of the Merciful Saviour for Crippled Children.

Lewis, M., & Brooks-Gunn, J. (1979a). *Social cognition and the acquisition of self.* New York: Plenum.

Lewis, M., & Brooks-Gunn, J. (1979b). Toward a theory of social cognition: The development of self. In I. Uzgiris (Ed.), *New directions in child development: Social interaction and communication in infancy* (pp 1–20). San Francisco, CA: Jossey-Bass.

Lewis, M., Brooks-Gunn, J., & Jaskir, J. (1985). Individual differences in visual self recognition as a function of mother-infant attachment relationship. *Developmental Psychology, 21,* 1181–1187.

Lewis, M., & Cherry, L. (1977). Social behavior and language acquisition. In M. Lewis & L. Rosenblum (Eds.), *Interaction, conversation, and the development of language: The origins of behavior, 5.* New York: Wiley.

Lewis, M., & Michalson, L. (1982a, June). *From emotional state to emotional expression.* Paper presented at the Symposium on Human Development from the Perspective of Person and Environment Interactions. University of Stockholm, Stockholm, Sweden.

Lewis, M., & Michalson, L. (1982b). The measurement of emotional state. In C. E. Izard (Ed.), *Measuring emotions in infants and children* (pp. 178–207). New York: Cambridge University Press.

Lewis, M., & Michalson, L. (1982c). The socialization of emotions. In T. Field & A. Fogel (Eds.), *Emotion and early interactions* (pp. 189–212). Hillsdale, NJ: Lawrence Erlbaum Associates.

Lewis, M., & Michalson, L. (1983a). From emotional state to emotional expression: Emotional development from a person-environment interaction perspective. In D. Magnusson & V. L. Allen (Eds.), *Human development: An interactional perspective* (pp. 261–275). New York: Academic Press.

Lewis, M., & Michalson, L. (Eds.) (1983b). *Children's emotions and moods: Developmental theory and measurement.* New York: Plenum.

Lewis, M., & Michalson, L. (1984a). The socialization of emotional pathology in infancy. *Infant Mental Health Journal, 5,* 121–134.

Lewis, M., & Michalson, L. (1984b). Emotion without feeling? Feeling without thinking? *Contemporary Psychology, 29,* 457–459.

Lewis, M., & Michalson, L. (1985). Faces as signs and symbols. In G. Zivin (Ed.), *Develop-

ment of expressive behavior: Biology-environmental interaction (pp. 153–182). New York: Academic Press.

Lewis, M., & Rosenblum, L. (1978). Issues in affect development. In M. Lewis & L. Rosenblum (Eds.), *The development of affect: The genesis of behavior* (Vol. 1, pp. 1–10). New York: Plenum.

Lewis, M., Sullivan, M. W., & Michalson, L. (1984). The cognitive-emotional fugue. In T. E. Izard, J. Kagan, & R. B. Zajonc (Eds.), *Emotions, cognition and behavior* (pp. 264–288). London: Cambridge University Press.

Lewis, M., Sullivan, M. W., Stanger, C., & Weiss, M. (1989). Self-development and self-conscious emotions. *Child Development, 60,* 146–156.

Lewis, M., Sullivan, M. W., Weiss, M., & Stanger, C. (1987). Self-development and self-conscious emotions. *Child Development.*

Lewis, M., & Weinraub, M. (1979). Origins of early sex-role development. *Sex Roles, 5,* 135–153.

Mahler, M. S., Pine, F., & Gerbman, A. (1975). *The psychological birth of the infant.* New York: Basic Books.

Olds, M. E., & Fobes, J. L. (1981). The central basis of motivation: Intracranial self-stimulation studies. *Annual Review of Psychology, 32,* 523–576.

Piaget, J. (1954). *The origins of intelligence in children.* (M. Cook, Trans.). New York: Norton.

Plutchik, R. (1980a). *Emotion: A psychoevolutionary synthesis.* New York: Harper & Row.

Plutchik, R. (1980b). A general psychoevolutionary theory of emotion. In R. Plutchik & H. Kellerman (Eds.), *Emotion: Theory, research, and experience* (pp. 1–40). New York: Academic Press.

Stern, D. N. (1985). Affect attunement. In J. D. Call, E. Galenson, & R. L. Tyson (Eds.), *Frontiers of infant psychiatry* (Vol. 2). New York: Basic Books.

Stipek, D. J. (1983). A developmental analysis of pride and shame. *Human Development, 26,* 42–54.

Sullivan, H. S. (1953). *The interpersonal theory of psychiatry.* New York: Norton.

Tomkins, S. (1962). *Affect, imagery, and consciousness: Vol. 1. The positive affects.* New York: Springer.

Watson, J. B. (1934). *Psychology from the standpoint of a behaviorist* (4th ed.). Philadelphia: Lippincott.

Wegner, M. A., Jones, F. N., & Jones, M. H. (1956). *Physiological psychology.* New York: Holt.

Werner, H. (1957). *Comparative psychology of mental development.* Chicago: Follet.

Zajonc, R. B. (1980). Feeling and thinking: Preferences need no inferences. *American Psychologists, 35,* 151–175.

Zajonc, R. B. (1984). On the primary affect. *American Psychologist, 39,* 117–123.

PART II

PROGRAMS TO PROMOTE COGNITIVE GROWTH AND PROGRAMMATIC ISSUES

[T]o the degree in which childhood education is thought of as endowed with its own genuine form of activity, and the development of mind as being included within that activity's dynamic, the relation between the subjects to be educated and society becomes reciprocal: the child no longer tends to approach the state of adulthood by receiving reason and the rules of right action ready-made, but by achieving them with his own effort and personal experience; in return, society expects more of its new generations than mere imitation: it expects enrichment.

—Piaget, Jean. (1970). *Science of education and the psychology of the child.* New York: Orion Press.

In the first chapter (6) in part 2, Feuerstein and Hoffman explain the theory of cognitive modifiability. One of the key components of the theory is the concept of mediated learning. Through the mediation of another person, such as a teacher, children develop new constructs and acquire new skills including the metacognitive self-control type. Instrumental Enrichment (IE) was developed for the express purpose of facilitating development by replacing deficient cognitive functions with effective new ones through use of material unrelated to the regular curriculum. Feuerstein's original purpose was to help teenage students who were retarded in mental functioning acquire the prerequisites to thinking. The learning experiences, which, for example, may involve temporal or spatial relations, are typically given under the close

111

guidance of a teacher trained to lead the students to higher level cognitive and metacognitive functioning. The objective is for these young people to develop self-confidence, improved self-esteem, and a greater degree of independence as a result of substantial advances in their ability to think and solve problems.

Some of those same objectives were shared by Gruber and Richard (chap. 7) in working with university students. After reviewing recent studies of highly creative people, Gruber and Richard examined the complex issues associated with the dilemma between the injunction to learn, and thus acquire the heritage of the past, and the injunction to think, and thus keep that heritage alive by infusing it with fresh ideas. Their research was conducted in universities where, in attempting to replace age-old teaching practices, they contended with academic mine fields. Those are presumably unavoidable whenever educators at any level, with children or adults, add to their goals for a course the enhancement of reflecting, creating, or any other cognitive process, including the metacognitive activity of reflecting on a particular process. In their case the mine-field took the form of how to "cover" adequately the material in a course and at the same time give equal attention to cultivating the thinking capacities of their students in Newark, New Jersey and Geneva, Switzerland.

Quality of teaching ranks high in Feuerstein's work with adolescents, Gruber and Richard's with university students, and no less so for Haywood and Brooks (chap. 8) with preschool children. Some who are skeptical about cognitive education question that teachers can actually carry out a program of instruction based on cognitive theory. They doubt that teachers as a rule possess the interest in and capacity to master theory for purposes of application. Haywood and Brooks argue that widespread beliefs about teachers in relationship to theory are erroneous. So too, they say, are claims that tend to underrate the usefulness or appropriateness of theory in the construction of curricula. They believe that to produce effective educational outcomes, programs must be rooted in theory, and teachers' involvement is essential, among other reasons because their unique frame of reference gives a different perspective when evaluating and revising a program. They applied their beliefs in connection with deriving, developing, and refining the Cognitive Curriculum for Young children.

Probably the most challenging task in promoting cognitive development is in attempting to transform a whole school system. That was the long-term objective in Ghent, Belgium. Starting with children of preschool and early grades, De Coster, De Meyer and Parmentier (chap. 9) found first that compensatory, add-on types of programs for educationally disadvantaged children did not suffice. Whatever changes they may have produced were temporary in duration and not generalized to other course content. Only by changing the objectives and methods of the regular school program and the practices of the teachers were worthwhile modifications achieved. Teachers and children were encouraged to be more aware of their behavior and achieve more control over it, in brief, to acquire metacognitive practices. For example, observations showed that problems in reading were rooted in such prerequisite skills as listening, remembering, analyzing, and synthesizing. Consequently, instead of following the usual instructional plan, experiences were designed to help children build and strengthen each of these skills, which were evaluated and further strengthened, if need be even before the children were introduced to reading. From their many years of experience, the authors share their impressions of what is essential to influence cognitive growth through the school curriculum.

This book bears the happy news that some attention is being given to making cognitive development one of the objectives of education in the life span. It also gives one the sober realization that we are at the infant stage of knowing what to do and how to do it. To deepen our understanding of cognitive development, Kagan (chap. 10) proposes that we free ourselves of some conceptual shackles. We know how to use thought but we don't understand it. Considering that an attempt to understand it is as formidable a problem as making sense of the origin of the universe, and that we have been involved in studying cognition for less than a century, it is not surprising that inquiry should be handicapped because it is still subject to untested presuppositions and handicapped by use of constructs that are not data based. That may be why the terminology of the science, like "knowledge" and "thought," are part of everyday vocabulary and limited in their usefulness in describing phenomena. The vocabulary in use is reflective of the thinking that is employed. If biology were to serve as a guide, the study of cognition and its development would be subject to more rigorous interpretations of data. It would also very likely open up psychologists to new concepts.

Chapter 6

MEDIATING COGNITIVE PROCESSES TO THE RETARDED PERFORMER – RATIONALE, GOALS, AND NATURE OF INTERVENTION

Reuven Feuerstein
Bar Ilan University, Ramat Gan
Director, Hadassah-Wizo-Canada Research Institute, Jerusalem

Mildred B. Hoffman*
Hadassah-Wizo-Canada Research Institute, Jerusalem

STRUCTURAL COGNITIVE MODIFIABILITY

The theory of Structural Cognitive Modifiability (SCM) argues that it is indeed possible to enhance and modify human intelligence. We view intelligence as the capacity to use previous experience to adapt to new situations more efficiently. We believe that the modifiability of the learning capacity, that is, an increase in the disposition toward learning to learn, is a basic characteristic of the human organism. Human cognitive modifiability has a structural nature, which can be defined by the three major characteristics of "structure" within a constructivist framework:

1. Part-whole cohesiveness: changes in a part will affect the whole to which it belongs.
2. Transformability: the process of change is itself subject to changes (e.g., in efficiency, rapidity, precision, conditions facilitating change).
3. Self-perpetuation and autoregulation of transformation: once change is introduced through external determinants, it will perpetuate itself in accordance with the self-regulatory rules of the structure.

Conceptual Framework

The theory of Structural Cognitive Modifiability and its emergent practices of assessment and intervention are firmly based on three major conceptual

*See Acknowledgments

frameworks. The first, and certainly the most important, is the theory of Mediated Learning Experience (MLE). MLE serves as an explicative system for the basic assumption of SCM and determines the principles, rules, and guidelines for constructing the types of interactions that will enhance modifiability.

The second major conceptual framework is provided by the description of a set of deficient cognitive functions in input, elaboration, and output, thought to be responsible for the failure of the low-functioning person to benefit from formal and informal learning opportunities (see Table 6.1) This failure is manifested in highly diverse situations: work or school activities, street culture, and even in antisocial delinquent behavior. The cognitive functions serve as prerequisites of thinking; and their deficiency hampers learning capacity either globally or in certain selected areas, depending on the nature of the stimuli, task requirements, and the locus of an individual's most marked deficiencies.

The third conceptual framework guiding the construction and application of an intervention program for SCM, Instrumental Enrichment (to which this chapter is largely devoted), is the cognitive map. The cognitive map represents an analysis of the task to be accomplished, or the problem to be ͜ͅlved. This analysis is guided by seven parameters:

1. Content;
2. Language;
3. Phase of mental act (input, elaboration or output);
4. Type of cognitive operation;
5. Level of complexity;
6. Level of abstraction;
7. Level of efficiency required by the task for successful mastery.

Mediated Learning Experience

The theory of SCM or MLE suggests the possible determinant or cause of the postulated modifiability of the human being (Feuerstein, 1977; Feuerstein & Rand, 1974). MLE is also a source of insight and guidance in the ways by which modifiability can be produced and increased in some individuals or reduced in others.

The Stimulus–Human Mediator–Organism–Human Mediator–Response (S-(H)-O-(H)-R) model implies the existence of two modalities of organism–world interaction: the interaction through direct exposure to stimuli and their active manipulation, and the Mediated Learning Experience (MLE). MLE interactions are considerably less pervasive, stretch over relatively brief periods of time and, if normal, usually include only a fragment of an individual's dialogue with outer- and inner-experienced reality. It is MLE

Input Level
1. Blurred and sweeping perception
2. Unplanned, impulsive, and unsystematic exploratory behavior
3. Lack of, or impaired, receptive verbal tools which affect discrimination (e.g., objects, events, relationships, etc., do not have appropriate labels)
4. Lack of, or impaired, spatial orientation; the lack of stable systems of reference impairs the establishment of topological and Euclidean organization of space
5. Lack of, or impaired, temporal concepts
6. Lack of, or impaired, conservation of constancies (size, shape, quantity, orientation) across variation in these factors
7. Lack of, or deficient need for, precision and accuracy in data gathering
8. Lack of capacity for considering two or more sources of information at once; this is reflected in dealing with data in a piecemeal fashion rather than as a unit of organized facts

Elaborational Level
1. Inadequacy in the perception of the existence and definition of an actual problem
2. Inability to select relevant vs. non-relevant cues in defining a problem
3. Lack of spontaneous comparative behavior or limitation of its application by a restricted need system
4. Narrowness of the mental field
5. Episodic grasp of reality
6. Lack of, or impaired, need for pursuing logical evidence
7. Lack of, or impaired, interiorization
8. Lack of, or impaired, inferential-hypothetical, 'iffy' thinking
9. Lack of, or impaired, strategies for hypothesis testing
10. Lack of, or impaired, ability to define the framework necessary for problem solving behavior
11. Lack of, or impaired, planning behavior
12. Non-elaboration of certain cognitive categories because the verbal concepts are not a part of the individual's verbal inventory (on a receptive level) or they are not mobilized at the expressive level

Output Level
1. Egocentric communicational modalities
2. Difficulties in projecting virtual relationships
3. Blocking
4. Trial-and-error responses
5. Lack of, or impaired, verbal tools for communicating adequately elaborated responses
6. Lack of, or impaired, need for precision and accuracy in communicating one's response
7. Deficiency of visual transport
8. Impulsive, acting-out behavior

that lends the human organism its flexibility, plasticity, and the tremendous capacity to become affected in critical areas by direct exposure to stimuli.

In MLE (see Fig. 6.1), it is the mediator(H)s, interposing themselves between the stimuli and the organism, who determine the nature of the stimulus by selecting it from a multitude of stimuli available to the individual. The stimulus is filtered, amplified, scheduled, and transformed according to the specific culturally determined needs of the mediator.

The stimulus and response in the MLE type of interaction differ radically from those experienced in a random, direct way. In addition to what the experience itself offers and the traces it leaves on the cognitive system of an individual, the MLE interactive event creates dispositions, orientations, and modes of functioning by which incoming stimuli can be organized. The need to understand and interpret the experience by relating events to each other results in categorically conceptualized relations that are ultimately applied whenever new stimuli are directly encountered. The MLE thus renders the individual penetrable by and modifiable through new experiences.

Lacking MLE, the individual will eventually adapt to events that have become familiar through overlearning or through their strong relationship to some immediate elementary needs. However, any change in the situation will require a totally new start as if nothing in the changed situation has ever been experienced and as if no relationship exists between the two experiences. And indeed, no relationship does exist between the two experiences unless it has been established through a volitional, conscious, and well-defined act.

MLE represents the quality of an interaction rather than its content. It is not what is going on between the two partners in the interaction, but rather how it is taking place. MLE can occur through any type of task or any kind of physical, motor, or mental activity; it will always have the previously described formative effect on the mediatee. MLE is also not contingent on

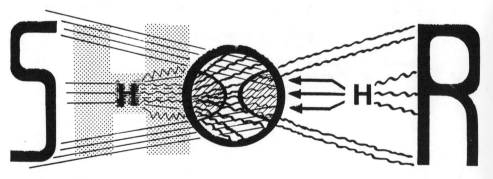

FIG. 6.1   Mediated learning experience model (MLE)

a particular language or modality of communication. This contention provides theoretical support for the quasi nonverbal, relatively content-free approach of the intervention program derived from the SCM theory: Instrumental Enrichment.

Criteria of Mediated Learning Experience

If it is neither content nor language, what then is MLE? The nature of MLE is best described by the following 11 criteria. They are as follows: Intentionality and reciprocity; transcendence; mediation of meaning; mediation of a feeling of competence; mediated regulation and control of behavior; mediated sharing behavior; mediated individuation and psychological differentiation; mediation of goal seeking, goal setting, and goal planning and achieving behavior; mediation of challenge: the search for novelty and complexity; mediation of an awareness of the human as a changing entity; and mediation of an optimistic alternative.

The first three criteria—intentionality (i.e., awareness of purpose), transcendence (i.e., transcending immediate experience), and mediation of meaning—are considered universal and are therefore necessary conditions for MLE interactions. They are responsible for the most common and characteristic trait of humans: structural modifiability. The other eight parameters of MLE are situationally, culturally, and experientially determined. In contrast with the first three, they are responsible for the diversity individuals and groups manifest in their modifiability, for the different areas of interest, motivation, cognitive styles, and specialization of skills.

Direct exposure to stimuli on the one hand and MLE, on the other, the two modalities of interaction, are directly responsible for structural cognitive modifiability. They account for the great diversity in human cognitive behavior, which is due to the many variations they bring into human–environment interactions. The plasticity they produce limits drastically the predictability of human development. Predictability, one of the major goals of psychology as a science, is even more limited and restricted once a purposeful theoretically guided and technically powerful intervention is instituted. This intervention should capitalize on what is known to be the determinant of cognitive modifiability and should be introduced as a phase-specific educational system. Education, unlike psychology, is not interested in predictions. Education must actively act against predictability by introducing those variations in the environment that will render individuals modifiable to the extent that their course of life will go in different directions from those predicted.

Structural changes are conceived of as the product of MLE interactions. Such changes are accessible to a broad and large group of individuals in need and are not limited (as postulated by other theoretical frameworks) to those who are genetically endowed with "the capacity to learn." Structural change is also considered accessible to individuals suffering from conditions usually described as hopeless so far as cognitive modification is concerned and who are consequently deemed ineligible for programs that have structural changes as goals. Modifiability is considered possible in human beings regardless of their age, stage of development, or the etiology of their condition and its degree of severity.

Furthermore, MLE is considered responsible for the constant widening of the need systems, the spheres of interest, types of motivation, and emotional/affective modalities of expression. The cognitive-affective impact of MLE goes beyond the manifest level of functioning and becomes established as a way by which culture shapes individuals and simultaneously is shaped itself.

Deficient Cognitive Functions and the Cognitive Map

Whereas the deficient cognitive functions describe the determinants of failure in an individual, the cognitive map describes the characteristics of the task that are responsible for the individual's failure to adapt to new situations. The explicative value of the cognitive map, and its meaning as a guide to where the most effort should be expended in order to better affect the individual, make it a powerful conceptual tool in the choices of means and ways for the construction and application of the intervention program.

The deficient cognitive functions and the cognitive map also explain the great diversity among individuals in the areas of their dysfunction, a diversity that is all too often obscured by the conventional monolithic psychometric and academic criteria used in assessment. Despite the diversity of success and failure in terms of its nature (as explained by the cognitive map) and its severity (as explained by both the cognitive map and the deficient cognitive functions), the common element shared by all retarded and dysfunctioning performers is a lack of or reduced modifiability when they are confronted with new situations they must learn and therefore adapt. It is this structural characteristic that distinguishes the culturally different from the culturally deprived, who manifest the same difficulty. (By "cultural difference" we mean individuals possess the products of their culture but not those of the dominant mainstream culture. By "cultural deprivation" we mean a condition resulting from insufficient mediation: the products of individuals' culture have not been transmitted to them.) The culturally different person learns and adapts, whereas the culturally deprived often does not learn and does not adapt, at least not without very meaningful help. This phenomenon can be explained by the fact that culturally different persons have been exposed to a culture that they have learned and that, in turn, has produced in them a readiness to learn, whereas the culturally deprived have been deprived of mediated learning experiences and thereby suffer from a lack of the transmission of their own culture.

APPLIED SYSTEM: LEARNING POTENTIAL ASSESSMENT DEVICE

The theory of Structural Cognitive Modifiability and its emergent theory of Mediated Learning Experience (MLE) have given rise to three major applied systems: the Learning Potential Assessment Device (LPAD), Instrumental Enrichment (IE), and shaping, modifying environments.

The Learning Potential Assessment Device is a dynamic assessment procedure whose major goal is to determine the nature and extent of change that can be produced in an individual, and the most favorable conditions for producing such changes. Through a test–teach (mediate)–test procedure, the LPAD determines the extent to which new structures can be established in the individual and assesses the effects of the new structures on the totality of the individual's behavior. It is nonpredictive and does not attempt to measure, but instead yields a profile of the individual's propensity for change.

The LPAD differs from static assessment procedures by changing the nature of the test instruments, changing the nature of the test situation, by moving from a product to a process orientation, and in its interpretation of the results of assessment.

LPAD tasks are oriented towards higher mental processes and address fluid rather than crystallized modes of thinking. They are ordered so as to permit the detection and registration of the most minimal changes in the cognitive structure of the examinee. Tasks are constructed so as to permit MLE to take place. The neutral examiner–examinee relationship that exists in static tests has been changed to one of teacher (mediator)–student (mediatee) in which examiners are vitally concerned with helping their student understand and succeed through active intervention. The individual's cognitive deficiencies will indicate the targets for intervention whereas the cognitive map will pinpoint the areas of difficulty requiring mediation. Mediation does not exceed the child's need to achieve and need for assistance.

A process, rather than a product orientation guides the selection of the content and organization of the mediational interventions. The emphasis is on determining the reasons for the individual's successes and failures and on describing them in terms of the nature, intensity, and quantity of intervention necessary for attaining structural changes. The LPAD deals with assessment rather than measurement, thus its results are expressed in terms of a profile of modifiability. Attention is paid to the domains of change, the quality of change, and the amount and nature of the intervention necessary to achieve the desired modifiability.

MLE Versus Social Interaction Theory of Vygotsky

LPAD, with its MLE interactions, is based on a theory that differs meaningfully from other theories dealing with the influence of the adult on the cognitive development of the child. For example, Vygotsky's social interactions are heavily laden with linguistic and other content, whereas MLE is neither contingent on content nor language, but is rather oriented to the quality of interactions. It is the mediated quality of the interaction that creates in the child a set of dispositions that enhance further learning and development. Partly because of its clinical and experimental origins, the MLE has been described and operationalized in a way that endows parents, teachers, and caregivers with the necessary criteria that can then be applied in a great diversity of content, life situations, and stages of development.

In the Vygotskian theory, there is a certain degree of limitation to the child's potential development. The Zone of Proximal Development is described by Vygotsky as the distance between the actual development level as determined by independent problem solving and the level of potential development as determined through problem solving under adult guidance or in collaboration with more capable peers. "The possibilities of the (child's) intellectual potential are not limitless, but change in a strictly lawful manner in accordance with the course of his mental development such that at each age-stage there exists within the child a definite zone of intellectual development connected with his actual level of development" (1984, p. 263). Thus, in Vygotsky's zone of proximal development, the potential seems to be there, with elements that are limited and quantifiable. Structures in the zone of proximal development emerge, develop, or are elaborated through adult intervention and the child's imitation of the adult behavior. With MLE, on the other hand, by sensitizing the individual, we not only develop and elaborate existent structures, but we actually produce them.

We deeply regret that Vygotsky was unable to capitalize on the large body of theoretical work that he had done and go on to develop an operationalized system of interactions. There is no doubt that there would certainly be a great deal of convergence between our theory of MLE and Vygotsky's theory of social interaction.

INSTRUMENTAL ENRICHMENT

What is the nature of a program whose goal is to produce new cognitive structures in the individual? Can such a program be offered to populations that are usually considered as inaccessible and therefore as ineligible for such an intervention? The Instrumental Enrichment (IE) program is presented as a paradigm of an applied system shaped and continuously guided in its various implementations by the theory that has engendered it. Instrumental Enrichment consists of about 350 pages of paper/pencil exercises distributed to the student page by page. Lessons take place in classrooms or individual tutorial settings 3 to 5 times weekly for a period of 2 to 3 years. The teacher specially trained to teach IE should preferably also teach other subject matter to the IE students, in order to insure the bridging of the modes of thinking and strategies acquired through IE to areas of curriculum and academic functioning.

Goals of Intervention

The goals of intervention, based on the theory of SCM, transcend the immediate manifest behavior and reach out to those components of human functioning that increase its flexibility and modifiability. These goals ensure that each encounter of the individual with external or internal stimuli will produce the type of changes we call learning. To a certain degree, the goals of such intervention can be seen as the necessary condition for the process of assimilation and accomodation described by Piaget as the basis for the development of intelligence and cognitive processes. Intervention produces the flexibility of the schemata that become enlarged and developed by the process of assimilation and accommodation. Once this flexibility is produced, changes in the organism become possible through direct exposure to stimuli, irrespective of their nature, content, or meaning.

Nature of Instrumental Enrichment

The declared overall goal of this program, consistent with the theory of SCM, is to increase the modifiability of the individual so that he/she will become able to achieve greater benefit from exposure to formal and informal opportunities for learning. Formulated in more familiar terms: the goal of this program is to make the individual able to learn and hence to be modified by stimuli wherever and whenever such opportunities present themselves.

What are the inherent characteristics of an intervention program that aims at this goal? Can such a goal be accomplished as the sole byproduct of activities oriented toward other goals, such as learning basic school skills or subject matter such as math, history, and so forth? This is indeed one of the questions that are often asked by those involved with the construction or the choice of intervention programs. Should the development of intelligence be directly attacked by a specially designed program that is applied in a distinctive way, or is it better to integrate the active components of the cognitive training program into other subject matter and instructional units that are taught by regular teachers?

The six subgoals of the program, by which the primary goal is achieved are, as follows: (a) To correct the deficient cognitive functions that are the result of inadequate and insufficient early mediated learning experiences; (b) to help the student acquire the concepts, vocabulary, operations and relationships, strategies, and skills necessary to complete the tasks; (c) to produce intrinsic motivation through the formation of habits. New strategies, operations and principles are consolidated and internalized so that they are used as a result of an internal need to do so; (d) to foster and create learners' insights into the reasons for their success or failure and the nature and utility of the various processes and strategies; (e) to create task-intrinsic motivation in which the reward for the successful completion of a task is being given another; and (f) to change students' perceptions of themselves from that of being a passive recipient of information to that of being an active generator of new information.

Instrumental Enrichment is an intervention program designed for a direct, specialized attack on those deficient functions considered responsible for individuals' limited capacity to be affected by the learning process to which they are exposed (see Table 6.1) Instrumental Enrichment therefore makes very little use of curriculum-oriented informational content. It is content-free in the sense that the content that is used for teaching cognitive functions has solely a secondary value; it only serves as a carrier for the techniques and didactics oriented toward the development of thinking processes. Thus, for example, organizing amorphous clouds of dots has very little to do with the subjects to which children or adults are usually exposed in school or in life. The same is true for tasks included in instruments such as Comparisons, Family Relations, and Representational Stencil Design in which there is no real content that must be learned. (See Fig. 6.2).

The question then must be: why not use real-life situations or the tasks required by school in order to develop aptitudes and capacities? Some of the reasons for the decision to use a content-free approach in shaping the IE program are as follows:

Content-free Approach

A program designed to increase the modifiability of low-functioning retarded performers must address, first and foremost, the prerequisites of thinking and those cognitive functions common to all mental acts, rather than a restricted set of specialized mental activities and operations that become too strongly associated with one or another particular task. All too often it is taken for granted that these 'elementary" cognitive functions, the prerequisites of thinking, exist and are equally efficient in all individuals. Thus, the failure to perform is usually not attributed to deficient functions, but to the inexistence or the deficiency of a given operatior. Piaget, for example, seldom interpreted the lack of conservation of matter or volume as being due to blurred perception, or to a lack of the use of two or more sources of information or to a lack of comparative behavior, but has attributed it, rather, to the immaturity of a cognitive system that does not include the reversibility necessary for the concept of conservation.

In contrast, Instrumental Enrichment stresses the role played by these discrete prerequisites of thinking and sets out to correct deficient cognitive functions on the input, elaboration, and output levels in a larger universe of contents, modalities, and mental activities. Any attempt to anchor the correction or development of the required cognitive function too strongly to a particular content may result in isolating this unit of content from the whole universe of contents to which it belongs. By this isolation, one of the most important characteristics of structural change will be abolished or weakened: namely, the part–whole cohesiveness. It is this cohesiveness that is responsible for the generalizability of the changes achieved in the individual's functioning to other tasks and modalities of functioning.

A second reason for the content-free nature of the program is the need to make it accessible to a variety of learners, irrespective of their degree of familiarity, interest, and motivation with one particular content. The formal aspects of cognitive functioning on the input, elaboration, and output levels, acquired through the IE exercises, are applied paradigmatically during the mediational phase of the learning. The teacher incites the learner to transcend the immediate tasks and apply the acquired learning to situations that are more remote, albeit still relevant to the universe of knowledge and the required mental acts. Instrumental Enrichment is never taught by itself, but always parallels a regular curriculum. By the same token, the program is never taught as part and parcel of the content curriculum. IE represents one shore of the stream of learning that parallels the shore of the regular curriculum; the mediational intervention of the initiated and intentioned teacher constructs a bridge between the two shores of IE and curricular learning. The content-free nature of the exercises makes it much easier to use their prerequisite components universally in other contexts than when they must be detached from all-too-specific content prior to their application to a new context.

Curriculum Independence

Basic prerequisites are best acquired in a content-free and curriculum-independent program. Any attempt to use specific content for the acquisi-

INSTRUMENTAL ENRICHMENT

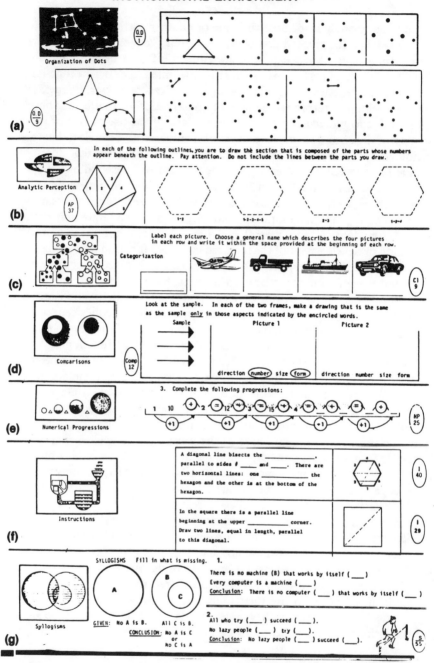

FIG. 6.2. Symbol and sample of: (a) Organization of Dots; (b) Analytic Perception; (c) Categorization; (d) Comparisons; (e) Numerical Progessions; (f) Insructions; (g) Syllogisms; (h) Orientation in Space I; (i) Orientation in

126

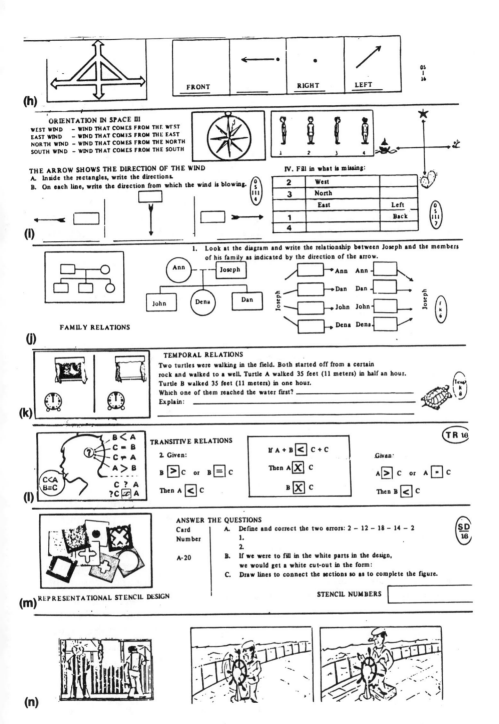

(h)

FRONT · RIGHT · LEFT ↗

ORIENTATION IN SPACE III

WEST WIND – WIND THAT COMES FROM THE WEST
EAST WIND – WIND THAT COMES FROM THE EAST
NORTH WIND – WIND THAT COMES FROM THE NORTH
SOUTH WIND – WIND THAT COMES FROM THE SOUTH

THE ARROW SHOWS THE DIRECTION OF THE WIND
A. Inside the rectangles, write the directions.
B. On each line, write the direction from which the wind is blowing.

IV. Fill in what is missing:

2	West	
3	North	
	East	Left
1		Back
4		

(i)

1. Look at the diagram and write the relationship between Joseph and the members of his family as indicated by the direction of the arrow.

Ann --- Joseph

John   Dena   Dan

Ann → Ann -
Dan → Dan -
John → John -
Dena → Dena -

FAMILY RELATIONS

(j)

TEMPORAL RELATIONS

Two turtles were walking in the field. Both started off from a certain rock and walked to a well. Turtle A walked 35 feet (11 meters) in half an hour. Turtle B walked 35 feet (11 meters) in one hour. Which one of them reached the water first? _____
Explain: _____

(k)

TRANSITIVE RELATIONS

B < A
C = B
C ≠ A
A > B

C < A
B = C
?C ⇄ A

2. Given:

B $>$ C or B $=$ C

Then A $<$ C

If A + B $<$ C + C

Then A $\boxed{X}$ C

B $\boxed{X}$ C

Given:

A $>$ C or A $·$ C

Then B $<$ C

(l)

ANSWER THE QUESTIONS

Card Number

A-20

A. Define and correct the two errors: 2 – 12 – 18 – 14 – 2
1.
2.

B. If we were to fill in the white parts in the design, we would get a white cut-out in the form:

C. Draw lines to connect the sections so as to complete the figure.

STENCIL NUMBERS

(m) REPRESENTATIONAL STENCIL DESIGN

(n)

Space II; (j) Family Relations; (k) Temporal Relations; (l) Transitive Relations; (m) Representational Stencil Design; (n) Illustrations.

tion of basic prerequisites will be met with a number of resistances. Students will resist the attempt to extract the formal prerequisites of thinking from the learned materials. They may display a materialistic attitude toward the studied subjects. They hate to learn and talk about; they want to deal with the thing proper. They express their resistance by tuning out each time they are asked to go beyond the stimuli or the event with which they are concerned. A second resistance is derived from the subject matter with which one attempts to modify cognitive processes. Subject matter such as mathematics, physics, history, or geography, have their own rationale, rhythm, and succession. Any attempt to impose the structure necessary for affecting the *learning capacity* of the individual on the subject matter may result in its dilution without really improving the thinking program's chances to fully develop all the ingredients necessary to become effective. By way of illustration: one of the subgoals of Instrumental Enrichment consists of correcting cognitive deficiencies on the input level (see Table 6.1). The IE program constructs tasks that require types of behavior such as gathering the data, using systematic precise accurate perception, and so forth, for mastery. Searching for such opportunities in subject matter may be totally superfluous or inappropriate to the particular structure of the subject matter.

Another example better illustrates the difficulties encountered when one attempts to impose the structure of the intervention program on subject matter. One of the subgoals of IE is to crystallize and automatize the acquired prerequisites of thinking so as to make their spontaneous adaptive use more probable and likely. Crystallization and automatization that lead to habit formation require overlearning through repeated encounters and reiterated operation and interaction. In order to escape the boredom and mechanization linked to reiterated responses to the same stimuli, IE has shaped the tasks so that their underlying rules and principles must be rediscovered while the tasks themselves are kept changed. The consolidation and crystallization will mostly affect the rules and the operations that are kept constant; the variation in certain critical aspects of the tasks (based on the same principle and operations) will increase flexibility and adaptability once the individual is faced with new dimensions. This is probably the best way to create the structural conditions for generalization and transfer. It is superfluous to say that it is impossible to thus manipulate the subject matter to be taught, or that such manipulation, if attempted, will interfere with the natural flow and succession of the units of information in the specific content.

The third resistance encountered in the integration of cognitive training and the curriculum is from teachers. Their commitment to transmit information and train specific skills makes them jealous guardians of the time allotted to the mastery of the subject matter they teach. In addition, they are not trained either to identify the difficulties created by some specific cognitive deficiency, or even less, to correct these deficiencies. To believe that a teacher, even an excellent one, will be able to improvise strategies and techniques and apply them systematically so as to reach the goal of cognitive training is certainly an act of naivete that may prove to be damaging. The author himself was guilty of this naivete when, in order to improve the children's level of cognitive and conceptual functioning (Feuerstein, & Richelle 1963), he offered teachers of immigrant culturally deprived children a set of paradigms for shaping a powerful program for teaching a new language. It was only after shaping the IE program, which required years of development, that the author realized how unrealistic it had been to expect so much from teachers.

Characteristics of Tasks

Another reason for using content-free material lies in the theoretically determined nature of the tasks to be included in the program. The first characteristic of the tasks is their high level of complexity. This complexity is not only related to the number of units in the task, but also to the types of mental operations and cognitive functions that are needed in order to solve the problem. Thus, in Orientation in Space I (see Figure 6.2h), the task requires reading the instructions, choosing the indicated position, placing the boy in the given position in the field, relating to the instructions, determining the object in the field that relates to the chosen position and then deciding on the relationship between the boy and the object. Despite its simplicity, the learner must perform a number of steps in order to master the task. The cognitive processes involved are also numerous: tracing the trajectory of behaviors and their succession; perceiving and registering the stimulus and its defining traits (orientation); using a representational modality of functioning; and, what is important, mentally reorienting the object. All of these create types of behaviors that have affinities with many other tasks, both in school and non-school activities, and serve as their prerequisites.

Another characteristic of the program's tasks is their limited use of concrete operations. Representational, abstract, and inferential thinking are involved instead. The learner must use a large network of cognitive functions and operations in order to master the task and produce the answer. The emphasis on production, that is, the generation of information, rather than on reproduction, requires that the task be presented in an abstract, symbolic way. If content-oriented material were used for this end, it would have to be all too task-bound; too contingent on specialized information that the disadvantaged learner would be unlikely to possess and therefore, too difficult; and, finally, too dependent on a verbal modality of presentation. A verbal modality, used mainly in academic-oriented activities, must be a hoped-for product of intervention, and not a precondition for its application. Indeed, many programs that address themselves to complex molar units of learning make verbal proficiency a sine qua non for their mastery. The limited, controlled, and goal-oriented language used in the IE program has often been misinterpreted as fostering solely nonverbal intelligence. It aims, instead, at producing a meaningful, well-defined and operationally used language through the communicational interactions triggered by the program. These communicational interactions use the verbal concepts underlying each task and the mediational interactions in the didactics of the teacher–mediator, and amplify them largely in the IE classroom discussions.

In addition, curriculum material should not be used for cognitive training because so many of those who need such a program have preserved a deep sense of failure in many of the contents and skills of academic studies. The use of these traumatizing experiences for attaining the goal of redevelopment is not likely to be successful.

For all the aforementioned reasons, the preferred approach to the issue of development of intelligence, that is , the increase of the modifiability of low-functioning individuals, is to use a specially designed content-free intervention program that aims at producing new cognitive structures.

THE PROCESS OF INSTRUMENTAL ENRICHMENT

IE represents an attempt to reproduce the MLE process and products in vitro and in a phase-specific way. This is done by presenting the learner with tasks of relatively limited familiarity, which creates a need and readiness for MLE even among initiated intelligent adults. The lack of specific content or language makes IE strongly resemble the characteristics of MLE, whose three first principles can be (intentionality, transcendence, and mediation of meaning) can be applied everywhere irrespective of the content that elicits the interaction or the language in which the interaction is expressed. The transcendent nature of the IE exercises is stressed in the mediational phase of the IE lesson by the rich interaction of bridging from the exercises into a larger universe of past or anticipated experiences. Thus, the mental activity of the individual is oriented toward convergent and divergent creative thinking processes. Activities developed in the course of the IE learning are solidified, automatized, and crystallized through creative variations in the learned task repeated numerous times. Motivation is ensured through the mediation of meaning and insight as to the role the acquisition of the prerequisites of thinking may have or the adaptability of the learner to life and its requirements. The mental activities are structured so that their mastery will be accompanied by the learners' awareness of themselves as changing entities. They will see themselves as persons able to generate new information and new stimuli rather than as only the recipients, or, at best, the reproducers of ready-made knowledge.

Once persons acquire this self-image, their cognitive structure will benefit from new experiences in the direction of more efficient adaptation to new situations, bringing about a self-perpetuation of the growth initiated by the MLE-based IE program.

IMPLEMENTATION
OF INSTRUMENTAL ENRICHMENT

There are a number of questions regarding the use of IE that must be answered.

Is Instrumental Enrichment useful only for retarded performers? Some of those active in the field of critical thinking and development of intelligence do not agree that the program should be implemented only with those defined as in need of learning to learn. They claim that the gifted, above-average, and average individual can benefit from IE no less than the low-functioning, disabled, culturally deprived individual. Although originally intended for adolescents, there has been both a downward and upward extension in the use of IE. The program has been and is currently being used with university students in preparatory classes and with adults in factory and work-place sponsored programs.

Does IE stand on its own, or does it need other programs as an integral part of its structure? A review of the previous discussion will not only show how important it is to have IE as a part of a more holistic program, but how little meaning IE would have if opportunities for bridging to more immediate and direct areas of adaptation were not provided parallel to the program.

Should one consider IE as oriented solely toward the acquisition of prerequisites of thinking so that it may have to be followed by other, more content-oriented programs? We firmly believe that programs such as Sternberg's (1982), Harvard's Project Intelligence (in press) Philosophy for Children (Lipman, Sharp & Oscanyan, 1980), and CORT (deBono, 1983) are beneficial for a population in need after it has been prepared and rendered modifiable by the MLE type of program. Sensitized by IE, the educable mentally retarded, the organically disabled, the culturally deprived and others will be better able to benefit from other programs that may be considered too difficult for them prior to their exposure to IE. The IE program may make them accessible to the valuable dimensions of curriculum-oriented programs.

What is the optimal length and intensity of the program? The intensity necessary in order to make a program effective in modifying the cognitive structure of the low-functioning individual is an important area of concern. Restricted types of goals, such as training in specific skills or mental activities, are short-lived and of limited generalizability; they can be attained with short-term programs of low intensity. However, if one must achieve a change in the cognitive structure, the optimum length of program should be spread over a period of time (2 to 3 years) with an optimum intensity of three to five periods a week.

Should the tasks of an intervention program be culled from diverse areas? The greater the diversity of mental functions, modalities, languages, operations, and levels of abstraction, the higher the number of affinities with other academic and life types of tasks that are involved. Indeed, IE has introduced a relatively large number of different types of tasks involving various cognitive functions. These range from purely perceptual tasks that can be solved only with cognitive assistance (termed elsewhere by the author as cognitive crutches for a limping perception") to highly sophisticated tasks that require representational and inferential forms of thinking.

What is the role played by the teacher in the successful implementation of the program? Many among those concerned with intervention program effectiveness consider that a dependence on the quality of teaching is a considerable drawback. These are the chronic pessimists who believe that a teacher is not modifiable even though they may believe the opposite for students. One of the arguments against the teacher's centrality is based on the fact that teacher training is expensive; therefore, in constructing programs, it is felt that one should strive to render them teacher-resistant. In our opinion, this view is highly questionable. The MLE model does not support the notion that direct exposure to stimuli, be they rich and exciting, will affect dysfunctioning individuals who have a reduced level of modifiability. They need a mediator in order to render them sensitive, perceptive and active in registering, manipulating, and interpreting the stimuli to which they are exposed. The teacher must act as the mediator even in tasks specially prepared to develop thinking. Teacher training is not only necessary in order to have teachers master the tasks and the specialized didactics of the program, but also to equip them with the most important determinant of success: the belief that indeed the program is necessary, that it is possible and that the chosen way has a meaning to look for! The belief in the modifiability of the child is not complete unless one believes that the teacher who must accomplish the task is modifiable as well. Far from being considered a burden, the teacher training imposed by the program should be considered strictly necessary and a most positive condition for a program to bring a meaningful contribution.

EFFECTS OF INSTRUMENTAL ENRICHMENT

Have the claims of the theory of SCM and its applied techniques material-ized? Have they been supported by controlled research studies? Instru-mental Enrichment is one of the programs that has been most researched by its authors and other researchers and clinicians (Nickerson, 1984; Nicker-son, Perkins, & Smith, 1985; Savell, Twohig, & Rachford, 1986). The work done with large and varied groups of individuals has given encouraging, though not pervasively equal support to the claim for SCM. The structural nature of the produced changes has been substantiated most dramatically by our individual clinical work, but is receiving strong support in empirical experimental data. The effects observed on various groups of autistic, psychotic, borderline persons; children and young adults with Down's Syndrome; and persons with organically determined disabilities, have also been a source of insight into the role cognition plays in certain affective conditions, and the way these conditions can be affected by cognitive remediation.

The findings on larger groups have yielded positive results despite the difficulties of field research, as contrasted with laboratory research. The accuracy of evaluational methodology, all too often insensitive to qualita-tive changes produced in the individual, makes the positive results obtained in many of the studies even more meaningful.

IE has been evaluated extensively on a broad range of populations in many parts of the world over a period of more than 15 years (Feuerstein et al., 1986). Here, only the original research and several more recent studies are reported.

One of several studies of IE in Venezuela was conducted in 24 schools in low-income sections of Caracas. About 1,400 students were given IE instruction 1 hour a day, 5 days a week for 13 months over a 2-year period. The 400 control students were in regular classes during that time. The dependent variable in the design was the score on the Mastery Project Tools Test, an instrument developed at Vanderbilt University to determine the degree of transference students achieve, presumably as a result of the IE experience. The results were significant in that 55% of the variance was attributable to IE (Ruiz-Bolivar, 1985).

In a more recent study, IE was given to seventh-grade students over a 2-year period (Tzuriel, 1989). The subjects were 186 children in schools that served an educationally and economically disadvantaged population. The experimental and control groups were found to be similar in demographic background. This study had several objectives, only one of which — validation of IE — is discussed here. A portion of the Learning Potential Assessment Device (LPAD) was administered before IE was taught. After the 2-year experiment, all subjects were given an LPAD test known as "The Organizer," which demands a high level of inferential thinking. Compared with members of the control group who showed little improvement, those in the IE experimental group improved their scores significantly.

The original research on the effects of IE was conducted in Israel and has been described elsewhere (Feuerstein et al., 1980). Both the initial research and follow-up studies have been replicated in Venezuela (Ruiz-Bolivar, 1985). Those and still other studies together offer important evidence for the attainment of structural cognitive modifiability.

The original Israeli research was conducted with 218 adolescents, aged 12–15 years, with IQs ranging from borderline to educable mentally retarded, and with a general level of scholastic deficits from 3 to 4 years behind their school peers. Many were functionally illiterate. The sample was divided into two groups: (a) One group received 300 hours of Instrumental Enrichment (IE) over a period of 2 years at the rate of 5 hours per week and were exposed to all 14 instruments of the program; (b) The second group was exposed to 300 hours of General Enrichment (GE) over the same period of time. After the first year, the two groups showed significant cognitive differences favoring the IE group. The inter-group differences increased in favor of the IE group at the end of intervention. The results of a battery of tests indicated that IE produced fairly substantial gains in performance, cognition, and intellectual tasks.

A follow-up study was conducted to ascertain whether the fairly substantial gains attributed to the effects of IE were sustained or even increased over time. Approximately 2 years after the cessation of the program, the students in both the IE and GE research groups were drafted into the Army. Of them, 184 (95 IE, 89 GE) were subjected to various Army intelligence and achievement tests. In seeking the differential long-term effects of IE, the IE and GE subjects were divided into high and low performers on the basis of their scores in the initial study and on the Army intelligence test results in the follow-up study. A complete discussion of the immediate and long-term effects can be found elsewhere (Rand et al., 1981). The most striking result was that 2 or more years after cessation of the intervention program, the differences between the two groups were not only sustained, but increased meaningfully. In certain cases, the inter-group differences even doubled.

This lends support to the contention that changes produced in the individual systematically exposed to IE are structural in nature. There is a part–whole cohesiveness, a transformability and most important, self-perpetuation. Intervention is not merely directed to an increase in the quantity of information but in a meaningful increase in the individual capacity to benefit from future learning opportunities. And that is indeed the goal of IE: to render individuals more modifiable and enable them to adapt to everchanging conditions in the world in which they live.

ACKNOWLEDGMENTS

This chapter is dedicated to the blessed memory of a beloved colleague and co-worker, Mrs. Levia Kyram, who contributed meaningfully to the development of FIE.

Upon the sudden passing away of Prof. Mildred B. Hoffman, our beloved co-author and co-worker, we also dedicate this chapter to her blessed memory.

REFERENCES

de Bono, E. (1983). The cognitive research trust (CORT) thinking program. In W. Maxwell (Ed.), *Thinking, an expanding frontier*. Philadelphia: The Franklin Institute.

Feuerstein, R. (1977). Mediated learning experience: A theoretical basis for cognitive human modifiability during adolescence. In P. Mittler (Ed.), *Research to practice in mental retardation* (Vol. 2, 105–116). Baltimore: University Park Press.

Feuerstein, R., Hoffman, M. B., Rand, Y., Jensen, M. R., Tzuriel, D. & Hoffman, D. B. (1986). Learning to learn: Mediated learning experiences and Instrumental Enrichment. In M. Schwebel & C. M. Maher (Eds.), *Facilitating cognitive development: International perspectives, programs, and practices*. New York: Haworth Press.

Feuerstein, R., & Rand, Y. (1974). Mediated learning experiences: An outline of the proximal etiology for differential development of cognitive functions. *Journal of International Council of Psychology, 9/10*, 7–37.

Feuerstein, R., Rand, Y., Hoffman, M., & Miller, R. (1980). *Instrumental Enrichment; An intervention program for cognitive modifiability*. Baltimore: University Park Press.

Feuerstein, R. & Richelle, M. (1963). *Children of the Melah, socio-cultural deprivation on its educational significance, The North-African Jewish child*. Jerusalem: The Szold Foundation for Child and Youth Welfare.

Harvard University, Bolt Beranek & Newman, Inc. & the Ministry of Education of the Republic of Venezuela. (in press). *A curriculum of thinking*. (Foundations of reasoning: Understanding language; verbal reasoning; problem solving; decision making; innovative thinking). Watertown, MA: Mastery Education Corporation.

Lipman, M., Sharp, A. M., & Oscanyan, F. S. (1980). *Philosophy in the classroom*. Philadelphia: Temple University Press.

Nickerson, R. S. (1984). *Report from the Excellence in Schools Task Force on Learning Strategies and Thinking Skills*. San Francisco.

Nickerson, R.S., Perkins, D.N., & Smith, E.E. (1985). *The teaching of thinking*. Hillsdale, NJ: Lawrence Erlbaum Associates.

Rand, Y., Mintzker, Y., Miller, R., & Hoffman, M.B. (1981). The Instrumental Enrichment program: Immediate and long-term effects. In P. Mittler (Ed.), *Frontiers of knowledge in mental retardation* (Vol. 1, 141–152). Baltimore: University Park Press.

Ruiz-Bolivar, C. J. (1985, Enero). *Modificabilidad cognoscitiva e irreversibilidad: Un estudio sobre el efecto a mediano plazo del programa Enriquecimiento Instrumental*. Publicacion No. 4. Ciudad Guayana: Centro de Investigaciones psicoeducativas. Universidad de Guayana.

Savell, J. N., Twohig, P., & Rachford, D. L. (1986). Empirical status of Feuerstein's Instrumental Enrichment (FIE) technique as a method for teaching thinking skills, *Review of Educational Research, 56* (4), 381–409.

Sternberg, R. J. (1982). Reasoning, problem-solving and intelligence. In R. J. Sternberg (Ed.), *Handbook of human intelligence.* Cambridge: Cambridge University Press.

Tzuriel, D. (1989). Dynamic assessment of learning potential in cognitive education programs. *The Thinking Teacher, 5,* (1, May), 1–5.

Vygotsky, L. S. (1984). Problema vozrasta [The problem of age.] In L. S. Vygotsky, *Sobranie sochinenii: Detskaia psikhologiia* (pp. 244–268). Moscow: Pedagogika. Cited in Minick, N. (1987), Implications of Vygotsky's theories for dynamic assessment. In C. Lidz (Ed.), *Dynamic assessment: An interactional approach to evaluating learning potential.* (pp. 116–140). New York, London: Guilford Press.

Chapter 7

ACTIVE WORK
AND CREATIVE THOUGHT
IN UNIVERSITY CLASSROOMS

Howard E. Gruber
Lucien Richard
University of Geneva

> It is, in fact, nothing short of a miracle that the modern methods of instruction have not yet entirely strangled the holy curiosity of inquiry; for this delicate little plant, aside from stimulation, stands mainly in need of freedom
>
> — (Albert Einstein, 1949 vol. 1, p. 17)

As scientists we are interested in understanding the growth and functioning of mental life from its earliest beginnings to its highest achievements. As educators we want to contribute to the development of people who are both cultivated and reflective — knowing the great heritage of the past and keeping it alive by their own independent thinking. These two goals are inseparable twins. One speaks in the voice of "learn" and the other in the voice of "think." Without one, the mind would be empty, without the other, dead.

In this essay we explore an approach to cognition and higher education that listens to both voices. It represents an effort toward synthesizing our research on very high-level creative thinking with our work as university teachers trying to help students to think better. We report some of our own teaching experiences in two universities — Rutgers University in Newark, and the University of Geneva, and we discuss related work by others. In our conclusion we discuss some problems to be faced if the widely agreed-upon goal of teaching students how to think better is to be approached seriously. If that goal really interests us, then we as educators will have to devote many times more effort to it than has so far even been envisaged.

Note: Howard E. Gruber is now Research Scholar at Teachers College, Columbia University.

COGNITION AND HIGHER EDUCATION

Although Einstein's remark in his *Autobiographical Notes,* already cited, seems to go very far in one direction, he, in fact, took a more balanced view. In another place, and speaking specifically about higher education, Einstein (1954/1936) wrote:

> The development of general ability for independent thinking and judgment should always be placed foremost, not the acquisition of special knowledge. If a person masters the fundamentals of his subject and has learned to think and work independently, he will surely find his way . . . (p. 64)

We begin with two guiding thoughts, one about creativity, the other about education.

There Is No Such Thing as a Free Launch

Probably the most easily documented and obviously visible fact about creative work is that it is difficult, requires maximum mobilization of resources, and takes a long time. When we want to break away from our earth-bound thinking of the past and put ourselves into a new orbit, there is no such thing as a free launch. Yet a great deal of the most common and popular thinking about creativity seems irresistibly drawn to quick and easy fixes, such as mysterious abilities, ready-made supergifted children, and magical moments of sudden insight. Whatever ways of thought we borrow from the study of creative work for use in a developmental and educational context, we must avoid this something-for-nothing magical thinking.

Whenever You Teach Adults Something You Deprive Him or Her of the Opportunity of Discovering It

This paraphrase of Piaget's often quoted remark about children seems, on the face of it, equally plausible for all ages. Why, then, is so little university teaching organized around a determined effort to allow students to learn by active work: doing, experiencing, thinking, finding out for themselves? Is there resistance, overt or covert, to the cultivation of independent minds? Must instructors come between the intellectual environment and their students by imposing their own accumulated knowledge? Can they not encourage curiosity and self-discovery?

THE EVOLVING SYSTEMS APPROACH
TO CREATIVE WORK

For the most part our work on creativity has taken the form of intensive case studies of indisputably creative individuals, such as Charles Darwin, Benjamin Franklin, William James, Jean Piaget, William Wordsworth, and Mary Wollstonecraft (see Gruber, 1978; Gruber & Davis, 1988; Wallace & Gruber, 1989). We have found it helpful to describe the creative person as a system composed of an organization of knowledge (both know-what and know-how), an organization of purpose, and an organization of affect. Each of these subsystems has a dual character: on the one hand it contributes to the internal milieu in which the others evolve, and on the other hand it is only loosely coupled with the others. Events in one subsystem do not uniquely determine the path taken by another.

A recurrent finding in our work has been the long duration of creative projects. Wordsworth took about 7 years to produce a first complete version of his long autobiographical poem *The Prelude,* and then he went on revising it for decades. From the time Darwin became a convinced evolutionist (that decision itself about a 6-year process), Darwin took about 2 years to construct a first version of the theory of evolution through natural selection, and then decades to write the *Origin of Species.* Even cases like Newton's where the process seems to have gone with miraculous speed turn out, under closer examination, to have taken years (see Westfall, 1980a, 1980b).

In the light of this knowledge about the time it takes to think, our understanding of incidents of sudden insight takes on a new meaning. Such incidents occur, not once or twice in a lifetime, but perhaps once or twice a week, or even more often—thus a thousand or more in a decade. They represent both a long series of breaks with the past and the steady functioning of a well-organized system. Creative work requires not only "The having of wonderful ideas" (Duckworth, 1987), but the skills and determination necessary to recognize them, exploit them, and assimilate them into valid structures. And these organizations of knowledge and purpose must be supported by an organization of affect (feelings, values, loyalties, etc.) adequate to sustain the work for the long reaches of time required.

Problem Solving and Divergent Thinking

There are two widespread ideas about creative work that we would like to deal with here, first, the notion that creative thinking is essentially nothing but problem solving and second, the notion that "divergent thinking" plays a very considerable role in creative processes.

The centration on problem solving is found in widely different works. Max Wertheimer's classic *Productive Thinking* (1959/1945) is essentially a collection of miniature case studies of problem-solving episodes. Indeed, Wertheimer's student, Karl Duncker, in his monograph written in the same vein, called it "On Problem Solving" (1945). In an entirely different vein, Bransford and Stein's *The Ideal Problem Solver, a Guide for Improving Thinking, Learning, and Creativity* (1984) is essentially a set of problem-solving exercises. These are both valuable books, but we emphasize that creative thinking, although it includes problem solving, is a much wider set of processes. In a customary way of thinking about the matter, it is said that we think in order to solve problems. We argue, instead, that people solve problems in order to help themselves think. For example, when we do not know what to believe about a certain matter, we sometimes set up a problem situation that will help us to explore the issue. In such instances the problem does not exist until we need it.

Our work on the improvement of thinking leads to the practical conclusion that the scope of our approach must be much wider than problem solving. In a way, this makes our task easier: some students are not very good problem solvers but can do other things quite well. Our broader focus is both more natural and more permissive in allowing students to operate from a position of their own strengths.

In spite of the vogue that the idea of "divergent thinking" recently enjoyed, there is little evidence that a large amount of it is an important part of the creative process. Exponents of divergent thinking advocate the production of many alternative proposals and approaches to the solution of a problem in order to select the best one, relegating the others to oblivion. One can imagine circumstances under which it would be necessary to suppress this kind of divergent thinking (see Fig. 7.1).

Most creative products require the harmonious fitting together of a number of components, with choices necessary for each. In a system having only three components, with three choices for each, there would be 27 pathways to construct and evaluate. If the number of alternatives at each choice point is 5, in a 5-component system, the number of alternatives rises to 125 pathways. As compared with the facile production of many solutions, these alternatives are not there for the asking but must be constructed, one at a time, and then evaluated — either retained or discarded. So it is far more important to have organizations of knowledge, purpose, and affect that guide the production of alternatives in such a way that the task remains feasible (See Fig. 7.2).

The Organization of Creative Work

Two practical points follow from our reconsideration of divergent thinking. First, the way in which the person organizes creative work must provide

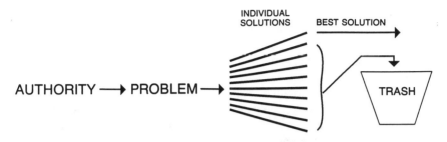

ONE "BEST" SOLUTION IS CHOSEN

FIG. 7.1. Standard divergent thinking paradigm. In the standard divergent thinking or "brainstorming" paradigm (a) the problem is supplied by an outside authority; (b) the emphasis is on an initial phase in which critical judgment is suspended and many solutions are proposed; (c) solutions are evaluated and one best solution is chosen; and (d) all the other solutions are thrown away. This corresponds to a grossly simplified version of the Darwinian theory of random variation and selection.

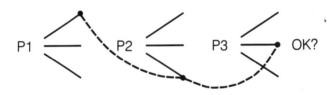

ONE OUT OF 27 POSSIBLE

FIG. 7.2. Finding a valid pathway with a workable number of choices. Imagine so simple a product as a three-term syllogism, with different possible meanings for each proposition, the validity of the syllogism depending on the correctness and harmony of all three choices. This would give rise to the three-component, 27 pathway situation discussed in the text. It is an interesting exercise to reexamine a well-known syllogism (e.g., Socrates is a man; all men are mortal; therefore Socrates is mortal) in this light.

time both for the generation of possibilities and for reflection upon them. To this it might be added that the process of reflection itself, once begun, probably generates more than enough alternatives. From all this it follows that the emphasis, among those studying divergent thinking, on the production of a *large* number of ideas may have been entirely misguided.

Second, creative work must be organized in such a way that the products of spontaneous play and variation can be captured in the web of ongoing projects; we call this organization of projects the "network of enterprise."

We have found that enterprises often have astonishing durations. Each creative person organizes a network of a number of enterprises. Consequently, at any one time some are active and some dormant. But if the person continues to work, a long dormant enterprise may surface when circumstances become appropriate.

In our competence oriented, "can do" society, it is often forgotten that Homo sapiens is a feeling organism. This neglect is reflected in the currently fashionable term "cognitive sciences." But emotions, values, ethical beliefs, and loyalties play a fundamental role in creative work. This organization of affect serves as a rudder in guiding the creative person through the reefs and shoals of his chosen domain. It serves also to keep him going in the face of discouragement, criticism, and isolation. And it serves to mobilize resources, to energize the whole system.

As young creative people gathers up their forces and shape their journeys they are liable to produce what their apologists later dismissively call "juvenilia." But these early products should not be dismissed by the student of creativity. They should be taken seriously, for they can reveal the lines of force, the fundamental vectors that will shape the whole life. An especially clear example of this kind can be found in the early writings of Jean Piaget—his prose poem, *la Mission de l'Idée* (1915), and his novel *Recherche* (1918). In his later years, Piaget himself became more and more driven to replace the errant thoughts of youth with very abstract formalisms. When Vonèche and I asked him for permission to translate the poem into English, he was quite reluctant, for it was "only" juvenilia. Fortunately, he finally agreed (see Gruber, 1982b; Gruber & Vonèche, 1977).

Historians of science, in an earlier phase of the growth of that discipline, tended to avoid close analysis of notebooks and early manuscripts, sticking rather to published texts as representing the ideas of their authors. This tendency entailed a neglect of the internal development of each thinker and also often concealed the intense social interactions that are vital parts of the creative process. Fortunately, we now have a number, although not very large, of close analyses of scientific notebooks, capturing thought on the wing. For example, see Holmes on Bernard (Holmes, 1974), and on Lavoisier (Holmes, 1985); see Westfall on Newton (Westfall, 1980a, 1980b). The Darwin case is particularly interesting. Until the 1950s his manuscripts were hardly touched. Now there are a number of studies going over them in the fine detail necessary to see a person at work, thinking (see Gruber, 1981; Kohn, 1985). Wallace and Gruber (1989) and their collaborators have produced a collection of twelve case studies of "creative people at work."

Resistance to looking at ideas aborning finds its parallel all too readily in the world of education. Teachers, especially in universities and especially in the sciences, don't have time to look at early drafts. They don't encourage their students to wander freely, to expatiate on themes of personal interest, to explore the metaphoric substrata of abstract ideas, to cultivate heroes and know something about their lives. Darwin said, "half my ideas come out of Lyell's brain." Without knowing something about that process of identification and sharing that goes on between mentor and pupil, we will never understand the other half of Darwin's ideas, those that came uniquely from Darwin's brain.

By the same token, by failing to give our students an inkling of the creative process we doom them to a spongelike absorption of the fruits of great men's thoughts. We deprive them of the life-long galvanization that comes from the thrill of participating in great intellectual episodes of discovery.

The question remains, can we, in an institutionalized setting such as a university, simulate this participation? Can we find means of giving our students a vicarious sense of engagement in the creative process? And will such vicarious experience and simulation be adequate to liberate the student's untapped resources? In a moment we address these questions by describing our own efforts as teachers. But before that we must add one last general idea about the study of creative work.

Deviation Amplifying Systems

Much of our thinking in psychology is rightly guided by the notion of adaptation considered as a set of homeostatic processes. Deviations from some norm or ideal are considered as errors to be eliminated. Errors are detected, their values fed back into the system, and counteracted. Thus we speak of "negative feedback." But if creative growth is to be understood, we need another way of thinking. In some episodes at least, deviations from preexisting norms must be detected, seized upon as opportunities for change, amplified and consolidated. In Maruyama's phrase, these are "deviation-amplifying systems" (1963).

Such deviation amplifying systems are not mysterious gifts with which some individuals are endowed. We conceive of them as special organizations of assets, assets that are shared by many if not all normal human beings. In some instances only a little effort may be required to transform the functioning of the whole system. Herbert Simon's (1981/1969) parable of the two watchmakers illustrates this idea dramatically.

There once were two watchmakers, named Hora and Tempus, who manufactured very fine watches. Both of them were highly regarded, and the phones in their workshops rang frequently—new customers were constantly calling them. However, Hora prospered, while Tempus became poorer and poorer and finally lost his shop. What was the reason?

The watches the men made consisted of about 1,000 parts each. Tempus had so constructed his that if he had one partly assembled and had to put it down—to answer the phone, say,—it immediately fell to pieces and had to be reassembled from the elements. The better the customers liked his watches, the more they phoned him and the more difficult it became for him to find enough uninterrupted time to finish a watch.

The watches that Hora made were no less complex than those of Tempus. But he had designed them so that he could put together subassemblies of about ten elements each. Ten of these subassembly, again, could be put together into a large subassembly; and a system of ten of the latter subasemblies constituted the whole watch. Hence, when Hora had to put down a partly assembled watch to answer the phone, he lost only a small part of his work, and he assembled his watches in only a fraction of the man-hours it took Tempus. (p. 200)

The transformation from one to the other, from the totally nonproductive to the productive organization of work, might perhaps be hard to conceive, but lies within the grasp of any watchmaker.

ON THE IMPROVEMENT OF COGNITIVE FUNCTIONS

Many citizens, policy makers, and educators are interested in encouraging methods that emphasize the goal of improving thinking as fundamental for modern education. As background for such effort, it would be valuable to have some perspective on the possibility of making a difference.

There have been two quite different sorts of scepticism about the possibility of producing important cognitive change by direct training. On the one hand, psychologists of a hereditarian persuasion believe that the person's cognitive fate is largely determined at the moment of conception, and environmental factors of all sorts play only a minor role. On the other hand, Piaget and his school of developmental psychology believe that little can be done, by means of direct training, to accelerate the spontaneous growth of particular mental structures. Nevertheless, the Piaget group and others associated with them have themselves demonstrated that, during childhood, cultural and educational factors can make something like a 2-year difference in the time of appearance of the concepts and structures that have interested that group.

In spite of these doubts, a body of knowledge has developed showing that important cognitive changes can be experimentally and educationally induced. We take up two kinds of evidence, experimental and case study material.

Experimental Studies of Cognitive Improvement

Some important changes in cognitive functioning can be produced by a minor change in the situation or in the person's approach. More often, probably, many hours of work are required. Here we take up a few examples touching on different aspects of cognitive functioning.

Memory

The publication of *Plans and the Structure of Behavior* (1960) by Miller, Galanter, and Pribram, marked a watershed in the study of memory. They reported a set of dramatic experiments on mnemonic processing, showing that quite ordinary people could perform feats of memory far outdistancing what had previously been thought possible—such as memorizing lists of 500 paired associates with 99% accuracy and excellent long-range retention. All that is necessary is for the subject to abandon the customary "I am a recording machine" posture of passive repetition and instead invent interesting images connecting the items to be paired. Instead of thinking of memorizing as slow, painful, and mindless, it could be seen as potentially creative, imaginative, and under the control of a thinking person.

Gruber, Kulkin, and Schwartz (1965) studied the length of time necessary for our subjects to form images useful in the task of remembering paired associates. To our surprise, we found that if less than 5 seconds was allowed for each pair, the subjects could not do it effectively. We were surprised because in the whole tradition of research on memory 5 seconds would be considered a rather long exposure time, but we found it minimal. In fact, we should not have been surprised, because professional mental calculators and memory wizards generally work at a comfortable, unhurried pace (Smith, 1983).

Ericcson, Chase, and Faloon (1980) showed that with about 200 hours of practice an average college student can be transformed into a person who can perform feats of memory almost at the level of a professional memory wizard. The comparison between my own work, cited earlier, and this result is interesting. Subjects given instructions to use mnemonic imagery performed only two or three times as well as subjects with a conventional rote-learning attitude. Thus, we could induce a detectable change with a brief paragraph of instruction, taking only a minute or two to explain. To reach the level of Ericcson's results took many hours; moreover, the practice was really intelligent coaching aimed at developing a repertoire of powerful strategies for remembering. While 200 hours seems very long compared to typical laboratory studies, it is actually a rather short time in the life of someone really interested in mastering a skill—in learning to play a musical instrument, practicing 2 hours per day, 5 days per week mounts up to 200 hours in only 20 weeks.

Controlling the Field of Attention

In all complex cognitive activities thinking subject must deploy their attention over a diversified terrain, keep several things in mind, and decide which aspects of the total set of possibilities to pursue at any given time. In our study of creativity, as previously mentioned, we have referred to this aspect of the organization of work as the individual's "network of enterprise" (Gruber, 1989). At the same time, there is a field of experimental research dealing with the processes of attention, emphasizing the study of the limits of attention.

At one time, based on research with relatively passive subjects in highly constrained and standardized situations, experimental results seemed to suggest that human ability to divide attention was relatively limited. But Spelke, Hirst, and Neisser (1976) argued that this was an implausible result, and probably an experimental artifact: the conductor of an orchestra, for example, can attend simultaneously to the sounds produced by many different instruments, to his complex score, and other things all necessary for the task at hand. Spelke and her colleagues designed an experiment to show how the field of divided attention can expand and differentiate with appropriate training. Their subjects began with simple tasks, such as marking all the occurrences of the letter *o* in a passage, while at the same time reading it for comprehension. With each session, the task was made more complex, and the subject encouraged to invent adequate strategies for dealing with it. With this approach, the subjects reached levels of performance previously unheard of in the experimental literature on divided attention.

From a methodological point of view, this research is interesting in the present context. In order to help the subjects attain this high level of performance, experimental standardization was abandoned. In preparing for each session, the experimenters took account of the subject's previous performance and invented a task appropriate to that individual's needs at that point in developing the desired skill. Just as undue, preconceived standardization of tasks across individuals limits performance in the laboratory, it stultifies growth in the classroom.

Causal Reasoning

Although causal reasoning is obviously an important part of many fields of endeavour, there is little direct instruction aimed at improving it. Kuhn and her associates, however, have shown that children can improve their performance significantly. In a typical study, the subjects were repeatedly given chemical combination problems of the same type—in a multivariable situation, to isolate the one variable responsible for a given effect. The problems used were similar to those used by Inhelder and Piaget (1958) in their study of adolescent thought. A typical experiment entailed 11 sessions, 1 per week. It is interesting to note that the main form of intervention by the experimenters was simply to present the problem and ask nonleading questions, such as "what have you learned?" Among Kuhn's many interesting results: (a) Subjects who have demonstrated in one session that they have a superior form of reasoning available to them do not necessarily use it the next time—it takes "brooding time" to stabilize new cognitive functions; (b) Subjects given an opportunity to test conclusions in actual experiments performed noticeably better than subjects who were required to work on a more abstract plane (devotees of computer substitutes for hands-on work, take warning) and; (c) Simple repetition of the same kind of activity, week after week, does lead to improvement. (See, for example: Kuhn & Ho, 1980; Kuhn, Amsel, & O'Loughlin, 1988.)

The game of "Twenty Questions" as usually played does not involve causal reasoning, but it does involve eliminating alternatives in a logical format similar to Kuhn's chemical combination problems. Two older studies of the game reveal the importance of allowing enough time for the person to think. In one study (Bendig, 1957), a shortened form of the game—only 5 questions allowed—was played for 3 games. No improvement was found. In another study (Taylor & Faust, 1952), a lengthened form of the game—30 questions allowed—was played for 16 games. Significant improvement occurred.

In these experiments, opportunity for repeated performance on the same task was used in two ways: to permit the investigator to get a better look at the actual processes involved; and to permit subjects to become more self-aware of what procedures they were using, and what possibilities existed for choosing and controlling them. This approach is quite unlike most research on problem solving, which focuses mainly on the solution and seems to take it for granted that once a problem is solved, it is solved once and for all. In the conventional university classroom, too, with its emphasis on "coverage" of a wide range of subject matter, there is no time for a leisurely going over of the same ground in various ways, and no time for attending to the thought processes of the students.

Case Studies of Gifted People

There have recently been two important studies of gifted people. Feldman (1986) carried out longitudinal studies of a small number of children gifted in music, chess, mathematics, and creative writing. Bloom (1985) studied a much larger number of mature individuals (in their thirties) who had attained high levels of performance at early ages; the subjects in this study were exceptional in the sciences, the arts, and athletics.

Two points emerge that are central for our present discussion. First, it is clear that the period of time from the first appearance of an exceptional ability to its first flowering in the form of effective, creative work or extraordinary performance is a matter of years. Bloom's retrospective method enabled him to conclude, with some plausibility, that the time involved is always about 10 years. Second, without recognition and support of the individual's talents, they will not develop to the fullest extent. The complexity of the effort to develop an adequate support system, tailored to the individual's needs, is well documented in Feldman's study.

Seeming exceptions come to mind—Mozart's or Picasso's precocity; Einstein's four great papers of 1905, when he was only 25-years-old and working in isolation. But as I have argued elsewhere (Gruber, 1982a), these are only seeming exceptions. The 10-year rule and the need for support stand up very well under the scrutiny of exceptional cases. Even the possible exception of child prodigies in the performing arts does not undermine our basic argument that extraordinary achievement requires recognition, encouragement, and years of hard work.

In Summary

We pause to draw a few threads together, and to draw a few somewhat speculative conclusions from the foregoing. First, it seems that improvement of thinking and creative work can be achieved in every component skill or in complex, molar performances whenever educational or training efforts are made toward that end. Although it goes somewhat beyond the available evidence, it is not going very far out on a limb to suggest that the results are proportionate to the effort.

Second, all high level skills depend for their development on protracted hard work. The pianist who practices 4 hours per day for 1 year accumulates over 1,000 hours at the keyboard. This is the work that lies behind the spontaneous magic of the public performance. Not brute force, rote learning, or unthinkingly repetitive drill, but intelligent work accompanied by good coaching, based on reflection about the needs of the individual or group. Third, modern education, at every level, is poorly organized and poorly oriented for such efforts.

IMPROVING THINKING
IN UNIVERSITY CLASSROOMS

They learn nothing there [at the universities of Europe] but to believe; first, to believe that others know that which they know not; and after, that themselves know that which they know not.
—(Francis Bacon, *Cogitationes de Scientia Humana*)

Innovative educators interested in changing their highly conservative institutions are caught between two voices, "learn" and "think." From the side of "learn" we hear that the rapid growth of knowledge requires more discipline and more pressure on students to learn — learn more rapidly, learn more, catch up to the Japanese, and so forth. This pressure generally leads in the direction of quantitative change: increasing the number of courses taught and the weight of textbooks assigned.

Meanwhile, from the side of "think," comes the recurrent refrain that our students are passive, don't know how to learn independently, are not taught to think critically or creatively. Institutionally, the side of "think" has less power than the side of "learn" — but it is by no means an inaudible voice. Its recommendations have usually led to restricted experiments that, although they do not modify the institution as a whole, do keep a vision alive. Sometimes the innovation is coupled with an expensive evaluation study that suffers from the apparent need to collect results immediately — in the first year or two of the study, before the innovative methods have been perfected and stabilized. These evaluations often show moderate positive results. The innovation usually disappears after a few years, leaving the conservative voice of "learn" in the ascendancy.

Proposals for the improvement of thinking have often taken a form emphasizing general cognitive skills and metacognitive knowledge, independent of particular content areas. De Bono (1970) and Bransford and Stein (1984) provided good examples of this type, and Mays (1985) provided an interesting historical review and commentary of "thinking skills programmes." In contrast, other proposals presuppose that thinking goes best when it is directed toward a particular subject matter, one that is important to the thinker. This emphasis on what is now often called "domain specific knowledge" is currently widespread among cognitive scientists. Interestingly, Bransford and his colleagues (Bransford, Sherwood, Vye, & Rieser, 1986), in what appears to be a volte face, have recently suggested that a blending of general and domain specific approaches might be desirable. Perkins (1986) took a similar approach.

A second way in which proposals aimed at improving thinking differ is in the length of time spent in any one activity. In our review of the experimental literature, we stressed the importance of this variable in efforts to induce cognitive change. There are programs in which a few minutes per exercise is envisaged. In our own courses, to be reported later, we use 1 or 2 hours per session, and usually one new exercise every session — although some very brief warm-up activities are sometimes used, and sometimes so much happens in one session that we carry over the same task to the next session, or introduce a closely related task. In the Newark experiment we used almost 100% of the time available in a semester course for these purposes. In the Geneva experiment we used about 50% of the time available (i.e., every other session) for these purposes. In some of Duckworth's studies (discussed elsewhere), the subjects worked on a single problem for a whole semester.

Proposals for the improvement of thinking vary in still another way, the pattern of social interaction elicited. In some instances, such as de Bono's, the entire emphasis is placed on individual work. In Duckworth's group of teachers, there is constant social interaction and very little individual work. In our classes, there is a movement from individual activity to dialogue, not unlike Hawkins' (1965) proposal.

Note that we speak of classroom experiments already performed as "proposals." That is, after all, what they are. We are only at the threshold of understanding how to improve thinking. To be sure, the innovators must have confidence enough to sustain long and difficult projects. But their best efforts are not proven products, only proposals. We turn now to the examination of three such efforts.

Duckworth: "The Having of Wonderful Ideas"

For some years, at Harvard University and MIT, Eleanor Duckworth has worked with experienced elementary school teachers in a small seminar situation. The teachers go through the protracted, exhilarating, painful experience of scientific thinking in an unstructured situation. In one group, meeting for a year, the central task was simply to find out as much as they could about the moon, primarily through direct observation and reflection, both individual and shared. Does the crescent moon always lie on its back? Does the concave side always face one way? Which way? Why? Even to read Duckworth's account is a chastening experience, as one realizes how thin and fragile is one's own knowledge acquired in conventional education. Duckworth found that the teachers in her experiment grew in self-confidence, in their will to think through an idea; and they applied what they learned from the seminar in their own teaching (Duckworth, 1987).

In another study, Duckworth (1986) applied the same general approach with a group that came to focus its attention on "what makes things float or sink" — in other words, what a properly educated scientist might call "density." After months of work, meeting once a week, the group came pretty close to inventing the concept of density. Not too bad, considering that the magnificent Archimedes found the problem of understanding density worthy of his attention: he ran naked in the streets, crying "Eureka!", when he solved it.

Duckworth's approach is important in showing both how difficult it is and how rewarding it can be for the participants to immerse themselves in a single problem area long enough to have a sense of making genuine headway through their own thinking. At the same time, her approach makes no attempt to cover the range and diversity of subject matter that characterizes a conventional course.

The Newark Experiment

The Newark Experiment was a protracted effort to develop ways of university teaching that would help students to think better. While the approach was being developed, quite a variety of students were involved. They ranged from unselected juniors and seniors at Rutgers-Newark (for the most part white, of lower middle-class origins) to professional people, some with masters and doctoral degrees. But from its inception the aim was to develop a program that would be appropriate for educationally deprived, ill-prepared students. In cooperation with the Academic Foundation Program at Rutgers-Newark with the special help of Dr. Bea Seagull, we were able to organize a course for the intended students.

For some years the course was given as a special section of introductory psychology. The teacher was Howard Gruber together with a succession of graduate assistants. The students were first-year undergraduates. Usually the class was divided into two groups, one directed by Gruber, the other by an assistant.[1]

Although it was not initially part of our plan for this project, one new goal emerged early in the course of the work; to develop methods that could be used in teaching the subject matter of a conventional course, if possible in any discipline at any level—methods that would respect both the voice of "learn" and the voice of "think."

Some of the major features of the approach to be described were worked out in a graduate seminar on cognition and creativity, at the Institute for Cognitive Studies of Rutgers-Newark. Other features developed as we went along. Here are the major aspects of the program:

1. *Openness.* When the students register for the course they are told that its main aim is to help them to think better, with coverage of subject matter a secondary aim. One of the requirements of the course is active participa

---

[1]Individuals who worked in this program include Camille Burns, Sarah Gruber, Hope Hartman, and Robert Keegan. Providentially, at nearby Essex Community College, David Griffiths was teaching an introductory course in physics, using similar methods, and we cooperated in various ways.

tion in classroom work. To avoid imposing the special goals of the course on anyone, the students are given an opportunity to transfer to other courses or other sections taught in a traditional way.

2. *Pluralism.* There is no one best way to think well. Activities, problems, and experiences are chosen with an eye to bringing out the natural diversity of students' thinking.

3. *Active participation.* Every student is expected to do all the work. Activities in class are done either individually or in small groups.

4. *Communication and self-explanation.* After each bout of individual or small-group activity, there is a round-robin in which each student is asked to describe what he or she did. During this phase the teacher makes notes at the blackboard, for the use of all. One invariable result in this phase is everyone's astonishment and usually pleasure at the diversity produced.

5. *Shared reflection.* After every individual has reported, a discussion is developed, examining differences, points in common, strengths, missed opportunities, underlying assumptions, possible future problems, and so forth. A main goal of this phase is to reiterate, as is done throughout the course, that it is not enough to have good, even wonderful ideas. They must be expressed, tried out, reflected upon, and elaborated.

6. *Teacher participation.* In the initial phase of each class meeting the teacher tries to get the experiential, active part going as quickly as possible, usually with a 5-minute introduction and explanation of the task for the day. When it is appropriate, the teacher tries to do the same work as the students. Even though the teacher has done it before while preparing the class, there is always some fresh nuance to be discovered, so the teacher can be a bona fide participant. Because the teacher is usually a more "experienced thinker" (John-Steiner, 1985) than the others in the room, this broadens the spectrum of available models of thought, but without imposing one model as the best way to think.

7. *Mini-lecture.* Often the teacher will see an opportunity to give a brief talk at the end of the class period, linking the experiences the students have just had with other information and reflections.

8. *Group planning.* Ideally, the class would—after the first meeting or two—plan its own future sessions. As this program is conducted within the confines of an ordinary American university structure, with classes meeting twice a week for 75–100 minutes, we have not often found it possible to do this. But we do have a reasonable substitute for it, to be described later.

9. *Production and reflection.* After all, the conduct of the class described earlier does have something in common with divergent thinking experiments. The teacher presents a problem, and then there is a relatively relaxed period of idea-production. But the all-important differences lie in the process of reflection: First, there is no effort made to find the best idea

or solution. Rather, the collection of ideas produced by the group becomes the object of reflection. Second, the process of shared reflection usually takes as much or often considerably more time than the initial, individual work. The difference is expressed graphically in the contrast between Fig. 7.1 and Fig. 7.3.

10. *Self-tailoring.* One fundamental principle of our approach asks that students should become aware of their own strengths and develop them. This happens spontaneously in the reiterated process of self-explanation and mutual comparison. In addition, we give the students a few exercises explictly aimed at this goal. These can take the form of asking everyone to develop an exercise that plays from that individual's own strengths — or that focusses on a felt weakness.

The following are a few examples of the activities we use.

Synaesthesia

In about 5 minutes, the teacher explains the basic facts of synaesthesia. Then the students are asked to close their eyes and listen. The teacher produces a more or less musical tone (sometimes vocally, sometimes with an alto recorder or a pitch pipe). Then we go around the room and students are asked individually to describe their visual experiences. We repeat this process a number of times, varying the sounds, and sometimes trying for a particular kind of experience (such as a pure color response). We then move from the phase of communication and self-explanation into the phase of shared reflection — trying to make sense of the rich array of "data" just accumulated, and noted down on the blackboard.

This is a good exercise with which to begin the course. It is nonthreaten-

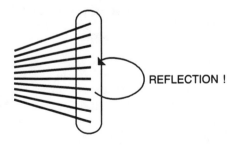

INDIVIDUAL WORK x SHARED REFLECTION

FIG. 7.3. Individual thought and shared reflection. The diversity of individual productions becomes part of the reflective dialogue of the entire group.

ing, because there is obviously no correct answer; it produces a great variety of responses (which the teacher welcomes openly); and it opens the way to discussion and later reading about standard topics in general psychology, imagery and cross-modal experiences. If the teacher can manage to stop the students' momentum, the last 5 or 10 minutes can be used to link up these fresh experiences with a mini-lecture about research on imagery and synaesthesia.

Patterns of Communication

After the students have had at least one experience, preferably two or three, with the basic approach, we ask them to think about and then draw a picture or diagram representing the pattern of communication in a conventional classroom. Then we go around the room asking students to show and explain their diagrams. Typically, different kinds of graphic skills are drawn upon. Almost everyone draws some version of a one-many, unidirectional pattern, that is, one teacher talks, many students listen. Some students will introduce a little cross-talk in the back of the room, and so forth.

We sometimes then ask the students to represent the pattern of communication at work in our own course. Here we get pictures showing much more complex sorts of interaction. At this point there may be a few minutes left in which the teacher can give a mini-lecture about research on patterns of communication, such as Leavitt's (1951), showing the respective merits of centralized and decentralized patterns.

These exercises can be followed up with an exercise on representing the system of feedback or evaluation in the ordinary classroom. This is more difficult and should not be squeezed into the same class period as the others. But it is very rich. If, for example, the principle of prompt feedback (or immediate reinforcement) is worth anything, what do the students make of the usual system of examination?

The Conservation of Matter

Every topic that can be lectured about can also be taught through an invitation to think about it. In a brief lecture — 5 or 10 minutes — Piaget is introduced to the students, and the teacher provides the basic facts about the development of the idea of conservation of matter in young children. Then the teacher explains that the key point is not whether children know the "right answer," but how they think about it. Typically, the conserving child can produce three standard arguments justifying the notion of conservation (identity, reversibility, and compensation — but we don't tell the students that). The students' task is to find those arguments. They are urged to find arguments that could be expected of a child, and especially, arguments that do not implicitly assume a grasp of the idea of conservation.

This task can be done individually, but it is also a good task for small group work (we like groups no larger than three or four). A typical university class—or a typical group of professionals in a workshop situation—will produce two legitimate reasons and some more that discussion reveals as unsuitable (e.g., unfair to expect of a child). All three of the reasons previously mentioned are rarely found, which opens the way for some of the discussion that follows.

If there happen to be some people present who have done some reading and know the right answer, there is a variant problem to occupy them so that they do not prevent the others from doing the work described. Are the three reasons "good"? That is, do they constitute a valid proof of the idea of conservation? This is a hard question. It can also be used as a follow-up to the first problem. Any subject can be raised to a level of difficulty that makes it worth thinking about.

We have avoided conventional outcome evaluation because we believe we are still in an early phase of developing the method. But we have enough accumulated experience to draw several conclusions: (a) With this approach we can cover almost the same ground as in a standard course in introductory psychology. To be sure, fewer topics are covered, but the range is not dramatically reduced; (b) Graduate assistants can be found who adapt readily to using this approach. Perhaps one-third are ripe for it, one-third need a moderate amount of encouragement and more coaching, and one-third are too thoroughly imbued with conventional values such as the goal of "coverage" and teaching the "right answers"; and (c) The students are enthusiastic. Regular attendance, spirited classes that spontaneously run overtime, and explicit student reactions all give positive signs. The greatest, but not insuperable, difficulty is the steady attention necessary if both voices, "learn" and think" are to be heeded.

The Geneva Experiment

At the University of Geneva we introduced the general approach described earlier in a course called "Genetic Psychology: Origins, Stages, and Future Perspectives of Piagetian Theory." Here we were somewhat more constrained in the choice of exercises than in the Newark experiment, because we were committed to the coverage of a fairly well-defined subject matter in an advanced course. And that is exactly what makes the challenge interesting. Can we use the method of active work in a course like that?

There is a certain irony in our having the opportunity to introduce an activity mode of instruction in the faculty founded by Piaget. He was one of the leading exponents of the idea that the single commanding factor in intellectual growth is the child's own activity. One of his best known remarks is that "every time you teach a child something you deprive him of the opportunity to discover it." But, as Gruber and Vonèche (1977) pointed out, there are a number of quite different interpretations of how to apply Piaget's theory to educational practice. To be consistent with the theory, each of them must stress the student's own activity as the central point. Yet it must be said that Piaget himself relied primarily on ex cathedra lectures as the means of instruction, and—with few exceptions—that is still the practice in Geneva. Moreover, the typical student, during a 4-year period, must takes 12 year-long courses at a time! The students' efforts are thus so fragmented that individual initiative is risky and must be taken at the expense of devotion to the prescribed syllabus. We do not say this to criticize Piaget. His lectures were excellent. Nor is the organization of study in Geneva unusual. With minor differences it can be found in universities all over the world.

The course we now report on, "Genetic Psychology: Origins, Stages, and Future Perspectives of Piagetian Theory" was a second-year course, taught by Howard Gruber in Geneva beginning in 1984–1985. Lucien Richard, one of the assistants, had previous experience with an "Activity School" at the secondary level in Geneva. To meet the circumstances, it was decided to alternate between lectures and seminars, the latter taking a form similar to that of the Newark Experiment. The lectures, given by Gruber, covered the development of key ideas in Piagetian theory, coupled with a historical-critical analysis of their origins and future prospects. There were about 60 students in the course; for the purpose of the seminars they were divided into two groups of 30. With one exception, each year we found a second assistant who could fall in comfortably with the activity method of the seminars. It is important that the person directing the seminar be open to the students, tolerant, flexible, and committed to the joint goals of conveying subject matter knowledge and improving cognitive functioning.

The students were informed at the outset that participation in the seminar would affect their grade. They had the choice of an oral examination on the contents of the course (such orals are common in this faculty) or a research paper coupled with an oral examination.

The general procedure followed in the seminar was similar to that described for the Newark experiment: initial presentation of problem by teacher; individual or small group work on problem; round-robin reporting on the previous phase; general discussion and reflection, both on contents and process. Because the subject matter of the course centered on the development of a theory, a number of the exercises presented brief texts with theoretical contents, the task being to interpret the texts, to discover differences between texts, to invent alternative formulations—in short, to do theoretical work. Thus, the theory became, not something to be learned, but something to be thought about and sometimes invented.

We give two examples of typical seminars, drawn from experiences in the academic year 1984–1985.

Memory and Representation

The students were asked to draw a map of a pedestrian path from Cornavin, the railway station of Geneva to "Uni Deux," the University building in which the faculty of psychology is housed—a 15–20 minute urban walk. For this task we asked the students to work in groups of three, with two students drawing maps while the other observed them. This produced lively dialogue and interesting confrontations between students using different strategies.

One of the two most common strategies was "step-by-step": the map-maker chooses a starting point and works from there. Typically, people using this strategy worked on too large a scale at first, leaving them with insufficient space on the paper at the far end of the map. The other main strategy was "holistic-deductive." The mapmaker first indicates the two endpoints of the path; usually a prominent midpoint, such as the point where the path crosses the Rhone, is then added, and then details are filled in. There were also differences in the sequence of drawing in streets and landmarks, and differences in handling the problem of orienting the map.

The round-robin demonstrated to the students the great variety of productions elicited by the task. The discussion centered on the constructive nature of memory and on the nature of representation in memory. Student participation and later commentary show that this was a rich and successful seminar.

Moral Judgment

The aim of this exercise was to provide the starting point for a discussion of moral judgment, egocentrism, and Piaget's notions of heteronomy and autonomy. The seminar leader presented a hypothetical international crisis arising out of the invention of a new weapon of mass destruction; the country that has invented this weapon is also signatory to a treaty forbidding it.

The students were assigned, in pairs, to one of eight different social roles, or points of view: military, diplomatic, pacifist, scientific, the people, the industrialists, the finance ministry. The pairs were given enough time to work out a statement of their positions. This arrangement produced a variety of points of view and a set of lively confrontations.

In the period of reflection that followed, a major point that emerged was the necessity for exposure to diverse perspectives in order to break out of one's egocentric starting point. In one of his lectures, Gruber discussed the misleadingly ahistorical way in which Piaget's theory is often presented, and the relation of Piaget's later thinking about moral questions to his earlier reactions to World War 1. The students were generally interested in looking for connections among the lectures, the reading assignments, and the seminars. The format of the course thus provoked considerable integrative activity on the student's part, much of this taking place in the framework of the seminars.

Some Extensions and Conclusions

In 1987–1988, the activity seminars in the course on Piaget's theory were conducted by Isabelle Sehl and Sylvie Pellet. Each student was required to keep a journal of experiences in and related to the course. About half of the students focussed mainly on a description of the overt or manifest events of the seminars; the other half reflected on the intellectual processes involved. Encouraging a synthesis of these two aspects would be an important new goal for our work. Asking the students to keep these journals may have imposed one burden too many on them, considering that they are each taking 11 other courses at the same time. In spite of this difficulty, journal keeping may turn out to be a very important part of the whole process of encouraging students to achieve a higher level of self-awareness of their own cognitive capacities.

The same year, Gruber and Sehl worked together in a third-year course on creative thinking in which we used approximately the same format.

The main conclusion we can draw at this point concerns the feasibility of our approach. The alternation of lectures and activity seminars seems to work out well, allowing for reasonable coverage of course contents, and repeated experiences in the process-oriented seminars. Contrary to dire predictions made by some of our colleagues, we met with little student resistance and considerable enthusiasm. When the number of students in an activity-oriented seminar rises above 20, the individual-oriented round-robin phase becomes too lengthy. Small group work and cutting the round-robin short are feasible substitutes. But we much prefer a setting in which every student expects to be heard from, is heard from, and finds that his or her contribution is valued. Often, the last student to speak has something valuable to add. The emphasis on understanding process rather than evaluating product makes it easy to be genuinely interested in and welcoming of every student's experience.

Of course we know that many teachers have used elements of this approach within standard courses. We believe that our systematic, repeated use of the activity mode, and the movement from individual work to dialogue, encourage the students to value their own intellects and to understand themselves as knowing systems. In a course with the two main goals we set for ourselves, it is important to work steadily at maintaining a good balance between conveying the contents and grasping the process.

CONCLUSION: IS THE NECESSARY CHANGE POSSIBLE?

Increasing attention to the goal of improving thinking in higher education is impeded by an institutional sense of satisfaction with a job well done. Honest self-congratulation is in order for the typical professors. Years of training and experience, excellent command of subject matter knowledge, and hours of preparation for each class — all these lead to the production of a series of lectures that systematically present to their students something of value, a disciplined, carefully chosen part of accumulated human knowledge. Many if not most university teachers would claim that they do aim to help their students to think better, and that the main way they do this is to expose them to some of the best products of human thought — in other words, to cover the subject matter of their courses. Thus coverage of subject matter becomes the main goal of each course, while various hoped for cognitive changes in the student becomes a set of "collateral" goals (in John Dewey's phrase).

It is this well-deserved sense of self-satisfaction that permits most university teachers to turn a deaf ear to the recurrent critical voices bringing evidence that delivering thoughts and knowledge to the student does not succeed in imparting that knowledge or inducing that thought in the student. It is the teacher, not the student, who does the hard work of preparing lectures, and by the iron law, output equals input, it is the teacher who profits the most. But teachers entrenched in a system that is tuned to the voice of "learn" do not, as teachers, listen to the voice of "think."

And yet in every decade, a number of researchers and teachers come forward to challenge the priorities of traditional education. Our claim is not that there is some best way to help people to think better. On the contrary, we believe that there are many ways, an extended family of them. Once teachers have rejected the traditional priorities and given equal weight to what are now only collateral goals, they will not find it extremely difficult to invent ways in which the new goal structure might be implemented. The main impediment does not lie in the paucity of invention of new classroom methods, but in implementing them steadily over the years, in working against the heavy weight of self-satisfied tradition.

The Ford Foundation Experiment

In the 1950s in the United States, the Fund for the Advancement of Education (a subdivision of the Ford Foundation) sponsored a nationwide investigation of different ways of giving students more responsibility for their own education. Gruber was responsible for an extensive experiment at the University of Colorado, involving about 20 courses in as many different departments (Gruber & Weitman, 1962, 1963). The main innovation was to reduce the number of class meetings from three per week to one in the experimental courses, always maintaining a comparison group meeting normally. In general, little or no difference between the groups was found in amount of course material retained, except that on a delayed posttest given a year later the experimental students did somewhat better. In some of the experimental courses there was good evidence that the students improved in their ability to learn independently and to solve problems they had never seen before.

These results even occurred in one course in physical optics in which the experimental group had zero meetings per week; the control group received lectures from one of the best professors at the university. Thus, at a minimum, the experiment showed that the heavily defended requirement of three 50-minute classes per week, or the equivalent, could not be justified; and it was probable that fewer classes would lead to a better result.

But our real point in recounting this story from the 1950s is not to recommend a particular change in ways of teaching, but to draw attention to the difficulty of introducing stable educational change. At the University of Colorado, when the experiment was over, Gruber interviewed the participating teachers. Even those who thought the experiment was a great success did not continue to use the methods that had been successful. Something similar happened in other institutions. Nationally, the Ford Foundation's experiment has disappeared into the dustbin of history.

Facilitating Cognitive Development: Problems and Next Steps

There are a number of chronic problems facing those of us who are interested in giving cognitive development its appropriate place in the goal structure of university education.

Active Learning Versus Coverage

There is no escaping the fact that it takes time to think. It takes more time to think through a problem than to read or hear about the solution. It follows that teachers who elicit more thinking must expect to cover less ground. There are various possible counterarguments. It might be said that we cover the same ground in a different way. Alternatively, we accept a change in our goals; in David Hawkins' phrasing, our task is not to cover the subject but to uncover it. True, and well said, but still an admission that certain cherished topics will not be taught.

General Cognitive Skills
Versus Domain-specific Knowledge

Planning a program for cognitive development at the university level requires some theoretical decision about the nature of cognitive growth. At this time there are certainly important differences among cognitive scientists as to the possibility of cognitive skill training outside the framework of an organized knowledge structure such as an academic discipline. But even supposing that general skill training is possible, why make that choice? In order to think at all, the student must think about something. Why not organize the problems and other activities so that, taken together, they correspond to the study of a disciplined field of inquiry?

It is our conviction that the most viable innovations will be those that respect the strength of the conservative voice of "learn." In other words, the realistic aim for the next decade or two should be innovations in which the desire for standard subject matter coverage is met, only modifying the approach to teaching it so as to embody the goal of "think." Special classes in how to think better, free of commitment to any domain-specific body of knowledge, and drawing, for example, on methods advocated by de Bono (1977/1970) or Bransford and Stein (1984) are valuable for exploring the terrain; we also need to learn how to exploit the results of these special efforts in the framework of existing disciplines and organized bodies of knowledge.

Perhaps midway between the abstract cognitive skills approach and the domain centered approach there is an older tradition of teaching "study skills." In recent years this field has been revitalized by connecting it with advances in cognitive science. Hartman's work is a good example of this type. In a recent article, moreover, Hartman pointed out that thinking skills programs typically ignore the relation of affect and cognition: "even well-developed, higher-order thinking skills are worthless to a student who is unmotivated to apply them" (Hartman, 1987). There may be many ways in which more could be done to connect thinking skills programs with the real concerns of students, including attending to their desire for subject matter mastery.

Individual Versus Group

In many thinking skills programs the normal social form of activity is the individual working alone. This corresponds to a conception of thinking and creativity as lonely processes. But this is a false conception. Thinking, even at its loneliest, is social to the bone. And, although the topic is neglected, most creative work includes some elements of collaboration. Here there is a series of choices to be made, but not very difficult ones. As our work has shown, it is relatively easy to arrange matters so that students move back and forth between individual work and various sorts of dialogue. Moreover, in some of our recent experimental work on the collaborative synthesis of points of view, we have found that such processes reach their highest development when the individuals involved oscillate between working alone and working together.

Is the necessary transformation of the university possible? There are two main factors to consider, the students and the teachers. Speaking first of the students: In many settings where we have discussed these issues we have been told that the students "here" are very passive, can't be activated, all you can do is lecture to them, hope for the best, and so forth. We have never found this to be true. In university courses taught in two cultures, in other adult education settings, and in a number of workshops in different institutions—the great majority of participants respond positively to our activity-oriented, experiental mode of teaching. Some few are apprehensive at first, but only briefly. A tiny minority resist participation: they require individual attention outside of class time.

As far as the teachers are concerned, we are less optimistic. They work under the heavy weight of tradition, and under institutional restraints that make even the examination of educational goals difficult, much less inauguration of explicitly goal-oriented change. They may well have in mind the real world their students will have to face—a world in which employers do not always welcome individual initiative, independent moral judgment, and creative thought. They have important investments in their own scholarly activities and are happy to to teach courses in which they can express themselves. Even though there are persistent criticisms of the quality of higher education, even though there are now flourishing networks and other enterprises aimed at moving higher education toward greater emphasis on cognitive development—the great majority of the professoriate remain unmoved.

What can be done about the teachers?

REFERENCES

Bendig, A. W. (1957). Practice effects in "twenty questions." *Journal of General Psychology,* *56,* 261–268.
Bloom, B. S. (1985). (Ed.). *Developing talent in young children.* New York: Ballantine.
Bransford, J. D., & Stein, B. S. (1984). *The ideal problem solver, a guide for improving thinking, learning, and creativity.* New York: W. H. Freeman.
Bransford, J., Sherwood, R., Vye, N., & Rieser, J. (1986). Teaching thinking and problem

solving. *American Psychologist, 41,* 1078-1089.

De Bono, E. (1977). *Lateral thinking, a textbook of creativity.* New York: Penguin.

Duckworth, E. (1986). *Inventing Density.* Grand Forks: North Dakota Study Group on Evaluation.

Duckworth, E. (1987). *"The having of wonderful ideas" and other essays on teaching and learning.* New York: Teachers College Press.

Duncker, K. (1945). On problem-solving. *Psychological Monographs, 58,* i-ix, 1-113.

Einstein, A. (1949). Autobiographical notes. In P. A. Schilpp (Ed.), *Albert Einstein: Philosopher-scientist,* 2 vols. New York: Harper & Row.

Einstein, A. (1954/1936). *Ideas and opinions.* New York: Bonanza Books.

Ericcson, K. A., Chase, W. G., & Faloon, S. (1980). Acquisition of a memory skill. *Science, 208,* 1181-1182.

Feldman, D. H. (1986). *Nature's gambit: The mystery and meaning of the child prodigy.* New York: Basic Books.

Gruber, H. E. (1968). The uses and abuses of negative results. In O. Milton & E. J. Shoben, Jr. (Eds.), *Learning and the professors.* Athens, OH: University of Ohio Press.

Gruber, H. E. (1976). Créativité et fonction constructive de la répétition. *Bulletin de psychologie de la Sorbonne: numéro special pour le 80e anniversaire de Jean Piaget.*

Gruber, H. E. (1978). Darwin's 'Tree of Nature' and other images of wide scope. In J. Wechsler (Ed.), *On aesthetics in science* (pp. 121-140). Cambridge, MA: MIT Press.

Gruber, H. E. (1982a). On the hypothesized relation between giftedness and creativity. In D. H. Feldman (Ed.), *New directions for child development: Developmental approaches to giftedness and creativity.* San Francisco, CA: Jossey-Bass.

Gruber, H. E. (1982b). Piaget's *Mission. Social Research, 49,* 239-264.

Gruber, H. E. (1989). Networks of enterprise in creative scientific work. In B. Gholson, A. Houts, R. A. Neimayer, & W. Shadish (Eds.), *Psychology of science and metascience.* Cambridge: Cambridge University Press.

Gruber, H. E., & Davis, S. N. (1988). Inching our way up Mount Olympus: The evolving— systems approach to creative thinking. In R.J. Sternberg (Ed.), *The nature of creativity: contemporary psychological perspectives* (pp. 243-270). Cambridge: Cambridge University Press.

Gruber, H. E., Kulkin, A., & Schwartz, P. (1965, April). *The effect of exposure time on mnemonic processing in paired associate learning.* Paper presented at the meeting of the Eastern Psychological Association, Atlantic City, NJ.

Gruber, H. E., & Vonèche, J. J. (Eds.). (1977). *The essential Piaget.* New York: Basic Books.

Gruber, H. E., & Weitman, M. (1962). Self-directed study: Experiments in higher education. *Behavior Research Laboratory Report No. 19.* Boulder, CO: University of Colorado.

Gruber, H. E. & Weitman, M. (1963). The growth of self-reliance. *School and Society, 91,* 222-223.

Hartman, H. (1987). Thinking about feelings. *Cogitare, 2,* 7-8.

Hawkins, D. (1965). Messing about in science. *Science and Children, 2,* 1-5.

Holmes, F. L. (1974). *Claude Bernard and animal chemistry.* Cambridge, MA: Harvard University Press.

Holmes. F. L. (1985). *Lavoisier and the chemistry of life.* Madison: University of Wisconsin Press.

Holmes. F. L. (1989). *Lavoisier and Krebs: Two styles of scientific creativity.* In D. B. Wallace & H. E. Gruber (Eds.), *Creative people at work: Twelve cognitive case studies.* New York: Oxford University Press.

Inhelder, B., & Piaget, J. (1958). *The growth of logical thinking from childhood to adolescence.* New York: Basic Books.

John-Steiner, V. (1985). *Notebooks of the mind.* Albuquerque: University of New Mexico Press.

Kuhn, D. Amsel, E., & O'Loughlin, M. (1988). *The development of scientific thinking skills.* Orlando, FL: Academic Press.

Kohn, D. (1980). Theories to work by: Rejected theories, reproduction, and Darwin's path to natural selection. *Studies in the History of Biology, 4,* 67–170.

Kuhn, D., & Ho. V. (1980). *Journal of Applied Developmental Psychology, 1,* 119–133.

Leavitt, H. J. (1951). Some effects of certain communication patterns on group performance. *Journal of Abnormal and Social Psychology, 46,* 38–50.

Maruyama, M. (1963). The second cybernetics: deviation amplifying mutual causal processes. *American Scientist, 51,* 164–179.

Mays, W. (1985). Thinking skills programmes: an analysis. *New Ideas in Psychology, 3,* 149–164.

Miller, G. A., Galanter, E., & Pribram, K. H. (1960). *Plans and the structure of behavior.* New York: Holt, Rinehart & Winston.

Perkins, D. N. (1986). *Knowledge as design.* Hillsdale, NJ: Lawrence Erlbaum Associates.

Piaget, J. (1915). *La mission de l'Idée.* Lausanne: Edition La Concorde (cover printed 1916). Partial English translation in H. E. Gruber & J. J. Vonèche (Eds). (1977). *The Essential Piaget.* New York: Basic Books.

Piaget, J. (1918). *Recherche.* Lausanne: Edition La Concorde. (Chapter by chapter summary in Gruber & Vonèche, 1977).

Simon, H. A. (1981). *The Sciences of the Artificial* (2d ed.). Cambridge, MA: MIT Press.

Smith, S. B. (1983). *The great mental calculators: The psychology, methods, and lives of calculating prodigies, past and present.* New York: Columbia University Press.

Spelke, E., Hirst, W., & Neisser, U. (1976). Skills of divided attention. *Cognition, 4,* 215–230.

Taylor, D. W., & Faust, W. L. (1952). Twenty questions: Efficiency in problem solving as a function of size of group. *Journal of Experimental Psychology, 44,* 360–368.

Wallace, D. B., & Gruber, H. E. (Eds. 1989). *Creative people at work.* New York: Oxford University Press.

Wertheimer, M. (1959). *Productive thinking.* New York: Harper & Row. (Original work published 1945).

Westfall, R. S. (1980a). Newton's marvellous years of discovery and their aftermath: Myth versus manuscript. *Isis, 71,* 109–121.

THEORY AND CURRICULUM DEVELOPMENT IN COGNITIVE EDUCATION

H. Carl Haywood
Penelope Brooks
Vanderbilt University

The relationship between theory and practice in any field is complex and usually poorly understood, with some practices growing up without apparent benefit of theoretical underpinning and much theoretical thought going without application. In fact, there is no necessity for theory to be applied or even to have potential application (see, e.g., Conant, 1947) so long as it helps us to organize and understand what we have observed and to give generalizable meaning to otherwise isolated data. On the other hand, applied fields such as engineering may develop in certain areas and even prosper in the relative absence of theory (even though the whole discipline certainly has its theoretical structure), but this situation is much rarer than is the existence of theory without application. In the usual case, attempts to make a practical difference proceed in a more efficient, effective, and orderly fashion to the extent that they are based on and derived from some organizing conceptual scheme. One could conceivably set about to solve all possible problems in the world, one at a time, in any or no order. To do so would require infinite time and effort, and if the history even of organized science is any indication the very solution of some problems would create others. In any event, no particular areas of applied work would advance in significant degree, except by accident, simply because a more-or-less random process of problem solving would leave critical knowledge gaps that would then have to await their random turn for solution. In the more usual order of the advance of knowledge, especially in applied areas such as education and mental health, practical problems in need of solution stimulate and challenge theory, which in turn yields possible solutions that can be tested in their application. (For a discussion of mission-oriented research and the relation of "pure" to applied science, with particular relevance to developmental sciences, see Conant, 1947, 1952; Haywood, 1977).

It is easy to agree that educational methods and approaches should be based as solidly as possible in relevant theory. One can then ask, "What theory?" It might be helpful to think of education as a set of developmental tasks. With that orientation, it becomes clear that educational practices need to be based in consistent theories of child development. Even that narrowing leaves too broad a theoretical field. The case that we have chosen for this chapter, cognitive education, helps us to narrow the theoretical field further. Methods in cognitive education should be derived directly from theories of cognitive development and cognitive modifiability. A theory of cognitive development would consist of the assumptions one would make, and their corollary hypotheses, about such questions as the following:

1. Are there generalizable (i.e., relatively content-independent) processes of thought that are important to the effective understanding and learning of a wide variety of content?
2. What cognitive processes are important to the learning of academic and social facts, relations, procedures, and generalizations?
3. When, under what circumstances, and in what sequence do these processes normally appear in the course of development?
4. What circumstances can be associated with acceleration or delay in their appearance?
5. Are there relevant social variables, for example, economic level, education of parents, immigrant status, or minority ethnic status, in the development of important cognitive processes, and if so how can these be dealt with?
6. Do these assumptions about cognitive development lead to or demand specific educational practices, materials, velocities, or curricula?

The curriculum that we have developed, begun to evaluate, and are now disseminating, the *Cognitive Curriculum for Young Children* (Haywood, Brooks, & Burns, 1986), was derived directly from a body of theory by a process that is communicable and replicable. Later in the chapter we describe that process in some detail. We should point out first that the relevant body of theory did not exist in a single place and had to be assembled, evaluated conceptually, and supplemented before work could begin in a coherent manner on development of the actual curriculum. Theory, although possibly valid in an explanatory sense, is neither useful nor useless except in relation to specified goals and purposes. The first step, then, in theoretical and curriculum development is to try to specify one's applied goals. In our case, we set out to develop a curriculum that would serve the following goals:

1. To enhance and accelerate the development of basic cognitive functions, especially those characteristic of concrete operatory thought.
2. To identify and remediate deficient cognitive functions.
3. To develop task-intrinsic motivation.
4. To develop representational thought.
5. To enhance learning effectiveness and readiness for school learning.
6. To prevent unnecessary special education placement.

These very goals dictated some aspects of the theoretical structure, and their expression revealed to us some implicit biases and assumptions that we held, almost without knowing it. For example, the goal of stimulating the development of important cognitive processes at or near the developmental time when they normally occur rests necessarily on the assumptions that such important cognitive processes exist across children, that they develop in an identifiable and predictable sequence, and that it is possible to do things that will accelerate or bring about their development. The goal of identifying and remediating deficient cognitive processes required the assumptions that cognitive processes are manifest in observable behavior, that such processes may fail to develop adequately under certain circumstances and in certain children, and that when that occurs, it is possible to do things later whose effect will be to bring about the redevelopment of those inadequately developed processes. The goal of supplying the cognitive basis for the learning of primary-grades content required the assumptions that certain fundamental cognitive processes may develop in developmentally hierarchical fashion, with simple ones preceding more complex ones, and that the combination of age (or developmental level) of the children and the nature of the content to be learned could be used to specify some of those prerequisite cognitive processes. The goal of enhancing the development of task-intrinsic motivation implies that (a) intrinsic motivation bears a systematic and important relationship to academic and social learning on the one hand and to development of cognitive processes on the other; (b) individual differences appear in this domain by 3–6 years of age; and (c) it is possible to change individual differences in intrinsic motivation. The goal of preventing special education placement rests on the assumption that the course of practical events can be altered by *changing the children* in important ways. Once those goals had been established, it was important to determine to what extent they were consistent with bodies of systematic thought that had guided our work up to that time and that could be integrated into a useful conceptual framework. Actually, the process was not quite that neatly sequenced, because the setting of those particular goals had certainly been determined in large part by what we thought to be both possible and desirable, and those estimates were clearly influenced by our prior theoretical orientations. Thus, the early development of our conceptual scheme, our applied goals, and subsequently our methods, procedures, and materials was a transactional process, with adjustments at each level of thought coming about as a result of developments at the others.

In this chapter we present a synopsis of the theoretical structure on which the *Cognitive Curriculum for Young Children* rests, followed by a discussion in some detail of the processes by which concepts were translated into "curriculum units" and those units were elaborated into classroom practices. Before doing that, we try to deal with some of the cognitive debris that impedes progress in theoretical development, in curriculum development, and in teacher training, especially in the field of cognitive education.

MYTHS AND MYSTERIES IN CURRICULUM DEVELOPMENT AND DISSEMINATION

In the course of trying to develop and disseminate the *Cognitive Curriculum for Young Children* we have encountered several destructive myths and a few mysteries regarding relations between developmental theory and educational practices. These beliefs are widespread, insidious, and constitute obstacles at all three levels of theory development, curriculum development, and teacher training. Some of the most prominent ones are discussed here.

Teachers Do Not Understand or Care About Theory

This is more a comment on the supposed intelligence of teachers than on the relevance of educational theory to educational practice. When we began to offer teacher training in cognitive education we were told by supposed experts that we could forget the theoretical instruction because teachers were interested only in methods and in any case would not understand the theoretical discussion. Because we were so enchanted with our own theoretical orientation, we presented the theoretical structure anyway; in fact, we devoted between 20% and 25% of our 40–48 hour workshops to considerations of the theoretical underpinnings of the *Cognitive Curriculum for Young Children* (CCYC). To our delight, teachers turned out to be interested and receptive as well as clearly capable of understanding what was presented. Throughout the remainder of the workshops they frequently related practices to conceptual principles, showing their understanding by the questions they asked and by their applications of principles in such activities as designing and planning lessons.

We have informally surveyed the reasons for their initial interest in the CCYC given by those who have written or telephoned to ask for further information or for instructions for enrolling in teacher training. The result was quite surprising: almost invariably such persons (usually teachers or program administrators) have indicated that they had become interested in our curriculum because of the attractiveness of its theoretical structure. Usually, they have characterized it as optimistic, respectful of the learning abilities of children, cognitive (and therefore efficient in the sense of teaching generalizable principles), and productive of effective methods of instruction, as well as broad in its encompassing of intellective, affective, and social-ecological variables.

We have typically ended our teacher training workshops by having the participants fill out workshop evaluation forms and then participate in an evaluative discussion of the various workshop sessions. On the forms, each session is identified by topic and instructor. For each session, the participants rate the session on a Likert-type scale (varying from 1 to 7 in early versions and from 1 to 5 in later ones), sometimes on two dimensions ("learned" and "liked") and sometimes on only one. We have combined data from the 30 workshop sessions into three categories: theory, information about processes, and hands-on or active-participation sessions (e.g., sessions in which the participants had to design a lesson and then get criticism on their efforts). Table 8.1 shows the mean ratings (converted to a common metric) of 146 and 157 participants in seven different workshops on these three sets of instructional sessions. We can see from Table 8.1 that theory sessions earned ratings at least as high as those of the other two

TABLE 8.1
Teacher Training Workshop Participants' Preferences for Training Sessions on Theory, Curriculum Information, or "Hands On" Experience

Measure	Component		
	Theory	Curric. Info.	"Hands On"
Mean Rating, "Learn"[a]	5.2	5.1	5.1
Mean Rating, "Like"[a]	5.2	5.1	5.2
Frequency of Choice as "Best" Session or Best Liked[b]	100 (64%)	16 (10%)	35 (22.3%)
Frequency of Choice as "Worst" Session or Least Liked[b]	4 (2.5%)	6 (3.8%)	5 (3.2%)

[a]Based on 146 participant ratings of 30 workshop sessions.
[b]Based on 157 participant ratings of 30 workshop sessions, not all participants expressing choices.

groups. These means also reveal that the respondents used very little of the available scale range, suggesting that they felt quite positively about all or most aspects of the workshop experiences. For that reason, we have examined data in a less aggregated form, taken from "free response" items in the evaluation questionnaire.

At the end of the workshop evaluation form, participants have been asked, "Which session was the very best?" and "Which session could be eliminated (or was the worst or least liked)?" Of 157 responses by participants who answered these questions, theory sessions showed up in "the very best" category 100 times, curriculum information sessions 16 times, and hands-on sessions 35 times. In the "could be eliminated" category theory sessions showed up 4 times, curriculum information sessions 6 times, and hands-on sessions 5 times. These data are also reported in Table 8.1. Open-ended comments have often included such statements as, "Thank you for not considering us too dumb to understand the theoretical aspects!", and "I am glad I have gotten a good theoretical basis, because now when I encounter new situations I will be able to figure out what to do."

Further informal evidence of teachers' understanding of the theory that underlies CCYC comes from our on-site observations of their classroom work, from viewing the in-classroom videotapes they submit for review and feedback, and from occasions when trained teachers have had to explain the curriculum to others (e.g., when integrating new teacher aides into the classroom or when presenting what they are doing at professional conferences or to visitors to their classes).

Teacher Training in Methods Is Sufficient, Without Theoretical Orientation

Occasionally, teachers have obtained the materials for this and other cognitively oriented curricula without having taken the training associated with use of those curricula. In some cases, they have taken parts of workshops, skipping the theoretical parts, or have taken whole workshops from instructors who themselves either did not think presentation of the theory to be especially important or who did not understand it well enough to do a good job of teaching it. It is impossible to know the "base rate" of these circumstances, and therefore the relative frequency of subsequent dissatisfaction with their theory-free training. What we do know is that we have received a substantial number of appeals for help from such persons. The appeal is always expressed in similar terms: "I was taught only the mechanics of implementing this curriculum, and that worked fine until I encountered situations that were not specifically covered in my training. Then I realized that I could not work out appropriate procedures without knowing the theoretical bases of the curriculum!" On the other hand, teachers who have had the full training experience, including theoretical orientation, have commented that it was not necessary to cover all possible classroom situations in the workshops because, having learned the theoretical bases of the curriculum, they could now work out conceptually consistent practices when encountering novel situations.

Theoreticians Do Not Understand the Real World

It is a fairly commonly held belief that theoreticians "live in ivory towers" and have little contact with the "real world." A corollary of that belief is that their theories have little validity or applicability in practical situations. Such a belief shows remarkable naivete about how theories come about! In the ideal case theories are simply statements about how things are that help us to organize in generalizable and efficient ways and to understand what we have already observed. Following certain rules of systematic thought, they do have formal requirements (such as internal consistency, specification of their parameters, assumptions, or limitations, logical progression of ideas, statement insofar as possible in "mathematical" terms), but they rest in the first instance on observations of "real world" events. Piaget's notions of the origins of knowledge came not from laboratory experiments in artificial situations but from observation of the development and behavior of live children. The same is true of Vygotsky and of Feuerstein, the other major theoretical contributors (besides ourselves) to the CCYC. In fact, there is a tradition in applied psychological research that says, "In the process of trying to do good things for people or to bring about social change, one encounters knowledge gaps. Then the thing to do is to go scurrying to one's theories to discover what *ought to* be true, and then to the laboratory to find out whether it is or not!" This intimate and reciprocal relation between theory and practice has been emphasized by Conant (1947, 1952) in the context of the physical sciences and discussed extensively by Haywood (1977) with respect to human development. In the present case, we had observed children in classrooms and other settings, had tried to work with them in clinical and research activities, and even so found it useful to seek the participation of teachers in testing the applicability of our theoretical structure and in deriving appropriate curriculum activities, sequences, and materials.

But You Don't Know My Children!

By making this statement, teachers are (a) acknowledging the fact of individual differences, and (b) denying the applicability of an approach to their children, thus defending themselves (and placing the blame on the children or on the child/theory fit) if it does not work. A good curriculum, then, must be broad in its theoretical base; that is, it must be based on a theoretical structure whose constructs apply to a wide range of individual differences. In addition, the curriculum itself must be flexible; in other words, it must allow room for variation in the specific procedures that can be used in classrooms to operationalize the same concepts. In our dissemination of the CCYC we have heard this statement often. In fact, it appears that almost all teachers of preschool classes have in their classrooms at least one child who does not seem to fit any mold, whose behavior defies management by the methods that work well enough with the other children, and who resists activities and incentives that are welcomed by the others. Our experience has been of two kinds. First, with many such children it simply takes more patience, more repetitions, more trying. The concepts often work, but not as rapidly as with other children. Second, it is important to recognize that classroom procedures cannot be expected to cure everything, and that the time comes with some children when group procedures do not work and when the teacher needs outside help. Thus, from a theoretical standpoint it is important to recognize the limits of the concepts and of their derived operations.

In the Heat of the School Day, the Teacher Must Do What She Thinks Will Work at the Moment

This is just another way of saying, "All that is fine, but when it comes down to moment-to-moment teaching, I'll just have to rely on my own judgment." Actually, relatively few teachers verbalize that attitude, but some practice it by taking workshops and courses, learning a conceptual approach, and then proceeding to do whatever they would have done in the first place. This is more likely to happen when theorists and curriculum developers ignore (or appear to ignore) the contributions that teachers can make to development of both theories and curricula. It is important to leave implementation decisions up to individual judgment of classroom teachers, along with the responsibility for making conceptually consistent judgments. For these reasons, in developing the CCYC we have tried to recognize choice-points in implementation and to leave room for individual teacher judgment. Examples include choice of particular activities to represent prescribed concepts, sequencing of events during the school day, and even design of activities during all but one critical period, "cognitive small group time," of the school day. We believe that we have observed that when teachers' experience and expertise are recognized they are less likely to be defensive about theory.

Good Theory Leads to Only One Possible Set of Practices

This one can only be combatted by taking an empirical approach and by working closely with teachers in curriculum development. Developmental theories generally describe how children change over time, but usually leave room for many different specific practices in education; that is, there may be many possible ways to bring about developmental change. It is up to the theoretician/teacher collaboration to determine which of several possible practices, all of which are consistent with one's conceptual structure, will actually work best with particular groups of children.

In our own case, the CCYC is being implemented in a variety of kinds of programs with a broad range of children, including a residential school for deaf children, several Head Start programs, several preschool programs for children from low-income families, a program for multiply handicapped children, and one in which the children have not yet acquired any facility in verbal communication, as well as programs for emotionally disturbed children, orthopedically handicapped children, and children with undiagnosed learning difficulties. In general, the children have developmental ages between 3 and 6 years, but that is about the extent of the similarity across programs. This diversity means that we have had to recognize multiple educational routes to the same cognitive goals. In a classroom in which the children do not have verbal communication both the questions and the answers might have to be provided by the teacher, or alternative ways of responding to questions might have to be entertained. Learning activities that require walking and running (in time with an external stimulus) might have to be replaced by activities in which these acts can be performed more symbolically, for example by rhythmic clapping. A principle that we have tried to follow in matching learning activities to individual differences in children and teachers is "start where the children are, but keep your eye on the cognitive goal," meaning that the specific activities may be varied but must ultimately serve the goal of modifying particular cognitive processes. The beginning points may vary widely, but the endpoints are stable.

Theoretical Consistency and Cognitive Education

We use the term *theoretical consistency* to refer to a consistent correspondence between concepts and practices. Of course, it is important that there be first the quality of internal theoretical consistency, which is logical consistency across parts of a conceptual structure itself. Without that, it would be difficult to achieve consistency between concepts and practices.

There are no cases in which those qualities are unimportant in the development and application of educational curricula, but theoretical consistency is especially important in cognitive education. If one is trying to teach children to think in logically consistent ways, then it is imperative that teachers behave in just such ways, and that means that they must model having what one does be a direct function of what one thinks. In other words, in cognitive education one tries to establish rational control over behavior, according to some set of principles of thought and rules of behavior. That is why it is especially important that correspondence between thought and behavior be modelled by cognitive teachers. In developing the CCYC we have tried to achieve theoretical consistency in four principal ways: (a) consistency between concepts of child development, especially cognitive development, and both the contents and the teaching methods that we prescribe in the curriculum; (b) consistency within the teaching that is directed toward a particular mastery goal; for example, it would probably not be advisable to try to teach reading by combining the "see and say" method with an analytic/phonics method; (c) conceptual consistency across educational functions; for example, content teaching and behavior management, or intrinsic motivation and the choice of learning incentives; (d) consistency across educators; that is, it is most helpful when the goals and methods of classroom teachers coincide with those of adjunctive therapists so that at least they are not working at cross purposes. To the extent that all persons connected with teaching the children understand the conceptual orientation of the curriculum, it will be possible to achieve consistency across the educational program. In keeping with this notion, we have regarded parents as part of the educational staff, and so have devised a parent participation component that is theoretically and methodically consistent with the classroom program.

DERIVATION AND DEVELOPMENT OF THE CCYC

Our principal task is to describe how the conceptual structure from which the CCYC was derived was translated into specific useful application. From that description readers will be able to see our work not only as a good example of how to accomplish this critical theory-to-application task but also as a series of examples of aspects that can now, given our experience, be done better. Before we can describe that process, however, it is necessary first to summarize our theoretical positions so that readers can see the conceptual raw materials from which the curriculum was constructed.

Summary of the Theoretical Structure of the CCYC

There are four principal domains of our theoretical structure. They are somewhat overlapping in similarity of concepts and certainly in their broad philosophical approaches to developmental processes. We have character-ized these as systematic views on: (a) the nature and development of intelligence; (b) the cognitive nature of preschool children; (c) the social nature of learning and the zone of proximal development; and (d) structural cognitive modifiability.

Nature and Development of Intelligence

Our basic view is a transactional one (Haywood, in press; Haywood & Switzky, 1986a, 1986b; Haywood & Wachs, 1981; Switzky & Haywood, 1984). According to this view, intelligence is multifaceted, not relying wholly on a "g" or general intelligence factor but admitting the functioning of a variety of qualities of intelligence. In addition, intelligence is multide-termined, but as we conceive of it intelligence is defined for our purposes as chiefly "native" ability, largely genetically determined, but influenced in its growth to some degree by genetic–experiential transactions. According to Haywood and associates (1986), "Thinking (cognition) is a product, then, of native (gene-based) ability and learned processes and strategies of thinking, perceiving, learning, and problem solving" (p. 130). Person-characteristic pathways and trajectories of development, established by gene action, may be abandoned to some degree as a result of traumatic developmental events, and these events may block the expression and application of intelligence. Salutary developmental events may remove obstacles to the expression of intelligence, but do not create new intelli-gence. Individual differences in intrinsic motivation help to determine to what extent environmental events will be used to greatest advantage to unblock expression of intelligence (Haywood & Switzky, 1986c). Further-more, we distinguish sharply between intelligence (as native ability) and cognitive processes (as necessarily acquired processes of thought), and it is to the development of the latter processes that we have addressed the curriculum. These differences are summarized in Table 8.2.

The Cognitive Nature of Preschool Children

In this area we have relied heavily on the systematic observations of Jean Piaget (e.g., 1952a, 1952b, 1960; Piaget & Inhelder, 1969) regarding the development of sequences of systematic and formal thought. We have borrowed from Piaget the notion of a usual and perhaps even necessary sequence in the acquisition of generalized understandings about the orga-nization of the world and of logical thought, as well as his emphasis on the acquisition of representational or symbolic thought in the early preschool years. Piaget's catalogue of "concrete operations," processes of logical thought that usually develop between 3 and 6 years of age, is reflected in our curriculum's emphasis on comparison, classification and class inclusion,

TABLE 8.2
Comparison of Intelligence and Cognitive Processes on Several Dimensions[a]

Dimension	Intelligence	Cognitive Processes
Source	Largely genetic	Must be taught/learned
Modifiability	Modest, with great effort	High, with teaching
Character	Both global and specific; equals ability to learn	Generalized across content domains
Assessment	Achievement; products of past learning	Process assessment; learning in teaching situations; dynamic
Composition	Intellectual aptitudes (verbal, spatial, memory, quantitative, etc.)	Mix of "native" ability, habits, attitudes, motives, strategies
Parents' Role	Genes, nutrition, health, safety	Mediated learning; active, directed teaching

[a]Reprinted from Haywood (1989), by permission of the American Psychological Association.

relations (seriation, transitivity, space, time, causality), conservation, and number. With respect to the dynamic processes of person-environment transactions, we have applied Piaget's notions of assimilation and accommodation. Piaget himself gave primary emphasis to assimilation, that is, the business of taking in new information and fitting it into preexisting cognitive structures. When new information is so discrepant from what is already in storage that it cannot readily be assimilated, one possible event is change in the organism itself. It is that process of accommodation to which this curriculum has been especially addressed; that is to say, we have sought to understand and to stimulate the processes whereby persons themselves may be changed in order to make them increasingly capable of seeking, absorbing, understanding, and applying new information.

*Social Learning Environments
and "Proximal Development"*

According to Vygotsky (1929, 1962, 1978; see also Campione, Brown, & Ferrara, 1982) the acquisition of cognitive structures through learning is a social process, with children experiencing their initial cognitive challenges and problems in the presence of adults. Adults play important roles in children's cumulative learning, beginning with modeling and continuing with guiding, correcting, and rewarding children's successive attempts to understand, structure, and gain some control over their world. The participation of adults becomes progressively less directive as the children acquire increasing independence and require less and less help from adults in structuring their cognitive world. One of the many ways in which adults give appropriate guidance to children in their cognitive development is to help them understand the requirements, parameters, and possible avenues of solution to tasks and problems, in such ways as to give the children some generalizable principles and strategies that can be followed in seeking solutions to similar problems. In that way, the adults help to define (and ultimately to reduce) the children's "zone of proximal development," defined as the "distance between the actual developmental level as determined by individual problem solving and the level of potential development as determined through problem solving under adult guidance or in collaboration with more capable peers" (Vygotsky, 1978, p. 86). The notion is of a definable region whose lower boundary is revealed by children's unassisted performance and whose upper reaches are suggested by children's performance after their social environment has been made more clearly available to them. Haywood and colleagues (1986) pointed out:

> For present purposes, two concepts are especially important: (a) the necessity of having an appropriate social environment that involves instruction in problem solving, and (b) the quality of the interaction between the social environment and the child. This emphasis on the quality of the social environment sets the stage for Feuerstein's description and further elaboration of the necessary characteristics of a social environment that enhances cognitive development. It is focused upon enhancing the parents' and teachers' effectiveness in reducing the discrepancy between children's typical performance and their potential performance. (p. 132)

Structural Cognitive Modifiability

Feuerstein's Theory of Structural Cognitive Modifiability (Arbitman-Smith, Haywood, & Bransford, 1984; Feuerstein, Rand, & Hoffman, 1979; Feuerstein, Rand, Hoffman, & Miller, 1980) is remarkably compatible with our views presented earlier on the nature and development of intelligence, including a common emphasis on the flexibility of the intellect and the necessity of acquiring cognitive processes through learning. There is a finite number of "cognitive functions" (compounds of native ability, learning history, attitudes toward learning, motives, and strategies) that are essential to effective learning and performance across a wide range of contents and contexts. Inadequate learning is most often associated with inadequate development of these basic cognitive functions. Cognitive functions are normally acquired through the twin processes of "direct exposure" learning and "mediated learning experience," so it is the failure or inadequacy of these processes that leads to inadequate development of the basic cognitive functions, ineffective learning attempts, school failure, and inadequate social learning. Mediated learning is the central concept in this theory. It refers to the process by which older and more competent persons help children to understand the generalized meaning of their successive encounters with events in their environments. Through the process of mediated learning, parents, grandparents, older siblings, and eventually other teachers help children to acquire logical structures by such events as stimulus selection, discriminating relevant from irrelevant aspects of stimulus arrays, focusing attention, attending to similarities across successive occurrences of events, naming and labeling events, objects, and persons, inducing explanatory and organizational rules by extracting essential similarities across members of classes, deducing appropriate applications of those rules, and understanding the processes by which one constructs logical rules. Parents typically rely on naturally occurring events as opportunities for mediated interactions with their children, while classroom teachers often deliberately construct situations that will yield opportunities to engage in mediated interactions. Feuerstein and his co-workers (e.g., Feuerstein & Rand, 1974) have specified the defining characteristics of mediated interactions between adults and children. The four most important and essential of these criteria are: (a) *intention* to use the elements of the interaction to produce cognitive change in the child; (b) *transcendence* of the intended change beyond the content of the immediate experience, that is, the mediator intends to produce a generalizable, structural cognitive change that will be useful to the children in novel situations; (c) *communication* of meaning and purpose, by which mediators communicate to children the long-range, structural, or developmental meaning and purpose of a shared activity—that is, explains why one is doing a particular activity in cognitive terms; (d) *mediation of a feeling of competence,* by which mediators acknowledge good performance but also specify the correct (or incorrect) aspects of that performance so children can be sure exactly what is being acknowledged and what should be repeated. From this emphasis on mediated learning experiences (MLE) in development, Feuerstein and others have developed, and we (e.g., Haywood, 1987) have elaborated on, a "mediational teaching style."

> Mediational teaching is characterized by awareness of the criteria of MLE and of the developmental needs of the children, by structural-cognitive goals rather than immediate correct-answer goals, by attempts to elicit process responses from the children, by challenging of both correct and incorrect responses, and by the use of extremely varied content material as vehicles for the teaching of cognitive processes and strategies. Mediational teachers are systematic, directive, focused on cognitive goals, and optimistic about the possibility of achievement on the part of the children. . . . The mediational teaching style is the essence of the method in a cognitive classroom, whatever content is being taught. (Haywood et al., 1986, p. 134)

These, then, are the elements of the theoretical understructure of the CCYC. In the next sections we describe some of the procedures by which these notions were translated into a curriculum and into classroom practice.

TRANSLATION OF THEORY TO CURRICULUM

The translation of any broad developmental theory into an application, such as an educational program, is a complex and difficult process. This curriculum evolved under the influence of theoretical constraints, but its development was influenced as well by commonsense help from teachers and by hundreds of difficult choices. In retrospect it appears to have been an orderly process; in reality, the pace of development was dictated by the progress of the children in our two local demonstration classes. After the initial phase, much of the curriculum was revised. Units were eliminated, combined, reordered, and added. Lessons within units were completely rewritten, and the format was significantly changed. These changes were based heavily on comments from teachers and observers who tried to implement the initial program.

In the next few sections we provide an orderly account of curriculum development that in fact was not so orderly. It could not have been otherwise, because there are few rules on translating developmental theory into educational practice. For purposes of this chapter, we divide the curriculum into four categories: units and lessons, procedures, teaching style, and day-to-day classroom activities.

From Theory to Curriculum Units

The theories discussed earlier had a great influence on the topics of the actual teaching units. The unit on Self Regulation was formulated on the basis of the work of Vygotsky, Wertsch, and others. The initial unit consisted of one principal game, "Busy Bee," in which the children made individual large rope circles to stand in, responded to leaders' directions to "Put your [part of body] on the rope," and exchanged circles when the leader called "Busy Bee" (adapted from Wirth, 1976). The goal of the game was to help children learn to follow rules as organizers of behavior sequences and to conform their body movements to external direction. This unit seemed a logical beginning for the curriculum because such self-regulation is thought to be prerequisite to later symbolic thought — and it is definitely required for organized classroom activities! (We were to change the order of games later, but this was the beginning and prototypic activity.)

The second unit, Quantitative Relations, was included in recognition of the children's later needs for quantitative skills. The content came primarily from Piagetian accounts of the development of the concept of number (Piaget, 1952b) and also from Gelman and Baillargeon's (1983) modification and Kamaii and DeVries's (1976) formulations.

Comparison, the third unit, evolved as a result of our conviction that the cognitive operation of comparison comes very close to being the cognitive atom of more complex thought processes. Comparing is itself a rather complex activity, depending on the relevant dimension(s). Piaget and his associates have included comparison as one of the criteria of developmental accession to concrete operations, and it appears to be a prerequisite to classification. Activities of comparison offer the opportunity to teach and learn complementary attitudes and habits such as attending to relevant cues, examining models, and looking back and forth between a model and one's own production. It is also an activity that can be done with both concrete/familiar and abstract/novel stimuli, a fact that offers the opportunity to progress developmentally within the context of a single set of activities. Finally, addressing the world in comparative terms is a function that can be performed without "props," using naturally occurring stimuli, so there were many opportunities for "bridging" classroom principles to events that would be familiar in the children's everyday lives.

The unit on Role Taking was included in response to the observation that the children we were instructing were seldom exposed to people in their immediate environment who modeled role-taking very well. The content of the unit was elaborated extensively until it now includes a collection of concepts from spatial role-taking, cognitive role-taking, and affective role-taking to reading other people's faces and looking for clues as to how people feel.

The Classification and Seriation units are based on thought processes and strategies that are essential prerequisites to more complex thought from Piagetian cognitive psychology. As such they help to define concrete operations. It was natural to install instructional units addressed specifically to these manifestations of operatory thought because we had already established competence in operatory thought as one of the principal goals of the curriculum. In addition, observation of children in the classroom had revealed that at 5 years of age most of them had not achieved understanding of these processes.

The last unit, Distinctive Features, is an adaptation of E. J. Gibson's (1969) concept of distinctive features as invariants to be picked up by the perceptual system. Conceived as a prereading, prewriting unit, it concentrates on such distinctive features of letters as the open–closed dimension, symmetry, straight–curved aspects, and vertical–horizontal dimensions.

Thus, all of the units have more-or-less firm theoretical underpinnings as to their inclusion in a cognitive curriculum for children. The order of units was also logically determined. In general, the later ones are based partially on the cognitive functions and operations developed by the earlier units. When teachers ask whether the order of units is to be rigidly followed, we advise them that they can teach the cognitive (Quantitative Relations, Comparison, Classification, Seriation, Distinctive Features) and social (Self Regulation, Role Taking) units in parallel but within those major groupings the order is important.

**Translation of Theory
Into Classroom Procedures**

The curriculum has some procedural dictates that have a basis in theory and common sense. These requirements involve scheduling of activities and, because of them, the curriculum falls firmly on the structured side of the unstructured–structured dimension. A day in the cognitive education classroom must have a planning time, a summary time, a small group time, a large group time, and a directed free choice time. Furthermore, these events should proceed in the same order every day unless a special exception is made and discussed. All these components are required because the predictable order of recurring, labeled events provides a structure or script for children who experience very few other recurring scripted events in their lives.

The day begins with a planning time and ends with a summary time—the "bookends" of the day. These were very consciously built in to provide conceptual contact across the past, the present, and the future. They give children tools with which to recognize predictability and to organize their behavior in accordance with the day's events.

A second part of the day that we thought was critical was a time when teachers had a relatively intimate "conversation" with a few (three to four) children. This time is called small group time and is the main vehicle of mediated instruction—when teachers have a chance to individualize the curriculum. It is for this social conversation time that the curriculum units were written.

Large group time is designated especially for content-teaching. It is the time when children learn the content prescribed by schools or states, for example, colors, numbers. During directed free choice, children work at supervised activities that provide practice at the cognitive functions being emphasized that day (discussed later).

Another major requirement of the day is a theme or topic. These are not content areas such as "colors" or "community helpers," but cognitive processes that include such topics as keeping two things in mind at the same time, using your senses to give you clues about what's happening, planning, and classifying. The teachers are instructed not only to engage the children's thought processes in the fashion described by the operations, but in many cases the children are asked to label what they are doing. They do not usually use the cognitive developmentalists' technical terms but they can explain their responses with appropriate phrases such as "I used two senses—taste and my eyes—to tell that the candy was chocolate."

There are four controversial issues regarding the teaching of such metacognitive concepts to such young children, as follows.

Why Teach These Concepts?

There are some data in cognitive developmental writings to suggest that young preschool children can use strategies to remember things (DeLoache, Cassidy, & Brown, 1985; Wellman, Ritter, & Flavell, 1975). The purpose of teaching these concepts would be to enable them, via the teachers' intervention, to manipulate cognitive processes: to call on them, to sequence them, to inhibit them, and most of all to generalize them, if the processes have a name that is known by the children and used by the teacher. There is ample theoretical and empirical precedent for the notion that representations arise from doing and these may, in turn, act as templates for subsequent overt behavior (see Vallacher & Wegner, 1985, for a brief summary of these connections). Thus, teachers can lead the children into thinking, give them the names for the processes, and tell them when to use them. They can remind the children to plan, to look systematically, to picture something in their heads, and the children know what the teachers are talking about.

How Did We Know What to Teach?

We started organizing the curriculum around the 20+ deficient cognitive functions that Reuven Feuerstein extracted from his clinical observations (Feuerstein et al., 1979, 1980). We changed them from "deficits" to "functions" because the CCYC is not essentially a remedial curriculum. Rather, we attempt to prevent deficits by teaching cognitive functions that are developmentally appropriate. We also reinterpreted and supplemented Feuerstein's cognitive functions into abilities that were appropriate for 4-year-olds instead of adolescents. Many more functions were added—some suggested by Piaget, some by cognitive research, some by our conversations with teachers. Our current list of functions is not exhaustive, inclusive, mutually exclusive, or systematic, but it is a good, workable list of cognitive functions that teachers can teach and many preschool children can understand. See Haywood (1986) for a discussion of cognitive functions.

Do the Children Learn the Cognitive Concepts?

Almost all of our teachers have been surprised at the ease with which their children could learn the concepts, and they have volunteered stories about the children's spontaneous and appropriate use of them. They tell of their children's reminding them to "make a plan," of children's telling each other to "change your perspective," to look carefully, to compare. Although we are not sure that all the children learn all the concepts, we can at least say that some of the children learn some of the concepts.

The "hard" data of such learning are more difficult to come by. We wish for a good test of metacognitive processes in children at this age. The best data available so far come from performance on standard intelligence tests, which have been very encouraging on a short-term basis—even when compared with other programs (see, e.g., Dale & Cole, 1988; Haywood, Brooks, & Burns, 1986). These are such an indirect index of a cognitive function targeted by the curriculum that even if there had been no increase in IQs, we would not have been seriously concerned.

Do the Children Generalize the Cognitive Functions?

This question leads into a discussion of the fourth prescribed feature of a "cog-ed day." Because generalization is critical to the cognitive education concept (i.e., we do not set out to teach domain-specific skills) we have included occasions during the day for "bridging" or generalization discussions. In these discussions, the teacher tries to get the children to recognize other contexts when they have needed or will need to apply the principles, operations, or strategies they have been learning; for example, to "make a plan," to "remember two things at once," to "compare two things," to "count in order to find out how many we have." At first teachers elicit recent examples from the classroom and give many clues. Later, children are able to think of applications at home, at the store, on the playground. In many lessons, activities are prescribed in which children are given other occasions to use particular cognitive functions.

We have no formal data on the frequency with which children do this. Many teachers have told us about creative responses to the questioning about other times when they have had to "plan" or "to look carefully," or to "share;" for example, one child volunteered that her family had to share space in the car when they went on a trip.

Translation of Theory Into Teaching Style

The translation of theory into teaching style has been the most challenging aspect of the curriculum development. The main task was to match the criteria for mediated instruction—intentionality, transcendence, communication of meaning and purpose, mediating a feeling of competence, regulation of behavior, and sharing of a quest for solutions—into "things that teachers do."

By way of mapping theory and practice, we asked an intermediate question: What can teachers do to motivate and manipulate children's thought processes? The best way to get children to think is to ask them questions that require mental operations to find an answer. Question-asking combines the compelling and motivational aspects of a social interaction with the opportunity to calibrate the complexity of the demand depending on the children's responses. These are not simple factual questions such as "what is this?" but rather questions such as "How did you know (which picture to pick, what to do)?" "What made you think that (a red square came next, she was happy)?" "What do we have to do in order to (go home, have lunch, go to the market for a pumpkin)?" "When is another time (you need to compare, we use models) at school?" "Why did you think (he feels that way, there is too much water in the jar)?" "What happens when (you don't plan, you share, you know the rules)?"

Of Feuerstein's criteria for mediated learning, the most difficult to operationalize has been "mediating a feeling of competence." We merged this criterion with "increasing intrinsic motivation" (one of the goals) and solicited suggestions from teachers. We also watched some teachers whose children seemed to undertake tasks, such as puzzles, as if they were intrinsically motivated. Here is a composite of the strategies we saw.

1. Teachers always worked with the answers they got from children. Most of the time they did not accept or reject a child's answer immediately.
2. They tried to adjust the level of questioning in accordance with what they thought the children could do with just a little effort.
3. They did not make a big issue over being correct as a product, but they did describe the appropriate thought processes that the children used: "Ethan looked at each choice carefully until he saw the one with the pizza in it and that was the one that finished the puzzle."
4. They promoted self-reward with phrases such as "You must feel good because you . . ."; "You looked at the puzzle carefully. Give yourself a pat on the back"; "Isn't it fun to finish a puzzle?"
5. They often used a mixture of social and self-reward. According to Vygotsky, self-reward originates as another's notice of one's success. Such phrases as "I'll bet you can't tell me . . ."; "O.K., you've got your jacket on right, let's see you button one of the buttons";

"Take the page home and tell your parents how you solved the problem" seem to mediate a feeling of pride and accomplishment.
6. They also watched their children carefully and gave the minimum boost when they faltered while undertaking a task. They reminded the children to look again at the model, to compare the two pictures before picking one, to remember the rule. When teachers do this they are letting the children themselves solve the problem. They are not giving hints about the answer but rather about the processes to engage in while looking for the answer.

From Prescription to Actual Classroom

Yet to be discussed are the pacing of lessons and the selection of activities that were actually used in the classroom. From the beginning we had theoretical direction about what to teach children and some general rules or guidelines for how to teach them. What remained was to put the two together so that a reasonable set of lessons could be written. This was accomplished by combining the efforts of psychologists—both faculty members and graduate students—and teachers together with the task of formulating some lessons that would be tried in the classroom. After a great deal of trial-and-error, these initial attempts would evolve into lessons in the curriculum. The plan was to have the developmental psychologists write theoretical papers that spelled out what children needed to know about a given topic, for example, quantitative relations meant one-to-one correspondence, counting scripts, counting rules, few/less versus many/more, and conservation. In collaboration with the model classroom teachers the group of teachers and psychologists constructed tasks and directions for interaction that they thought would facilitate the learning of the concept. For example, one of the early units was called "social problem solving." It was decided that the first major topic would be "sharing"—first of space, then of toys, tools, food, and finally of time as in taking turns. The second major topic was cooperation—first working together for a common goal, then helping. When this "Friday morning group" met, it was decided that the children first needed to be given examples of each kind of behavior that could serve as a common anchor and something that teachers could bridge to. One member suggested that each new concept might be introduced with a skit about the concept with the teachers as actors. One teacher would narrate while the other and an aide or parent acted out the skit. In time, the children could substitute for the adults. Another group member suggested the topics for the skits and the group thought that negative behavior should also be acted and discussed. Then the group started day-by-day planning of the units. The planning varied in generality from "acting out a skit about children sharing" to specifying items on worksheets that exemplified a particular principle, for example, the nature of buffer items in a matching task. In the beginning we even made a list of questions for teachers to ask during the lesson; for example, Lesson 1 (Comparison Unit): What do we have on this page? What do you think we are supposed to do on this page? How do you know? When we are looking for a shape that looks like the model, how will we look? Why would it be better to go in order? What does it mean to "go in order?" Games, activities, and songs that exemplified cognitive factions were contributed by the teachers. All members suggested variations that would better suit the cognitive function or would adapt the activity up or down to fit the children's level. One rule that we followed at each planning session was to determine, in advance, some bridging for the teacher for each lesson. For a lesson on taking turns, the teacher was to discuss other times during the day when they had to take turns, for example, on the playground, at home, and during bus rides. Some of the examples were written in the lesson plans. These Friday meetings were 2 hours long, but during the next week the group members would observe in the classroom and take notes on what the teacher did. If plans were not working, an emergency meeting was held to change the plans. Most of the time, the teachers adapted the original plans as they went along so that observers saw a smoothly flowing classroom that deviated somewhat from the plans. Occasionally, the deviation was not in a desirable direction so we had to get together to reinstate the appropriate procedure. This was most likely to happen when some activity was not working and teachers would revert to their previous style of teaching. Sometimes the teachers were too constrained by the plans and carried on some activities too long because they were determined to get the children to a more desired level. Much of the final curriculum was a product of these trial-feedback-rewrite sessions involving the teachers, psychologists, and children. The curriculum benefited from this process. One activity that was eventually discarded was one in which teachers acted out undesirable social behavior in the skits. While the children's attention was riveted to the performance and their enjoyment was obvious, they were apparently learning new ways to misbehave.

The curriculum is now complete and the various (still not enough!) evaluations are quite positive—at least for short-term gains on several standardized tests and observation scales. It is a curriculum that, when delivered according to plan, apparently holds benefits for children. It is a unique curriculum in several ways. It is probably more theory-governed than other preschool curricula. It provides structure for the children but flexibility for the teachers. For any observer, it is easy to distinguish a cognitive education classroom just by walking by the door outside the classroom (Dale & Cole, 1988), because teachers are questioning the children and discussing thinking. Like any curriculum, it cannot meet every need; for example, we cannot yet teach teachers the clinical sensitivity to assess how much a child knows and how much help to give. In Vygotsky's concepts, it contains no guidelines on how to accurately determine a child's zone of proximal development. At least the teaching strategy it proposes allows teachers to see the formative products of children's thinking and to work with those products. Furthermore, it provides children with the tools they need — "the how-to" as well as the "what" of schooling.

THE PROGRAM-PROLIFIC NATURE OF GOOD THEORY

From an applied perspective, one criterion of the value of theory is the number and quality of applications it has generated. From that standpoint, we are convinced that the underlying theoretical structure of the CCYC is indeed good theory. Various aspects of the conceptual schemes of Vygotsky and Piaget have led, of course, to their own independent applications. When we combine these with our own transactional view of the nature and development of intelligence and the role of intrinsic motivation in cognitive development, and add Feuerstein's theory of structural cognitive modifiability, we can point to a variety of useful applications. In this latter combination may be found at least five fairly well-formulated and structured applications. These are discussed briefly.

The Cognitive Curriculum for Young Children (Haywood, Brooks, & Burns, 1986) is an educational program designed for use with children at a developmental level of 3 to 6 years, and with mentally retarded children up to about 8 years of age. It is a full preschool curriculum of 1 year's duration that can be offered to the same children, if necessary, for a second year, using suggested variations on the prescribed daily activities. It is cognitive in the sense that its primary goals are to enhance the development of the formal processes of thought and to lay the cognitive base for the content learning that will occur in subsequent school years. It is now being taught in 58 replication sites across North America, as well as in Europe, to about 2,500–3,000 young children. Preparing to teach the CCYC requires about 30–40 hours of intensive instruction, assuming that one begins with certified preschool teachers, and benefits from subsequent advanced teacher training after a period of classroom experience with it.

Instrumental Enrichment is a cognitive educational program designed for use with older children, adolescents, and young adults. Developed by Feuerstein and associates (Feuerstein, Rand, Hoffman, & Miller, 1980), it is supplemental to the regular content curriculum. Its goals are both remedial (to redevelop cognitive processes that are found to be inadequately developed) and preventive/developmental (to enhance cognitive development at developmental level). Instrumental Enrichment is structured around specific cognitive functions and makes use of verbal interchange as well as paper-and-pencil exercises. The full program consists of 16 "instruments" (curriculum units) that, given one class period per school day, require 2 to 3 school years to complete. It has been implemented with many thousands of children and adolescents, as well as with adult soldiers, prisoners, and chronically unemployed persons, in four major national applications (Israel, the United States, Venezuela, and Canada) and in many other countries in more limited experiments. It is commercially available. Training of already certified teachers requires about 40 hours of instruction, with a recommended additional 40 hours following classroom experience.

The Learning Potential Assessment Device (LPAD) is a dynamic approach to the assessment of learning potential that is based on, and has stimulated the further development of, Feuerstein's Theory of Structural Cognitive Modifiability. It differs from the two foregoing programs in that its application is assessment, not education itself. Its 15 available "instruments" (tests) can be used with older children, adolescents, and adults with an intellectual range from moderate mental retardation to superior intellect, and several of those instruments can be group administered. The LPAD requires teaching of generalizable cognitive and precognitive principles and strategies, and assessment of both the amount and quality of help required for subjects to reach more adequate performance, and the subjects' response to that help. Workshops of about 40 hours prepare examiners who are already qualified in psychometrics, and follow-up workshops are recommended following initial clinical experience. The LPAD is not yet commercially available (see Feuerstein, Rand, & Hoffman, 1979; Feuerstein, Haywood, Rand, Hoffman, & Jensen, 1984).

Other Dynamic Assessment Procedures

The same set of theoretical considerations has given rise to three other groups of dynamic assessment procedures, both for use with quite young (preschool and primary) children and handicapped children. One group of such instruments has been developed by Tzuriel and Klein (1985, 1987; Tzuriel, 1989), another by Vye, Burns, Delclos, and Bransford (1987), and another by Lidz (1983; Lidz & Thomas, 1987), whereas Mearig (1987) has adapted LPAD instruments for use with young children. The general principles of dynamic assessment are the same as in the LPAD, but the target population is developmentally younger.

Cognitive-Developmental Psychotherapy is a system designed by Haywood and his students (Haywood, 1989; Menal & Haywood, 1985) for the psychoeducational treatment or prevention of learning disorders, behavior disorders, emotional distress, or social maladjustment. Based on the premise that many psychological and psychosocial problems are less the result of classical psychopathology than of inadequate development of basic processes of thought, cognitive-developmental psychotherapy is a combination of cognitive education, using either Instrumental Enrichment or the Cognitive Curriculum for Young Children, and individual psychotherapy. One of the main purposes of the psychotherapy component is to help clients to apply in their everyday lives the principles and cognitive concepts learned in the cognitive education component. In addition, therapists establish an affective climate in which clients become able to confront their own thinking processes and engage in metacognitive work. Thus, the cognitive and affective aspects of their (mal)functioning are addressed simultaneously and in complementary fashion. So far, this system has been used primarily with adolescents and young adults, but is applicable to young children as well.

SUMMARY AND CONCLUSIONS

Applied psychoeducational systems are generally more effective and more generalizable to the extent that they are based in clear and consistent theories of development and developmental change. This is particularly important for "cognitive" systems, because logical thought can be taught partly by example.

Widespread notions about teachers' relationship to theory are discussed and shown to be erroneous. These include: the mistaken notion that teachers do not care about educational theory but want only to hear about what to do and how to do it; the idea that successful teacher training can be carried out in an atheoretical context; the notion that theoreticians do not understand the "real world"; the defensive statement that any one teacher's children are unique in ways that make general theory inapplicable; the notion that pragmatic teaching is best because theoretical approaches are impractical "in the heat of the school day"; and failure to recognize that good theory leads to multiple possibilities for application.

Participation of appliers (teachers, in the present case) in the development of educational applications of good theory is essential in order to get the most useful products. The experience and unique points of view of teachers help in the evaluation of applications and in the revision of theory. Similarly, good theoretical grounding of teachers equips them to devise on their own some theoretically consistent solutions to problems that cannot be anticipated in every case and taught to them.

Derivation, development, and refinement of the Cognitive Curriculum for Young Children is described in detail, including how relevant developmental theory has been turned into a broad curriculum concept and into curriculum components, how specific classroom activities were developed in concert with the underlying theory, how a characteristic teaching style became an essential part of the curriculum, and how a sequence of day-to-day activities evolved to become consistent applications of theoretical principles.

The four major theoretical components of the Cognitive Curriculum for Young Children are described in summary form: Haywood's transactional view of the nature and development of intelligence and cognition; Piaget's descriptions of the cognitive nature of preschool children; Vygotsky's "social learning environments" and "zone of proximal development"; and Feuerstein's theory of structural cognitive modifiability. This combination of theoretical structures has produced a number of useful applications, including psychoeducational assessment systems, cognitive education systems, and at least one system for psychoeducational treatment of learning and social/behavior disorders.

REFERENCES

Arbitman-Smith, R., Haywood, H. C., & Bransford, J. D. (1984). Assessing cognitive change. In P. Brooks, R. Sperber, & C. McCauley (Eds.), *Learning and cognition in the mentally retarded* (pp. 433–471). Hillsdale, NJ: Lawrence Erlbaum Associates.

Campione, J. C., Brown, A. L., & Ferrara, R. A. (1982). Mental retardation and intelligence. In R. J. Sternberg (Ed.), *Handbook of human intelligence* (pp. 393–490). New York: Cambridge University Press.

Conant, J. B. (1947). *On understanding science: An historical approach.* New Haven, CT: Yale University Press.

Conant, J. B. (1952). *Modern science and modern man.* New York: Columbia University Press.

Dale, P. S., & Cole, K. N. (1988). Comparison of academic and cognitive programs for young handicapped children. *Exceptional Children, 54* (5), 439–447.

DeLoache, J. S., Cassidy, D. J., & Brown, A. L. (1985). Precursors of mnemonic strategies in very young children's memory. *Child Development, 56,* 125–137.

Feuerstein, R. (1970). A dynamic approach to the causation, prevention, and alleviation of retarded performance. In H. C. Haywood (Ed.), *Social-cultural aspects of mental retardation* (pp. 341–377). New York: Appleton-Century-Crofts.

Feuerstein, R., Haywood, H. C., Rand, Y., Hoffman, M. B., & Jensen, M. (1984). *Examiner manual for the Learning Potential Assessment Device.* Jerusalem: Hadassah-WIZO-Canada Research Institute.

Feuerstein, R., & Rand, Y. (1974). Mediated learning experiences: An outline of the proximal etiology for differential development of cognitive functions. *International Understanding, 10,* 7–37.

Feuerstein, R., Rand, Y., & Hoffman, M. B. (1979). *Dynamic assessment of retarded performance: The Learning Potential Assessment Device, theory, instruments, and techniques.* Baltimore: University Park Press.

Feuerstein, R., Rand, Y., Hoffman, M. B., & Miller, R. (1980). *Instrumental Enrichment*. Baltimore: University Park Press.

Gelman, R., & Baillargeon, R. (1983). A review of some Piagetian concepts. In P. Mussen (Ed.), *Handbook of child psychology* (4th ed., Vol.3, pp. 167-230). New York: Wiley.

Gibson, E. J. (1969). *Principles of perceptual learning and development*. New York: Appleton-Century-Crofts.

Haywood, H. C. (1986). On the nature of cognitive functions. *The Thinking Teacher, 3* (1), 1-3.*

Haywood, H. C. (1977, March). Research with a mission: Science or evangelism? Keynote address, Tenth Annual Gatlinburg Conference on Research in Mental Retardation, Gatlinburg, TN.

Haywood, H. C. (1987). A mediational teaching style. *The Thinking Teacher, 4* (1), 1-6.*

Haywood, H. C. (1989a). Multidimensional treatment of mental retardation. *Psychology in mental retardation and developmental disabilities, 15* (1), 1-10.

Haywood, H. C. (1989b, August). *Cognitive-developmental psychotherapy*. Paper presented at the 2nd International Conference on Mediated Learning, Knoxville, TN.

Haywood, H. C. (in press). L'Education cognitive des enfants d'âge préscolaire: Une application de la théorie transactionnelle-développementale [Cognitive education of preschool children: An application of transactional-developmental theory]. In M. Hurtig, J.-L. Paour, & E. Schmid-Kitsikis (Eds.), *Penser à penser, apprendre à apprendre [Think about thinking, learn to learn]*. Brussels: Mardaga.

Haywood, H. C., Brooks, P., & Burns, S. (1986). Stimulating cognitive development at developmental level: A tested, nonremedial preschool curriculum for preschoolers and older retarded children. In M. Schwebel & C. A. Maher (Eds.), *Facilitating cognitive development: Principles, practices, and programs* (pp. 127-147). New York: Haworth Press.

Haywood, H. C., & Switzky, H. N. (1986a). The malleability of intelligence: Cognitive processes as a function of polygenic-experiential interaction. *School Psychology Review, 15*, 245-255.

Haywood, H. C. & Switzky, H. N. (1986b). Transactionalism and cognitive processes: Reply to Reynolds and Gresham. *School Psychology Review, 15*, 264-267.

Haywood, H. C., & Switzky, H. N. (1986c). Intrinsic motivation and behavior effectiveness in retarded persons. In N. R. Ellis & N. W. Bray (Eds.), *International review of research in mental retardation* (Vol. 14, pp. 1-46). New York: Academic Press.

Haywood, H. C., & Wachs, T. D. (1981). Intelligence, cognition, and individual differences. In M. J. Begab, H. C. Haywood, & H. Garber (Eds.), *Psychosocial influences in retarded performance, Vol. 1: Issues and theories in development* (pp. 95-126). Baltimore: University Park Press.

Kamaii, C., & DeVries, R. (1976). *Piaget, children, and number*. Washington, DC: National Association for the Education of Young Children.

Lidz, C. S. (1983). Dynamic assessment and the preschool child. *Journal of Psychoeducational Assessment, 1* (1), 59-72.

Lidz, C. S., & Thomas, C. (1987). The Preschool Learning Assessment Device: Extension of a static approach. In C. S. Lidz (Ed.), *Dynamic assessment* (pp. 288-306). New York: Guilford Press.

Mearig, J. S. (1987). Assessing the learning potential of kindergarten and primary-age children. In C. S. Lidz (Ed.), *Dynamic assessment* (pp. 237-267). New York: Guilford Press.

Menal, C. A., & Haywood, H. C. (1985). *Psychothérapie cognitive-développementale: Étude*

---

*Available from Cognitive Education Project, Box 9 Peabody, Vanderbilt University, Nashville, TN 37203.

d'un cas individuel. [Cognitive-developmental psychotherapy: A case study.] Unpublished manuscript, Vanderbilt University, Nashville, TN.

Piaget, J. (1952a). *The origins of intelligence in children*. New York & Paris: International Universities Press.

Piaget, J. (1952b). *The child's conception of number*. London: Routledge & Kegan Paul.

Piaget, J. (1960). *The language and thought of the child*. London: Routledge & Kegan Paul.

Piaget, J., & Inhelder, B. (1969). *The psychology of the child*. New York: Basic Books.

Switzky, H. N., & Haywood, H. C. (1984). A biosocial ecological perspective on mental retardation. In N. E. Endler & J. McV. Hunt (Eds.), *Personality and the behavioral disorders* (2nd ed., Vol. 2, pp. 851–896). New York: Wiley.

Tzuriel, D. (1989). Dynamic assessment of learning potential: Novel measures for young children. *The Thinking Teacher, 5* (1), 9–10. (See footnote * on previous page.)

Tzuriel, D., & Klein, P. S. (1985). Analogical thinking modifiability in disadvantaged, regular, special education, and mentally retarded children. *Journal of Abnormal Child Psychology, 13,* 539–552.

Tzuriel, D., & Klein, P. S. (1987). Assessing the young child: Children's analogical thinking modifiability. In C. S. Lidz (Ed.), *Dynamic assessment* (pp. 268–282). New York: Guilford Press.

Vallacher, R. R., & Wegner, D. M. (1985). *A theory of action identification*. Hillsdale, NJ: Lawrence Erlbaum Associates.

Vye, N. J., Burns, M. S., Delclos, V. R., & Bransford, J. D. (1987). A comprehensive approach to assessing intellectually handicapped children. In C. S. Lidz (Ed.), *Dynamic assessment* (pp. 327–359). New York: Guilford Press.

Vygotsky, L. S. (1929). The problem of the cultural development of the child. *Journal of Genetic Psychology, 36,* 415–434.

Vygotsky, L. S. (1962). *Thought and language*. Cambridge, MA: MIT Press.

Vygotsky, L. S. (1978). *Mind in society: The development of higher psychological processes*. Cambridge, MA: Harvard University Press.

Wellman, H. M., Ritter, K., & Flavell, J. H. (1975). Deliberate memory behavior in the delayed reactions of very young children. *Developmental Psychology, 11,* 780–787.

Wirth, M. J. (1976). *Teacher's handbook of children's games: A guide to developing perceptual-motor skills*. New York: Parker.

Chapter 9

PRACTICAL PERSPECTIVES ON CHANGING SCHOOLS TO STIMULATE COGNITIVE DEVELOPMENT

Willy De Coster
University of Ghent, Belgium

Armand De Meyer
Educational Center of Ghent City, Belgium

Roger Parmentier
University of Ghent, Belgium

It is of obvious practical importance that one should be able to stimulate cognitive development. This goes not only for the stimulation of socially disadvantaged children, but for that of all children. Indeed, the spontaneous experience that all of us can gain is likely to be less than what is optimally desirable. Moreover, current knowledge and technology, and Western society in general, have become very complex. This necessitates adult mediation and facilitation of learning for the upgrowing generations (Bruner, 1960; Bruner et al., 1966; Feuerstein, 1980). Investigations to activate cognitive develoment are also significant for the setting up of theories as they shed light on the distinctive nature of cognitive functioning and on the factors that influence it. The successes as well as the failures of practical applications constitute an essential test of the cognitive hypotheses used. It is also clear, however, that the underlying explicit and implicit theory, with its structure of hypotheses, constitutes the inevitable basis and inspiration of any type of stimulative strategy and of any kind of legitimate pedagogical practice.

Unfortunately, in terms of cognitive stimulation there has so far been insufficient reported accounts of interactions between theory and practical application. Often theories make insufficient allowance for the operational aspect, that is, their orientation towards the practical problems is insufficient. As a result, it is often difficult to translate outcomes of laboratory research into meaningful, practical action in schools.

On the other hand, practice, and particularly school-based practice, shows too little interest in the theoretical framework and in the scientific data available. All this is compounded by the fact that cognitive development, learning processes, and cognitive functioning to an extraordinary degree prove to depend also on extracognitive factors, the precise nature and influence of which are insufficiently known.

Learning, at school, depends on a particularly complex multiplicity of factors, in which emotional, motivational, interactional, and social factors are of essential importance. Therefore, a better understanding of the psychology of the classroom is indispensable to setting up a strategy for "learning to think." For example, a strategy for cognitive facilitation in the field of learning at school, designed for the beginning of primary school, resulted in conspicuous reduction in the number of children with reading problems when applied in a child-centered school with project learning and explicit team-work. Also, the children proved to like reading, and they read much more and with a greater critical sense. However, when transferred to other schools, and in spite of program guidance given to the teachers, this strategy turned out to be almost without any result. This goes to show how ineffective general educational reform programs can be, how complex the problem is in practice, and how many factors are at play.

Acting in an intelligent way comprises the discovery, the development, and the use of problem-solving methods, based on insight. In this cognitive functioning, the child's constitutional basis is of course of fundamental importance. But, there are reasons to assume that experience and "learning" have a major influence as well:

- The contemporary psychophysiological study of the brain points to the influence of experience, of the degree and form of the activity, on the physiology and the morphology of the brain, so that further learning is conditioned by it.
- Psychological and pedagogical observations bear out the great and determinative significance of the earliest development phases. Still, this does not preclude a remarkable degree of plasticity in later stages of life and the possibility of compensation, in so far as proper experience is offered and on condition that the "sensitive period" is not over yet.
- In a sense, understanding evolves from memory, therefore from experience. The emergence of the first understanding, during the second half year of one's life, consists in the child's ability to foresee the result of a process or an action on the basis of a mental action, though such a mental action is, for the time being, only a vaguely conscious one. The perception that an out-of-reach object can be brought closer by means of a stick, means for example that the

young child, on the basis of its experience, is able to conceive of the action, motorically and visually, at least in its essentials.

- Therefore the action is performed mentally (even if, in a first stage, vaguely), before the action as such is carried out in reality. This is an ability to anticipate the effectiveness of certain actions for the attainment of certain goals. And this is precisely what understanding means. It is obvious that experience lies at the basis of this ability to foresee and of this mental action, which will gradually gain in structure and clarity. By way of these interiorized experiments, the child learns, in a subsequent stage, how to make a choice between several possibilities, between different plans of action by which a goal may be reached. The subsequent step consists of mental experiments in which several of the patterns discovered earlier (or parts of these plans) are combined. In this way, relatively new problem-solving methods are found for relatively new situations. Solving mathematical problems, for instance, is usually an example of this approach.

- In the meantime, abstraction, conceptualization, and verbal experiments will allow further structuring, with the immediate goal-centered application of known relations. Clearly, experience always remains present. The perceptual structures and the problem-solving methods that have been developed are made into automatisms in their entirety, a process in which only the starting-point (the assignment set, the situation) and the outcome (the goal) remain as conscious stages. These "automatized" problem-solving methods can be used as entities in wider-ranging mental actions and experiments. Thus broader and more abstract problem-solving systems can be developed. The process of thinking is not associative, but neither is it completely creative.

- Considering the role of experience in shaping cognitive structuration, it is not surprising that the problem-solving methods that one acquires are to a large extent topical, so much so that their transfer is relatively difficult. Cognitive functioning may be made even more topical, that is, tied up with contents, because of the orientation of a person's interest and motivation.

- Building up meta-structures and meta-problem-solving methods is probably facilitated by drawing attention to the process, by making explicit the effectiveness of earlier experiences for bridging the gap between starting-point and goal. These are crucial mediating roles of the teacher despite the fact that the nature of these meta-structures and of the way in which they can be acquired is far from clear. At any rate, at all levels it is essential that attention should be given to the structure of the means used, as the path leading to the solution. Through such activity, it seems likely, children develop meta-cognitive practices.

- By now it should be evident that constitution and learning are both of essential importance in development of cognitive functioning. There is no point in trying to find out what the relative share of each plays in development. It is the constitutional factor that offers a range of possibilities for "learning." This range differs in each individual, not only as to the level, but also as to the extent of and the individual's sensitiveness to experience. However, these individual differences do not mean that fairly general strategies for stimulation should be impossible.

- The stages of development as described by Piaget (1970) do appear to correspond in their entirety with reality, although they seem to be more sensitive to stimulation and experience than Piaget originally assumed. As such, it may be possible for young children to function appropriately at the level of the distinctive stages, and to do so at an earlier age than is generally assumed, at least in so far as contents are concerned that match their real experiences. It must be clear, however, that this real experience is influenced by the attained level of assimilation. Our data suggest that the transition from one substage to another can be stimulated, and that even a certain degree of transfer is possible. However, it did prove to be difficult to demonstrate the continuity, the ongoing significance of stimulation. Actually, research in this field is hampered by the blurred boundaries of each substage, because the substages are not as clearly outlined as one tends to assume.

- For the sake of comparison, our own findings suggest that, at least for children in the age-bracket of 4 to 6, cognitive stimulation in school may be continous, only if it is actually continued. If not, the environment and (or) the original rhythm of development may become again the primary influential factor. Moreover, the specific content area for stimulation may well be of secondary importance; whether one concentrates on seriation, classification, or conservation, the outcome of sustained guided interactions with the child may enhance the likelihood that the child becomes more thoughtful and inquisitive.

- On the basis of observations and case-studies, we would tend to believe that, for practical purposes, the constitutional as well as the developmental basis of cognition chiefly concerns the number of elements that can be surveyed and combined, which can be coordinated and subjected to a mental experiment. This comes close to reformulating the old definition of intelligence as *Kombinationsfä-higkeit*. However, we do not now have at our disposal any hard test data to support this belief in an experimental sense. Should the number of data that can be combined really turn out to be a distinctive characteristic of the individual, this would not preclude further differentiation of intelligence. There is not of necessity a fully linear relation between for example the following aspects:

- The number of elements that an individual can survey and incorporate in a synthesis.
- The number of steps in which an individual can follow a strategy in a mental experiment.
- The number of problem-solving methods that an individual can compare by following them in a given series of steps (compare Case, 1985). Within these confines, the building up of problem-solving methods retains its fullest significance, and the possibility remains that the application of strategies is topical, that is, that it is strongly tied up with contents.
- After all, the human brain functions like a computer, with hardware and built-in software, processing more divergent information and integrating more feedback than any other computer in the world: and, on top of all this, on the basis of this experience the brain develops (to a certain extent) differentiated additional software for the conception and realization of particular goals in given situations.

PERSPECTIVES ON
A COGNITIVE STIMULATION STRATEGY
IN SCHOOLS

With support of the Bernard Van Leer Foundation (The Hague) and in cooperation with the State University of Ghent, the Pedagogical Center of the City of Ghent, and the Belgian Ministry of Education, a project was undertaken to facilitate cognitive development and school readiness of 4- to 7-year-olds in schools of the City of Ghent's network (the second and third year of preschool, and the first year of basic school). In so doing, socially disadvantaged children came in for special attention.

In designing the project, compensatory programs as devised in the United States did not prove to be particularly helpful to us, probably because for one thing the context was rather different, because social-economic conditions in Belgium are rather less extremely different from one social class to another, and because the virtually general attendance of kindergarten helps the children to certain experiences and fills certain gaps.[1] Designing a well-considered program for compensation or stimulation was made more difficult because we were unable to tie in with the fundamental character- istics of the socially disadvantaged child. For project purposes, we consid- ered the state of deprivation and the individual reactions to such conditions of life too varied. In spite of systematic examinations, we were unable to find clear-cut characteristics, both cognitively and socially—and for ex- ample with regard to the self-image—of these children.

Moreover, it would have been erroneous for us to have provided a one-sided interpretation of the achievements and the experiences of the socially disadvantaged child, as "deficiencies," by comparison with middle- class children. In our setting, we got the impression that the deprived child did not only seem to merely possess a lesser-degree of experience, but might also have a different experience; and we thought that part of the very frequent failures of these children from the first grades onwards may also have been due to the apparent fact that the schools did not make any link with the experiences of socially deprived children.

Actually, the problem of socially disadvantaged children was not con- fined to the cognitive area. Their life typically had been marked by poverty and by the lack of social security. The reactions and the expectations of these children, also in social intercourse, appeared to be different from what one typically found with middle-class children. Seemingly, their reactions and their expectations do not match those of the teacher, and the result was emergence of various misunderstandings that adversely affected interaction with the teacher as well as integration in the school and the child's record. This misunderstanding was such that it may have very well contributed to the vicious circle of failures and maladjustment.

Finally, the contacts between the school and the socially deprived parents were very scant. Such parents considered the school an unsafe place, although it is precisely the close contact between the school and the child's home that ultimately may prove essential to the adequate functioning of stimulation programs at school.

Compensatory Kindergarten Project

The first stage of our project was concerned with the prefinal kindergarten classes (age bracket of approximately 4-year-olds) of eight schools (four in 1970 and four in 1971); in each school, we selected 12 children in the socially disadvantaged group. Randomly, they were distributed over a project group

---

[1]Belgian practice generally contains day cribs and day-care centers until 3 years; toddler centers from 1,5 until 3 years; preschool from 3 years until 6 years (admittance tolerated from 2,5 years on); basic school from 6 to 12 years.

and a nonproject group. The children from the project group were provided a compensatory program, two half days a week during 2 years, with a specially trained teacher. An outline of elements of the program was:

1. The perceptual-motor program, based on the work of Frostig (1967): eye-motor coordination, figure-ground discrimination, form constancy, perception of position in space, perception of spatial relations.
2. The language-thought program, largely based on a number of Dutch compensatory programs (e.g., Utrecht and Haarlem).
3. Language development and refinement of verbal (largely oral at this stage) competencies:
   • learning new words and implicit concepts, developments of active and passive vocabulary;
   • learning morphological rules;
   • learning syntactic rules;
   • making oneself familiar with the written language;
   • knowing that something spoken can also be written and vice versa;
   • familiarity with the direction of writing;
   • general recognition of their own written first name;
   • looking at picture storybooks;
4. cognitive activities and exercises:
   • making collections (sets);
   • working with two or more collections;
   • relational concepts of place, time, proportion, causality.[2]

These different elements were offered to the children in the form of games whenever possible. Throughout the project, our activities aimed at observation, experience-based learning, expression, and specific cognitive exercises of particular linguistic structures (again frequently in the form of games). Finally, serious efforts were made to establish the greatest possible degree of parent involvement.

In view of the interdependence of the different capacities, the project policy was not to deal with one entire target-area at a time and then move on to the next. Exercises provided for the different objectives were worked at in rotation; thus, we first tried to achieve a certain level of perceptual consistency and then concentrated on the observation of spatial relations. When a certain level had been reached, we then proceded to other exercises, including one for enhancing the child's mastery of perceptual consistency.

---

[2]More details about the methods, procedures, and curricula used in this program can be obtained by contacting: Willy De Coster, department of Psychology, University of Ghent, Henri Dunantlaan 2, B-9000 Ghent, Belgium.

Summary of the Evaluation

Each year, both the project group and the control group were subjected to a series of pretests and posttests: the Leiter International Performance Scale, the AKIT test (Amsterdam Child Intelligence Test), and the Frostig Developmental Test of Visual Perception. From pre- and posttesting, several observations can be noted here. First, with exception made for the perceptual tests, the scores were markedly different according to the social-cultural level of the child's family. Second, many Frostig scores may have been influenced by the training given, one of the probable reasons being that evaluation and training were relatively similar. Third, AKIT IQ scores as well, may have been influenced by training, in contrast to the scores obtained on the Leiter test.

Positive results were apparent in the project group, at the end of the projects' first year but the gains seemed to have lessened after the summer vacation, after additional testing. It is mainly the spontaneous development of the nonproject group that was at the basis of this equalization. The resumption of the project brought the project group ahead again, though in a less pronounced degree than the first year, and again the vacation period resulted in a leveling-off effect.

All in all, one might think that the developmental phase that was to follow next in the normal course of events was accelerated by the project, though there actually was no further positive evolution. Besides, as we pointed out, the positive effect after the first year of training was confined to the initial project groups. Conceivably, additional factors, such as the motivation of the teachers during the initial start-up of the project may indeed have played a part here, apart from the cognitive strategy as such.

Generally speaking, over time, we had to abandon the idea that children from the lower social-economic strata could be made more successful at school by just simply administering a compensatory program at the kindergarten level.

The learning situation being very complex, a large number of situational variables naturally can have effects on children's learning output. In a way, this practical reality seems to have been overlooked in the evaluation of some compensation programs. As such, very little is known about specific circumstances in which compensatory programs were implemented. Despite this situation, though, it goes without saying that teachers have often been trained for the application of compensation programs; the training may very well result in a better relationship between the teacher and the pupils, and in a more effective general approach to the subject-matter to be taught. Hence generalization of findings to regular classrooms indeed may be difficult. In short, we believe that the effects of programs may not only be due to instructional content, but also to the characteristics of the broader educational context. In fact, the latter may be a condition sine qua non, to the former.

Of course, another objection might be that IQ tests are not the most appropriate tools to evaluate results of compensatory and stimulation projects, because these tests have been designed to measure something that should be insensitive to training to the greatest possible extent.

Kindergarten Curriculum

Our experience with the compensatory program led us to the conclusion that direct instruction may be relevant mainly for specific skills. Thus, it appeared desirable to remodel "training" and compensation into a general enrichment program, which was to embed actual stimulation, within a framework of normal activities and experiences, and was to do so in a systematic, yet spontaneous and natural way.

Yet, we believed that experiences occurring in the regular classroom could be structured, so as to be responsive to children's individual needs, although we recognized that the mediating role of the teacher would be vastly different.

Therefore, we attempted to mount a program in which children had opportunity to be active explorers of their environment. We aimed at a general frame within which specific instruction could be included.

The new strategy was applied in the regular classes of 5-year-old children of municipal schools, initially in 20 classes, pending a more generalized application. The program was designed in an experience-oriented way, in the form of a project. In order to benefit from the experience and the interests of the children, the activities were largely centered round the children's points of interest. The program occurred within a yearly frame; the central themes, covering 14-day periods, were broken down into a number of specific activities. The yearly frame determined the underlying relation between the central themes.

The first central themes accentuated the exploration of the child's relation to its immediate environment, that is, school and family. Once this relation was established, the horizon of the child's exploration was progressively widened: from "me, school and family" to "I live in a house. Who lives with me in that house? I live in a street with a number of houses. Many streets form a city. What do the people do in the city. You can also leave the city and go to the country. Back to school but to a new class, teacher and friends" and back to "me, school and family." Working with the progression from one theme to another, within the yearly framework, had several apparent advantages. For one the teacher was able to easily situate activities in relation to the general objectives. For another, the child was able to relate different activities to each other.

The project provided for support to teachers, who had at their disposal a description of points of interest with detailed examples. In so doing, the relation between the activities and interventions proposed and the objectives was made explicit, in order to further purposeful action.

After the first year, the results were not positive: in spite of the support given, the teachers seemed to have lost their self-confidence. Our observations suggested that the teachers started to doubt the efficiency of their usual ways of doing, before reaching sufficient security in the practical application of the new methods. This led to feelings of insecurity and a less effective, hesitating attitude in the classroom, which may have hampered the close humane contact that we were striving for. Again, this shows how important the teachers' commitment is (as Haywood and Brooks stressed in chapter 8) and how difficult it is to implement general educational reforms.

As a result of the first year's disappointing experience, guidance and support were intensified, both in order to secure the child-oriented aspect of the project, and to help with the concrete organization of the activities. A permanent concern was for the teachers to continue to be aware of the relation between the activities organized and the ultimate objectives. To this end, further observation training sessions were conducted to emphasize the importance of observation. In the children too, we tried to strengthen purposefulness, a well-considered approach to the activities, and the conscious use of experience. The teachers made sure that all the children achieved the basic objectives. As a result, the child-oriented approach was clearly strengthened, as was the project's orientation towards stimulating the children.

Summary of the Evaluation of the Adjusted Project

In 10 project classes and in 10 nonproject classes, six children were subjected to a Nijmegen school ability test (as pretest) and to a large series of posttests. The results were subjected to factor analysis. Preliminary results suggest that the project may have had a positive influence, primarily in the language area.

Introducing Direct Instruction in Kindergarten

In the next stage, and in view of the major problems encountered in reading instruction in the first grades, the preschool project was extended with specific training for preparatory reading. Activities were concerned with learning to listen, remember, analyze, and synthesize: for example, to indicate the first or the last or the longest word of a sentence, form sentences, divide words in two parts, indicate the first and the last phoneme of a word, and to make an auditive synthesis.

Events suggested that it may well have been a combination of general enrichment with specific training, that was highly influential on readiness for reading. In the group of children belonging to the risk-group (as determined by pretests), progress was as considerable as in the riskless group. Both the risk and the nonrisk children proved to benefit from the program. Without the general enrichment program, however, the specific training program did not yield any positive results.

At a more general level (scores in a traditional scholastic maturity test), progress again proved to be minimal and to occur particularly in verbal competence, and further only in areas linked up closely with the training given. It was considered by us to have been desirable to have evaluated effects of a continued enrichment program on problem solving, because here too topical effects, bound up with contents, may be in evidence. However, we concluded that problem-solving research is carried out more easily with older children, whose general and cognitive disposition has to a large extent been fundamentally shaped. In the actual functioning of problem solving, though, there does appear to be room for stimulation: general cognitive attitudes and more specific problem-solving methods (possibly with some transfer in the application) can be acquired until well in adolescence and even later, in so far as self-image and motivation do not constitute barriers to new acquisitions.

Reading Instruction in First Grade

The project was generalized and continued in the first grade, using a reading method that relied primarily on auditive analysis and synthesis. Moreover, emphasis was on comprehensive reading (completion of sentences, finding words that fit in the story, logical ordering, etc.). For the basic skills the pace of the slowest children was followed, although in other instances there was a very high degree of individualization, in part to cater to the needs of the brighter children. It appeared that the children began to take to reading, and to read critically. Results indicated that the number of reading failures dropped from 25% to 5%. This effect seemed to have persisted, at least until the level of reading fluency was reached.

The Day-Nursery Project

In view of the importance of the first years of life, we also set up a project in a group of day-nurseries (children between 0 and 3-years-old). Thanks to the experience gained earlier and to systematic observations, we defined a number of aspects pointing up deficiencies that might influence the children's later development. These included our beliefs about the following matters in our setting:

- Child-centeredness and human contact often remained insufficient. The nursery-staff was mainly paramedically trained and therefore inclined to material and hygienic care and less to emotional contact. They tended to underestimate the importance of this emotional contact or they didn't possess skill to realize it. They overlooked possibilities of establishing such a contact during nursing and feeding. .
- Insufficient stimulation of experience and insufficient attempt to use experience were seemingly prevalent. When working with day-nurseries, an experience-oriented approach implied that children were stimulated to activity by means of offering them materials, but that free activities were thought to be indispensable before a more structured form of stimulation was possible.
- There was not enough purposeful action with these children:
  - Here too, objectives were hardly made explicit.
  - Activities were conducted without staff being aware of the potential significance of these activities for the objectives to be attained; as a result, chances for stimulation may be used inefficiently.
  - For the child, too, the relation between the means and the goal were not made explicit enough in the form of a problem that was adapted to their age; the starting-point was too rarely an analysis of the situation, a comparison with earlier findings, or a target-centered experiment.
- Team-work in the nursery and parent-involvement were considered inadequate. All in all, the problems seemed to reside in the day-nursery staff, including its inadequacies in mediating childrens' cognitive and emotional experiences. Consequently, refresher training was provided for them. The importance of the factors already mentioned was underlined and practice-centered training sessions tried to demonstrate the way to improve these points. In so doing, the relation was emphasized between the different forms of activity and the targets that could be attained in the child's development.
- The starting-point of the training was to set up sessions for observation-training and for interaction-training in order to make the nursery-staff aware of the behavior, signals, and attitudes of the children. Therefore, we used the observation-scheme constructed by Beller (unpublished report) in view of evaluating the different levels of development as a basis for a more stimulating interaction. Moreover, staff members were asked to look for means to use the

child's best developmental areas for stimulating the less good ones. This training for observation seems to have affected the quality of the observations of the children made by the nursery-staff. It also seems to have improved the child-centeredness of the staff, the contact between the staff and the child, and it heightened the stimulation of the children's level of activity.

- The result of such improvements was, for example, that children from a nonstimulating environment were observed to actually open up and exhibit new positive behaviors. Relatedly, the nursery-staff's interventions seem to have acquired considerably more purpose. Such an evolution, clearly, was important for the children's further development, including their cognitive development and cognitive application.

- In order to correctly evaluate the results of the project, it was necessary to train special observers. Apart from the children's forms of activity and behavior, the observers were to note, among others, eye-contact between the child and the staff, physical contacts, responses to calls, elicitation of activity, the stimulation of the use of experience by the child, and so forth. Although these data are still being computer-processed in the time of publication of this volume, we expect them to point up a higher degree of child-centeredness and, concomitantly, a direct effect on the child's emotional, social, and motivational attitudes. Normally speaking, this should also improve the chances for a better cognitive development, but we have as yet no certainty that the available observational data will be sufficiently large to permit the evaluation of this cognitive evolution.

Impressions

Based on our experiences in changing schools to stimulate cognitive development, we offer the following recounted observations:

- Stimulation and enrichment, it seems, must be implemented, on a continued basis; if not, the benefit gained risks being lost.
- General stimulation is not achieved easily and may best be initiated as early as possible; even at a later age, there is potential for cognitive facilitation.
- Teachers can be assisted to be more effective mediators: to be child-oriented, to foster intensive contact with the child, and gain understanding as a result of extended observation and training. This social climate, provided by the teacher along with self-image and

motivation, may well determine the outcome of training and enrichment.

- Cooperation with the parents and family seems to be important, along with social action to help achieve a more favorable attitude toward the school.
- Also important is experience-oriented education, with explication of experiences, in which the relation between experience and later applications is highlighted.
- Working with contents, and with assignments that are clearly understood to be problems, seems necessary.
- Team-work and individualization, education for independence, and positive self-image are all essential objectives.

CONCLUSIONS AND PROPOSALS

Our experiences have led us to suggest that a number of adjustments can be effected in schools, in order to optimalize cognitive functioning. We are fully aware that we have to deal here with a good many prerequisites, and also that in the area of cognitive facilitation, considerable systematic and well-coordinated research is required—inspired by an overarching vision of theoretical as well as practical problems and hypotheses.

Cognitive functioning and the effect of cognitive facilitation may strongly relate to self-image, feelings of security, and social interaction. Enrichment programs, therefore, may require a child-centered educational approach and positive, high-quality human interaction. The concrete form that can be given to these requirements changes, according to the child's age, but it can be considered a vital aspect, even though, at every level, there needs to be allowances for influences from preceding life-stages (particularly negative influences) that may have led to fixations that are harder to reduce as the child's age advances: Not only the available problem-solving techniques depend on experience, but children obtain a view of the world that determines the experience of a situation. The first years of life are of essential importance, but any age may give rise to emotional and interactional problems resulting in inhibitions.

Stimulation, facilitation, and enrichment of development may best begin from the earliest age onwards, and it may be necessary to continue them uninterruptedly. Nevertheless, even in adulthood, we believe that opportunities still exist for acquiring relatively general cognitive attitudes and problem-solving methods based on understanding.

Another important aspect of cognitive development seems to be hierarchical integration of executive structures. In this regard, we concur with Case (1985), when he identified four major stages of executive development: the stages of sensorimotor, relational, dimensional, and vectorial operations. What differentiates these stages, is the type of mental element acted upon. In particular, a basic point seems to be that each new stage integrates the preceding structures. At the vectorial or formal-operational stage the adolescent develops an abstract and, in principle, scientific thought system, which, however, consists of a higher-level integration of dimensional or concrete-operational systems.

At the dimensional stage (roughly the early school years) most problems solved have to do with the isolation of properties of objects and actions. These include compensatory and reversible effects of different dimensions, and the detection of operations that change certain properties. These dimensional systems, however, build on relational systems acquired in preschool. The basic units of preschool thought might well be relationships between objects and actions. Besides this, a central accomplishment is the acquisition of the linguistic code of the community, and its use for the representation of knowledge about objects and interesting actions upon them. Of course this relational stage can easily be conceived of as a higher-level hierarchical integration of the sensorimotor stage (infancy and toddlerhood) where the basic units are sensory objects and motor actions.

If this kind of view is meaningful and practical, a consequence might be that the blocking of cognitive development at a certain level can be fully remediated only after mastering the systems from the lower level. Of course, in practice, we knew already that remediation of a failing system through direct teacher-centered instruction can hardly be accomplished and leads to superficial and unstable accomplishments.

At all age-levels, success at school, and the effect of enrichment programs may be influenced by close contacts, understanding and cooperation between school, parents, and family. It seems that, with such interactions, the child will be integrated better, its self-image can be more positive, conflicts between the different influences can be reduced, the teacher can assume a more understanding and positive attitude toward a child when relevant family background is known, and the parents may indeed possess increased understanding of school operations and curricula and will, therefore, be in a better position to support the school.

The educational staff may benefit if they function effectively as a team. However, a teamlike approach is hard to achieve. Team development has to begin with a commitment of each team member, otherwise team-meetings may do more harm than good.

Our experience leads us to recommend that instruction be experience-based and oriented towards problem solving:

- It links up with the existing experience and helps to structure it.
- It introduces further necessary experience in a systematic, though nonartificial way.
- It considers relations and plans of actions from the point of view of

their effectiveness for problem solving; it accentuates and interio-
rizes the linking scheme between the situation (the problem) and the
goal (the result) fostering metacognitive practices and skills; and
possibily it demonstrates transfer.
- It is strongly centered on testing and control;
- It makes clear that the nature of the tasks presented is that of a
  problem.
- It analyses (new) problems accurately and tries to systematically
  draw on experiences that might be used; draws up a plan and tests
  it consistently, as much as possible by means of mental experiments.
- It systematically introduces and explicates its potential for application (if possible with its opportunities for transfer). Any kind of
  learning may link up with a real problem (initially with concrete
  problems, later with more abstract structures) and be motivated.
  The learning of contents and structures of which one does not see
  the sense can have a negative effect.[3] The eagerness to learn can be
  preserved and may be activated if possible.
- Any kind of school must formulate its final aims and its intermediate goals, and make them operational. This implies, among
  others, that the structure of the problem-solving methods to be
  acquired must be determined allowing for the transfer expected, and
  that the most efficient way to proceed from the methods acquired to
  new ones must be outlined. The indispensable foregoing experience
  can be carefully analyzed for each substage. Making allowance for
  the children's age, one will try to make them aware of the structure
  of the method used, and of the structure of larger entities of
  formation—essential mediating activities of the teacher.
- Therefore, we propose a school with a strongly structured approach
  to cognitive formation, but with a large degree of naturalness and
  spontaneity in the mediation of learning. Our plea for purposefulness and structure in the action of stimulation and in the operating
  procedure that we try to foster in the child, must not prevent us from
  stimulating the child's natural experience and its potential for

---

[3]As an illustration of a problem-solving approach at the level of advanced education, we cite
the following experience with a geometry course (in particular the ability to apply the
knowledge thus gained) in the training of skilled workers. The results proved to be totally
different according to whether the course started off by explaining concepts, properties,
combinations and formulas, to eventually reach the stage of practical application, or whether
the elementary concepts were allowed to grow as logical answers from practical problems, and
were next analyzed, after further insights could be introduced on the basis of new real
problems. The brief moment of rediscovering the useful strategy, of rebuilding knowledge,
remains a major pedagogical instrument, which is strictly indispensable if one is to give sense
to the learning process.

spontaneous structuration, and to exploit these to the full: they too are of essential importance. Furthermore, every point of the program must have been fully absorbed before transition to another point. Continuous evaluation, paired with a great concern for the self-image and for motivation, is fundamental and will make the teacher's intervention more effective and more understanding.

- Verbal skills will be in the forefront of attention, but they will always be directly related to other goals. The important point here is to have the child discover the functionality of language for purposeful communication, for ordering and storing information, for planning mental and external actions, and for representing knowledge.
- The school must leave room for individualization and teamwork. Learning should turn into learning to look for things, into rediscovering, into attempts to transfer and combine problem-solving methods that one has already mastered and to which one has added critical systematic evaluation of the hypotheses used.
- The training of teachers and educational staff can be usefully reconsidered and special attention be given to the following matters:
  - The ability to observe the child, and the orientation toward such observation, and not only of the child, but also of the "others" in general, as a starting-point for better understanding.
  - Skills of interaction.
  - Knowledge of the child's development and of the possibilities to stimulate this development. Above all, one must try to transfer theoretical contents into concrete educational situations. Special attention should be given to the possibilities to individualize, not an easy task for a teacher responsible for a group of 25 children.
  - The ability to work in a group which functions as a team.
  - Team-work and individualized approach with the child.
  - Interest for "learning to think" and for a problem solving, rather than a pedantic, approach. It is important to acquire appropriate general attitudes in the area of cognition as well as to develop proper problem-solving methods (along with their transferability if possible). Conceivably, it may be possible to argue that what one learns is less important than how one learns it. Probably, the how is very much related to the building up of general cognitive and metacognitive attitudes and possibly also of really effective problem-solving methods.
- All in all, it remains difficult to deduce, on the basis of the scientific data and in a critical way, a well-founded and coherent strategy to be applied to the educational practice. Still, important guidelines

can be formulated. But the modalities of their application continue to be essential, and naturally in this area different roads can be taken. Anyhow, humane interaction, besides the stimulation of genuine problem-solving attitudes, is of paramount importance.

ACKNOWLEDGMENTS

This action research was realized with the support of the Bernard Van Leer-Foundation (The Hague, The Netherlands) and the State Department of Education (Brussels, Belgium), with the collaboration of the administration of the city of Ghent (Belgium).

REFERENCES

Bruner, J. S. (1960). *The process of education*. Cambridge, MA: Harvard University Press.
Bruner, J. S., Oliver, R. R., & Greenfield, P. M. (1966). *Studies in cognitive growth*. New York: Wiley.
Case, R. (1985). *Intellectual development. Birth to adulthood*. New York: Academic Press.
Feuerstein, R. (1980). *Instrumental enrichment. An intervention program for cognitive modifiability*. Baltimore: University Park Press.
Frostig, M. (1967). *The developmental program in visual perception: Advanced pictures and patterns*. Chicago: Follet Publishing.
Piaget, J. (1970). *Science of education and the psychology of the child*. New York: Orion Press.

ON COGNITIVE DEVELOPMENT

Jerome Kagan
Harvard University

In every society a small number of Platonic ideas is surrounded with mystery and awarded such extraordinary significance that no one would ask why a contemplative adult was trying to understand more completely the idea and its most direct actualizations. The Greeks awarded such status to morality; early Christians tried to comprehend God; 17th-century Europeans sought to discover the natural laws that described physical phenomena. Contemporary natural scientists seek insight into the essence of matter and the forces that will explain the origin both of the universe and life by assuming that a small number of special instantiations provide the clearest picture of the idea. The outputs of a linear accelerator, for example, presumably reveal optimal understanding of the idea of atomic particles. Among psychologists, human thought, but oddly enough not skill or repentance, possesses an equivalent amount of mystery. The clearest signs of thought are believed to be captured by event-related potentials, answers to questions on tests, and, in infants, differential attentiveness to familiar and unfamiliar pictures or sounds. A century earlier, reaction time and sensory acuity were equally preferred sources of evidence. That is why a large part of the history of each scientific discipline is captured by changes in the referents of the longer lasting ideas. Stated differently, an important basis for change in a science, in addition to new theory, is invention of a new source of information.

Thought, which we know how to use but do not understand, poses as formidable a problem for inquiry on the origin of the universe or the evolution of vertebrates. Rigorous scientific inquiry into human cognition is less than a century old, thus it is inevitable that deep a priori presuppositions will retard progress in the same way that Ptolemy's idealized conception of the proper relation between earth and sun and the latter's circular orbit influenced inferences about the cosmos. That is why a philosophical analysis of cognition and cognitive development can be as useful as a synthetic review of what we have learned, especially when such excellent reviews exist in many places. Even though some of that knowledge will be reviewed here, the thrust of this chapter is a constructive critique of our assumptions about the development and measurement of cognitive processes.

THE NEED FOR A BACONIAN FRAME

The constructs that name the basic units of a scientific domain originate in informed intuitions, dominant theoretical prejudice, and empirical observations. Although early theories in biology and chemistry began with units that had their roots in theistic ideas, the extraordinary progress following the Enlightenment was facilitated by a Baconian mood insisting that evidence, not a pleasing idea, was to be the source of units. The idea of the cell, biology's most fundamental entity, provides an exemplar case. It is doubtful if the most imaginative 16th-century naturalist could have imagined a diverse class of irregularly shaped structures bounded by a partially permeable surface membrane, dotted with chemical receptors, containing a nucleus of interlaced chromosomes embedded in a cytoplasm dotted with tiny factories manufacturing a variety of proteins. This Rube Goldberg conception would have been rejected by both scholars and their scientific community because of its asymmetry, structural heterogeneity, and uneven assignment of functional responsibilities. Perhaps that is why physicist Richard Feynman warns us not to expect our initial explanations to conform either to our wishes or our phenomenology, because nature, in Feynman's view, is "absurd."

Despite the fact that a few areas of psychological research have matured to a stage where data are the major source of constructs, this advance has not yet occurred in the cognitive sciences or its subfield of cognitive development. The chapter headings in books and essays continue to be abstract dictionary terms that do not stray very far from the comprehension vocabulary of the educated community. The title of this year's *Annual Review* chapter on cognition, for example, is "Concept, Knowledge, and Thought" (Oden, 1987). The use of such a small number of terms—perception, language, memory, symbolic representation, problem solving, and intelligence—to name the diverse set of events comprising cognition is reminiscent of the Greek's parsing all of nature into air, water, fire, and earth. For reasons that are not clear, many psychologists remain reluctant to accommodate to robust observations that challenge the probable inutility of these popular, overly abstract constructs. For example, the correlation among the performances on a battery of procedures assessing recognition or recall memory for verbal or pictorial information is relatively low, especially in children. This suggests that memory is not a unitary process and, therefore, a more constrained construct combining recognition or recall memory with a particular class of information would be more powerful (Kagan, 1981). Furthermore, recent neuropsychological studies of memorial processes suggest that connections among association cortex, limbic structures, thalamus, and various areas of the prefrontal cortex contribute differentially to varied memory performances (Mishkin & Appenzeller, 1987). For example, the ventromedial prefrontal cortex participates in a major way for recognition memory for objects, whereas the dorsolateral prefrontal cortex participates in memory for the spatial location of an object (Bachevalier & Mishkin, 1986). Memory is not a unitary phenomenon occurring in a particular place but a set of varied functions, each mediated by a specific set of relations among different parts of the brain.

Years ago, Michael Moore and I studied 35 dyslexic boys and 35 matched controls 8- to 12-years-old. We found that although the recognition and evaluation of simple perceptual events was as efficient for dyslexics as it was for boys with normal reading ability, the former were less efficient in evaluating the meaning and validity of oral sentences composed of familiar words (Moore, Kagan, Sahl, & Grant, 1982). The dyslexics displayed unusually long response times (800 to 900 ms) before they affirmed or denied the validity of single sentences like, "Black is the color of coal," or "A watch is bigger than a football," compared with 600 ms for the controls. However, the two groups performed similarly when they had to detect 15 different occurrences of the word *to* embedded in a long tape-recorded story along with the words *two* and *too*. Moreover, there was no correlation, for either dyslexics or controls, between recall of a series of orally presented words and a series of pictures ($r = -.12, .22$), nor any relation between recognition memory for numbers (in six-digit strings) and recognition memory for words in an orally presented story ($r = -.13, -.18$). Thus, terms like *evaluation of meaning* or *recall memory* are specific to a class of information and do not name unitary processes. Why is there a resistance to analysis?

Pragmatic criteria can always be defended as a basis for collapsing or differentiating among performances. But if dyslexic boys are similar to normal boys in evaluating the correct meaning of the word *to* in a series of oral sentences, but differ in their evaluation of the validity of a series of oral sentences it seems reasonable to argue that we should invent constructs that preserve and communicate these differences in what some scholars treat as a unitary cognitive function.

THE GENERALIZATION
OF PROCESS PREDICATES

One reason why psychologists write about human characteristics as if they reflected abstract qualities that did not change in important ways across time, place, or target of action is because the targets of their inquiry are processes rather than things. Biologists study the characteristics of physical objects that can be observed either easily, like flowers and bones, or with difficulty like bacteria and viruses. They summarize their observations with sentences that consist of a noun phrase referring to the entity followed by a predicate that describes some of the entity's features. Most objects in nature are unique in some ways, consequently many advances in the natural sciences consist of discovering a feature that makes it necessary to discriminate between two classes of objects that had been regarded as belonging to the same class, for example viruses and retroviruses. But the targets of inquiry for psychologists, and especially cognitive scientists, are processes. Processes like thought, memory, or perception are predicates typically generalized across context and information rather than parsed into finer categories. Consider the following three short sentences:

1. Trees grow.
2. Insects grow.
3. Children grow.

Despite the extraordinary differences in the details of growth in the three objects, the same predicate is used, tempting readers to conceive of the growth process as consisting of the same core set of events for all living organisms. Most descriptive or theoretical constructs in cognitive development refer to mental processes, thus there is greater resistance to differentiating them into a set of finer classes than to differentiating among the entities participating in these processes.

The practice of generalizing predicate terms for cognitive processes leads behavioral scientists to write as if memory or representation were essential processes that did not change their core meaning, even when the age of the organism and the informational context did. Frege (1979) recognized this problem and attributed it to the tendency to treat the separate syntactic elements of the sentence as basic units, as linguists do, rather than treat the entire sentence as a unit. Frege argued that the basic unit in scientific description is the proposition, not the noun phrase representing a topic or the predicate describing it. Frege suggested that propositions assumed the form of function or argument. A function stated a general abstract relation among variables, whereas the arguments were the references that gave different meanings to the function. A psychological example, which Frege would not have used is:

1. Organisms experience internal states to unexpected events.

The function in sentence 1 obtains its truth value by taking on specific arguments. Hence,

2. "One year old infants experience a state of fear to strangers" is true. But,
3. "Newborn infants experience a state of fear to strangers", and,
4. "One year old infants experience a state of guilt to new toys" are both false.

Although the theoretical meaning of psychological processes and, therefore, their truth value require specification of context and the characteristics of the organism, these constraints are typically ignored in most psychological studies of cognitive development. Reports are written as if there were only one argument for a function, implying that perception, memory, and reasoning are, like paint colors, autonomous essences that transcend time and location and can be applied to any object that happens to be near the brush.

Consider several illustrations of this style. Patients with bilateral lesions of the occipital and temporal lobes, called prosopagnosics, will tell an examiner showing them photographs of family members that they do not recognize these familiar people. Their performance indicates serious failure of recognition memory. But if the test procedure is repeated while the patients' galvanic skin reflexes are being recorded, they show a GSR to the familiar, but not to the unfamiliar, photos (Tranel & Damasio, 1985). This surprising fact implies that the phrase "recognition memory for familiar photographs" has one meaning when verbal statements of recognition are the evidence and a different meaning when galvanic skin reflexes represent the data. This pair of phenomena lose their paradoxical quality if we assume that connections among the hippocampus and parts of the visual association and temporal cortex are more seriously impaired in prosopagnosics than connections between the amygdala and cortex. Existing data and theory imply that hippocampal structures evaluate the relation between past and present visual inputs, while the corticomedial division of the amygdala responds to unexpected sensory inputs with discharge to the autonomic nervous system (Mishkin & Appenzeller, 1987).

In a study with a similar conclusion, Kenneth Livingston (unpublished) found that when children were tested with four different procedures designed to assess their knowledge of the concept "animal" or "living thing," almost every child understood both concepts when asked to name a set of animals or living things, for all children could name at least a half dozen of each type. However, when the measurement context was an inference test, clustering words in recall memory, or proactive inhibition, a large number of children failed to show evidence of possessing the same two concepts. As a final example consider the fact that a 3-day-old infant will recognize a previously presented novel auditory stimulus (an English word) following a 2-minute delay if it hears a stimulus on postnatal days two and three, but a 3-day-old infant who hears the stimulus for the first time on day three cannot tolerate a delay as long as 2 minutes and fails to show recognition (Zelazo, personal communication). This fact means that "recognition performance" is a function of both the strength of the trace (the familiarity of the event) and the delay between familiarization and test. There is no absolute length of delay an infant of a particular age can tolerate; that value varies with the familiarity of the stimulus to be recognized. Thus precise generalizations about infant recognition memory will be, at the least, propositions describing interactions of event familiarity and duration of delay, and perhaps other factors as well. The most robust generalizations about recognition memory the future owes us will pertain to specific members of a family of processes now called simply *recognition memory*. I suspect that the construct *allergy* is at the same epistemological level as recognition memory, for the most powerful generalizations are for specific allergies, like hives, asthma, and poison ivy; few involve the superordinate concept *allergy*.

Although it seems obvious to me that the popular function terms in cognition are too broad, our shared intuition is jarred by the suggestion that the units in cognitive theory should be as restrictive as "recognition memory for familiar photographs with GSR as the index of recognition," or "concept of animal when clustering is the source of evidence." Yet, in one sense, the results of these studies reflect an accepted state of affairs in quantum mechanics. One of the deep assumptions in modern physics is Bohr's axiom that the scientist cannot know which aspect of the evidence reflects the entity in nature he/she wishes to understand and which part reflects what the procedures (or apparatus) have done to the entity. So, too, with experiments in cognition. When a subject in a proactive inhibition procedure cannot remember any of the three animals presented in the third trio of animal words we cannot say precisely which part of that performance reflects the structure of the concept *animal* in the subject's mind and which part the procedural probe. That is why a statement declaring that most 6-year-olds do or do not possess the concept animal must stipulate explicitly the procedural source of the data.

CONSTRUCTS SHOULD REPRESENT UNITS
CUM PROCESSES

If biology is taken as a fruitful guide to the study of cognition, and I acknowledge that there may not be consensus on that suggestion, the sense meaning of a construct for a cognitive process should also refer explicitly to the type of cognitive unit that participates in that process. For example, the biological process of meiosis applies to gametes, not somatic cells, and the process of synaptic transmission refers to neurons, not glia. I believe psychological theory will be advanced if we assume that the to-be-discovered generalizations about the processes of recognition, recall, or transformation of information when applied to schemata will be different from the generalizations that involve concepts, even though McClelland and Rumelhart (1986) reject the idea of schema as a basic unit.

I view schemata as partially veridical representations of experience that need not be part of a complex meaning network (for example, representations of 100 unfamiliar faces or 100 unfamiliar melodies played on a lute). I view concepts, however, as networks of related symbols. Thus, a person *recognizes* a face as familiar or unfamiliar through assimilation of that face to a schema, but *understands* the meaning of a frown or a shrill voice by relating the event to a network of symbols. Obviously, many events can be represented either as schemata or as a networks of symbols, or both. Frege would have approved of this suggestion for he argued that a sentence has a sense meaning (Sinn) derived from the meaning of its component concepts, whereas a perceptual experience may not. That is why the predicates *understand* and *recognize* have different theoretical meanings. There is empirical support for this claim.

First, the fact that interference effects in recall memory are much stronger for concepts than for schemata is one bit of evidence for their separate status. Second, 1-year-old infants, in most cases, will look longer at an unfamiliar than at a familiar event when both are presented simultaneously. But if the experimenter should say the name of the familiar picture (for example, cup) the child is likely to look longer at the cup than at the unfamiliar object. Third, the meanings of sentences in an orally presented short story, which are contained in a set of related concepts, are retrievable after a much longer delay than the representations of specific words or the tone of voice of the person reading the story. Fourth, concepts have complements (good-bad, boy-girl), whereas most schemata do not. Finally, violation of a conceptual expectancy (reading an incongruous word at the end of a sentence) is accompanied by a negative wave in the event related potential at about 400 msec, but violation of a schematic expectation is accompanied by a positive wave in the event related potential. If the functions that describe the recognition of a prior experience mediated by schemata turn out to be very different from the functions that describe the understanding of the meanings of a prior event we should not use the same predicate (e.g., *recognition*) for both cognitive activities. No biologist uses the word *birth* as a technical predicate to describe both the division of an amoeba into two cells and a human mother delivering twins.

If investigators who study cognition added dependent variables that reflected the motivational and affective processes that accompany perception, memory, and inference, they would invent new concepts with a different meaning. For example, most subjects show a dilation of the pupil and a small rise in heart rate when storing information in short-term memory for later retrieval. But there is a great deal of variation in the frequency and magnitude of these sympathetic changes. This extra evidence adds information about the processes accompanying the mental work being done by the subject. Two identical recall performances—two subjects recall 40% of the words presented—could have different profiles of pupillary and cardiac change. As a result, the construct that explains the performance should take this fact into account.

Unlike physics and biology, which have advanced because of new data provided by machines and apparatus, psychology has not invented many new devices that necessarily create new evidence and new constructs to account for the evidence. Psychologists, especially those who study cognition in humans, may be resistant to this strategy, as if straying too far from natural behavior was dangerous. I offer the speculation that when psychologists become more friendly to new classes of evidence they will see the necessity of new constructs. When that happens the split between hot and cold cognition will vanish for all cognition is warm, some a bit warmer.

The Metric Used

Metrical considerations also favor differentiating between the processes that involve schema and those that involve concepts. Schemata are not described typically as a composite of their separate dimensions, while concepts are often so described. Like a schema, each member of a set of structurally related steroids is a unique pattern in which the various members differ from each other in the arrangement of only one or two chemical elements. Chemists do not apply the metric "degree of steroidness" to describe or quantify the structural variation in members of the set. Rather, the value assigned to a particular member is based on its biological consequences with respect to some target tissue (for example, potency to produce muscle growth in the larynx). Because schemata, too, are coherent patterns, it is difficult to invent a metric that refers to a continuous characteristic that is inherent in the pattern, even though a quarter-century ago psychologists tried, unsuccessfully, to quantify visual patterns as varying in complexity. Rather, schemata are quantified with respect to their behavioral consequences, at least in infants (for example, duration of fixation to a visual event provides one metric for inferring a schema in infants).

However, some investigators describe concepts as a combination of a set of differentially weighted dimensions (e.g., the concept stone has fewer dimensions than the concept weather). J. Maynard Smith (1985) suggested that nature uses two basic strategies in creating phenomena—jigsaws and waves. Jigsaws are the result of putting smaller pieces together; a construction of a protein from amino acids is an obvious example. Waves, however, are holistic events that cannot be constructed by fitting together a set of smaller elements. Many concepts seem to be more like jigsaws; schemata are more like waves. In a recent review, Oden (1987) noted that, "Concepts are represented by nodes that are connected by labeled links corresponding to properties and relations. The result is equivalent to a collection of propositional expressions with complex concepts being composed of simpler ones combined with various operators" (p. 205). That definition sounds like a jigsaw.

There are, of course, occasions when a phenomenon can be viewed as a jigsaw or a wave depending on the question asked. For example, the ability to process speech syllables as adults do is a competence that has been recently awarded to the infant (Eimas & Miller, 1980; Kuhl & Meltzoff, 1982; Miller & Eimas, 1983). An additional claim purports that the processing of speech is context-dependent. Eimas and Miller reported that perception of the speech syllable *ba* or *wa* depends not only on the duration of the initial formant transition but also on the transition duration in relation to the duration of the entire syllable (Eimas & Miller, 1980; Miller & Eimas, 1983). There are two ways to interpret the data on which this inference rests. Eimas and Miller prefer the interpretation that because no percept is fully determined by the information in the signal, the stimulus is referred automatically to a larger frame, a conclusion reminiscent of the early Gestalt writings on perception. The mind evaluates the stimulus with reference to the larger frame in which the signal is embedded.

However, a somewhat different description of these data is possible. When the syllable *ba* is described as an event composed of variations in the durations of initial formant transitions and completed syllables, and investigators manipulate each of these dimensions separately, they find that the infant's perception of the syllable *ba* or *wa* under one formant transition duration depends on the duration of the syllable and conclude that there is context-dependent perception. This is a proper inference. But the infant's central nervous system may not analyze the stimulus *ba* in the way the experimenter intended. Therefore, it is also proper to state that the infant perceives *ba* as a unitary event under one set of conditions and perceives *wa* as a unitary event under another. The physicist Pierre Duhem (1906), writing on the distinction between qualities and quantities, stated that if a new value on a dimension can be formed by addition—like loudness—the dimension can be regarded as a quantity. But if a new phenomenon cannot be formed by adding the separate values on a selected dimension—like the syllable *ba*—it should be regarded as a quality. Every event contains many different dimensions, some of which can be conceptualized as continuous quantities, others as discrete qualities. The preference for conceptualizing an event as a quantity or a quality depends on the question being asked and, therefore, the theoretical interest of the scientist. Eimas and Miller are interested in how the central nervous system discriminates among the sounds of human speech. It is useful for that question to view the stimulus events as continua. But for investigators interested in the schematic representation of events, it may be more useful to regard the entire syllable as unitary, with a distinct quality. A pathologist seeking the causes of a new viral disease looks for the unique qualities of that pathogen; but a geneticist interested in classifying pathogens into their proper categories will search for continuous characteristics among a group of related viruses.

MATURATION OF COGNITIVE FUNCTIONS

The last two decades have been witness to an increased concern with the maturation of cognitive talents that appear to be separate from language. When we say a cognitive competence matures we mean that structural and/or chemical changes in the brain have made possible the processing and transformation of experiences that permit a particular cognitive product to be actualized. It is assumed that the "product" is derived from the experiences acting in combination with the altered brain.

Infancy

The growth of the central nervous system in the first year, especially the frontal lobe and limbic structures, is accompanied by a lawful increase in the ability to recognize an event over delays of 30 to 60 seconds by 3 to 4 months of age, and enhanced recall memory at 8 to 12 months of age. The former talent is accompanied by the appearance of the smile to the human face; the latter by object permanence and stranger and separation anxiety.

In a comparison of human and monkey infants, Adele Diamond (1987) showed that both 1-month-old monkeys and 8-month-old infants make the "A not B" error if the delay between hiding and permitting the infant to reach is not more than a few seconds. Moreover, both monkey and human infants improve dramatically in the next few months, so that 4-month-old monkeys and 1-year-old humans do not make the "A not B" error. Maturation of the dorsolateral prefrontal cortex and hippocampus and their connections provide a basis for the improved ability. First, bilateral lesions of the principal sulcus of the dorsolateral prefrontal cortex of the adult monkey destroy the ability to solve the "A not B," as well as delayed response problems. In addition, a circuit involving hippocampus, amygdala, thalamus, and prefrontal cortex seems to be involved in maintaining a representation of an event for delays greater than about 10 seconds. Thus, the phenomenon called the object-concept requires brain maturation. I suspect that the contribution of sensory-motor manipulation of objects, which is treated as absolutely necessary in Piaget's explanation of object permanence, may be less critical than many psychologists assume.

It is of interest that changes in behavior on a different task occur during the same developmental era. In a second task, the infant can see an attractive object within a rectangular transparent box that is open on only one side—top, front, right, or left side. Adult monkeys with frontal lesions fail to retrieve the object because they always reach for it on a line corresponding to their direct line of sight, as do 7-month-old human infants. The infants show a sequence of behavioral changes over the next 5 months that is so predictable it fits a Guttman scale with a reproducability coefficient of 0.93. Seven-month-olds, like lesioned monkeys, cannot retrieve the object from an open side if they see it through a closed side because they cannot inhibit reaching in the direction corresponding to their sight of the object, even if one hand is touching an opening in the box on the right side. One month later, by 8 months, infants will begin to look at the toy through different sides of the box; they may lean over to see the toy through the top of the box. However, they still reach only toward the locus they are fixating. At 9 months they first begin to succeed and will reach into an opening, even though they were looking through the closed top of the box. By 10 to 11 months infants will reach successfully through an opening, sometimes without even looking at it, because tactile information informed them of the open side. By 1 year, performance is close to perfect. Infants will now use the tactile information to guide them and they rarely return to a side that touch told them was closed. Infants are now able to retrieve the information indicating that a particular side is closed and can integrate visual and tactile information. (Diamond, 1987)

These data imply that the emergence of the ability to retrieve the immediate past and to integrate two sources of perceptual information are a result of growth changes in prefrontal cortex and limbic structures as well as the connections between these areas and the diencephalon and sensory association cortex (Mishkin & Appenzeller, 1987). Manipulative experience with objects may be less important in these victories than some psychologists have surmised. It is also likely that the ability to integrate information originating in two different modalities over a period of a few seconds requires maturation of the connections between prefrontal cortex and amygdala (Mishkin & Appenzeller, 1987). Hence, the claim for inter-modal schemata in infants under 6 or 7 months may be suspect. The ability to retrieve schemata established in the immediate past and to relate that information to the present may be necessary for separation anxiety (Kagan, Kearsley, Zelazo 1978; Kagan, 1984). That is, separation anxiety may be a result of the new ability to retrieve the schema of the mother's former presence, to compare it with the fact of her absence, and an inability to understand why the two representations are discordant.

The next 12 months contain other maturational victories, one of the most important being the appreciation of symbols and, soon after, comprehension and expression of language. Although the use of objects as tools by chimpanzees was hailed as evidence for a less disjunctive relation between the psychology of hominids and apes, the human addiction to the application of symbols must be as one of our most distinguishing qualities. The earliest stone carvings reveal how easy it is for humans to consider a single perceptual feature as representative of a complex idea or concept (for example, a circle as representative of the sun's beneficial effects on the earth). And 2-year-olds from different cultures have no difficulty in selecting the larger of two pieces of unpainted wood when asked, "I have a mommy and a daddy, which one is the daddy?", indicating that relative size is treated as a feature of the concept of gender. A year or two later simile and metaphor emerge. The profound difference between ape and human children can be seen if ball-point pens and paper are given to both. The latter automatically create a set of lines that symbolizes something. The apes scribble a few unclosed, irregular curved lines in the middle of the paper (Boysen, Bernston, & Prentice, 1987).

Psychologists who study inter-modal perception are suggesting that 7- to 11-month-olds have a component of this symbolic talent. The evidence still does not meet Savage's criterion of a "between-the-eyes-effect." But, on occasion, the infant's looking patterns at visual stimuli are in accord with the hypothesis that they can extract a dimension from one modality (like connectedness) and detect it in another. One of the more famous studies demonstrated that infants who heard an intermittent sound would be more likely to look at a discontinuous line than a continuous one; but would look longer at the continuous line if they had heard a continuous sound (Wagner, Winner, Cicchetti, & Gardrer, 1981; see Kagan, 1987 for a discussion of this issue). If the infant under 1 year is prepared to treat one feature of an event as representative of a concept that transcends modalities, the emergence of language is a little less of a mystery.

The Second Year

By the second birthday, two other distinctive human characteristics appear. They are an appreciation of right and wrong behaviors and self-awareness (Kagan, 1981; Lewis & Brooks-Gunn, 1979). The former is inferred from concern with flawed objects, shame, and anxiety over possible failure. The latter competence is inferred from the use of pronouns to refer to self, in both deaf and hearing children, recognition of self's reflection in the mirror, and an increase in directing the actions of others for its own sake. The recognition of the self's reflection in the mirror even occurs in children who do not have prior experience with mirrors (Priel & DeSchonen, 1986). Awareness of self's intentions and feelings is as much a cognitive product as is the enhancement of retrieval memory, despite the reluctance of some to regard internal feeling tone as information to be processed, categorized, and transformed.

An empirical example of the serious influence of internal state on cognitive performance comes from our research on inhibited and uninhibited children. We have been following a group of children who were selected in the second year to be extremely shy, timid, and fearful, or bold, sociable, and outgoing. All of the evidence indicates that the former group has a lower threshold for limbic arousal to stress — novelty and challenge. At 7½ years of age the inhibited, compared with uninhibited, children showed a much greater deterioration in recall memory performance following a series of mildly stressful cognitive tests. Furthermore, the inhibited children made significantly more errors when judging pairs of drawings as either identical or different when the picture portrayed emotional scenes but not when their content was neutral. Thus, a state one might call uncertainly or anxiety affected both memory and perceptual discrimination.

The Transition at 5 to 7 Years

Although it is likely that many other significant talents mature between 2 and 6 years, they have not yet been discovered; hence, most investigators jump from the second year to the emergence of concrete operations.

The fact that important cognitive changes occur between the fifth and seventh years of life was recognized by mothers in rural societies, the Catholic church, and English common law long before Piaget and Freud tried to analyze the essence of these changes. Piaget has come closest to articulating the nature of the new talents. The most important are the abilities to relate two concepts and to appreciate that their relation can change with context and, therefore, is relative. Consider the robust fact of conservation of liquid. When the liquid from one of two beakers has been poured into a tall, thin cylinder and the examiner has asked the standard conservation question, the 7-year-old with an introduction to the arithmetic idea of equality has two conceptual appreciations of the array. One originates in perception, the other in the recently developed concept of equality between two perceptually dissimilar events. The concrete operational child appreciates the related meanings of the question, "Which has more liquid?", and infers the one intended by the examiner. At a birthday party, the same child might make a different choice. That is the implication I take from the work of Tversky and Kahneman (1973), who claim that college students do not always apply statistical rules they know in a laboratory setting. However, they are likely to do so when they are buying a house or selecting a surgeon. The ability to infer the mind of another is also present in class inclusion problems for the child must appreciate that the examiner has made the improbable and counter intuitive request to relate a part and a whole. Few adults expect to be asked, "Which act has more virtue: Saving a drowning child or acting morally?"; or, "Are there more insects in the world or more living things?" Hence, when 5-year-old children are asked, "Are there more red balls or more balls?" they unselfconsciously choose the former, because they assume the question is about the relative numerosity of red and white balls. But by 7 years of age, when children can both monitor questions more carefully and can relate a part to the whole, they realize the possibility of two answers and offer the correct one (see Flavell, Spear, Green, & August, 1981).

Winner (1988) suggested that appreciation of irony does not appear before 6 or 7 years because the younger child cannot infer the intention of a speaker who, on a hot July day declares, "Isn't it refreshingly cool today"? The ability to detect the relation between or among categories also permits the child to nest hierarchically ordered categories properly and, therefore, to know that dogs, pets, animals, and living things form a nested set of concepts. This is one reason why it is not until age 7 that American children begin to worry about catastrophes, like war, kidnapping, and vandalism, for such apprehensions require the child to be able to relate the abstract concept of environmental danger to the concept of self. Additionally, the concrete operational child who can now seriate (that is, apply a magnitude dimension to a set of events and detect their relation) can compare self with others on qualities like degree of beauty, strength, and intelligence. As a consequent, important new components of the self-concept that could not be established earlier begin to grow.

Formal Operations

Piaget's suggestion that adolescence is marked by the emergence of fundamentally new cognitive competences is one of the most original ideas in any theory of human nature and provides insights about adolescent behavior that challenge traditional explanations. The abilities to deal with hypothetical situations, to sense the inconsistency in a set of related beliefs, and to know when one has exhausted all solution possibilities are generally absent from the repertoire of the average 9-year-old. These abilities help to explain the rise in suicides during the adolescent years, for in order to develop a state of depression deep enough to provoke a suicide attempt the person must hold the belief, whether valid or not, that all attempts to solve a personal problem have failed and, further, no constructive action is possible. Second, the ability to detect inconsistency among a set of personally held and related beliefs contributes to some of the rebellion, anger, and anxiety characteristic of adolescents, especially in modern societies with pluralistic philosophies. Among modern adolescents some important pairs of inconsistent themes include: Illicit sex is morally wrong yet pleasant; dependence on parents brings security but one should be independent of one's family; and parents are wise and potent but have serious flaws of character. Recognition of these and other inconsistencies demands a resolution and either rejection of one or synthesis of a compromise belief. During the period when this mental work is being accomplished the adolescent can experience serious dissonance and uncertainty. I interpret these insights from Piaget, as I did the earlier competences of infancy, to mean that many of the major milestones in universal emotional growth follow the maturation of cognitive processes. This view is not only the reverse of Freudian theory, it is, in a real sense, a fresh discovery about human nature.

Awarding influence to maturation of the brain does not imply a friendliness to reductionism or a committment to the assumption that eventually all statements in cognitive science will be translated into sentences with biological words. I remain loyal to the philosophical position claiming that although natural events are a unity scientists parse them into conceptual domains, each in a different language and at a different level of generality. In addition, it is often the case that the phenomena at one level are emergent from those at another. This position implies that although knowledge of the physiology of the brain can aid understanding of cognitive functions, it is not necessary to translate all psychological sentences into physiological ones. Furthermore, it is not possible to do so without some loss of theoretical meaning. The elegant laws of planetary motion illustrate emergent phenomena and they have not been replaced with statements in which the atoms comprising the planets are the basic entities.

So, too, with statements in cognitive development. The 1-year-old's ability to tolerate a 1-minute delay in an object permanence context is an emergent phenomenon derived from the growth of the brain and experience with objects. It is difficult to imagine the replacement of a function that has, on the ordinate, the duration of delay on which successful reaching occurred and on the abscissa the child's age with a function that relates discharge patterns in motor neurons to density of synaptic connections among visual, frontal, and limbic areas. Even if such a figure were possible at some time in the future, I doubt if it would be preferred to the one with psychological labels on the axes.

It is odd that some biologists, and even some philosophers—Patricia Smith Churchland (1986), for example—are insistent on the reduction of psychology. No one claims that the theoretical statements in evolution can be replaced with propositions that only have biochemical terms, like gene, protein, or amino acid, because unpredictable environmental events—like climate changes—must be included in an explanation of evolution. The expansion of mammals 60 million years ago was an event emergent from adaptive mutations in small rodents and alterations in ecology that eliminated large reptiles.

It is unlikely that we will be able to translate the descriptions of psychological growth into biological sentences, even though the biological knowledge enhances understanding in a major way. Perhaps that is why Stent (1987), in reviewing Churchland's book, wrote, "I doubt that a complete reduction is de facto possible. My cardinal hunch is that a significant residue of unreduced psychological as well as neural biological theory will remain with us long into the future" (p. 992).

A major lacuna in theories of cognitive development is our inability to state explicitly the critical environmental conditions that are necessary to actualize the cognitive competences made possible by growth of the central nervous system. No child locked in a closet would become operational. Consider, as an example, the conservation of mass. The fact that the earliest age of conservation is about 5 years, regardless of environmental context, suggests some maturational changes are absolutely necessary for this performance. But the fact that unschooled children in many isolated communities do not achieve conservation until adolescence—if at all— suggests that certain experiences that are not part of daily life are also necessary. School instruction, which emphasizes categories and classes, is one contributing factor; exposure to counting and the varied ideas of amount are others.

The literature suggests that some competences will appear in almost any environment with people and objects. Mayan Indian children living in northwest Guatamala, who have no radios, televisions, books, or pencils, develop some of these universal competences, even though their appearance is delayed by a few years. These isolated Indian children were able to solve a culturally fair version of an embedded figures test despite no familiarity with pictures, paper, or crayons (Kagan & Klein, 1973), and were able to perform as well as American children on a test of recognition memory for photographs of unfamiliar objects (e.g., typewriters and golf clubs), and, at adolescence, were able to generate reasonable replies when asked what would happen if the lake they see every day were to dry up.

It is necessary, therefore, to differentiate between highly prepared and less prepared cognitive competences. The former set seems to require only the experiences that are part of living in the natural world. The less prepared competences — multiplication and conjugating verbs — require special tutoring. Linguistic contrasts provide an example. Children find it easier to learn the contrasts between one and many than between several and many; between up and down; than between right and left; between in and on than between near and far. The less prepared competences — multiplication and conjugating verbs — always require special tutoring. Preparedness does not imply a rigid schedule of times when structures will develop; it only implies that some structures-cum-processes are easier to acquire than others. Nature gives to the young organism the potential for acquiring a large number of abilities and lets experience control the small number that will be actualized. The final pattern of brain synapses is a nice illustration of this principle.

This abbreviated review of a few of the obvious maturational milestones has listed only cognitive talents and, thus, contrasts with the milestones described by Piaget and, more recently, by Fischer, both of whom award major importance to the maturation of sensory-motor structures in the first year, and less to enhancement of recognition and retrieval memory. Fischer's ontogenetic schedule involves the assumption of a deep connectedness in a sequence that begins with the coordinated acts of infancy and moves, in turn, to representations of events, coordinations of representations, propositions for abstract ideas and, finally, coordinations of abstract ideas (Fischer & Silvern, 1985). The basic premises in this frame are, first, implementation of motor skills is necessary for the later cognitive competences and, second, the appearance of a new class of cognitive unit is followed by the emergence of the ability to coordinate and relate other members of that class. Although both premises are reasonable, the former remains in more dispute than the latter.

FINAL SPECULATIONS

I wish to make two final points. First, the meaning of theoretical propositions about cognitive functioning depends on the source of evidence, which I alluded to in the introduction. The reader will recall that when simply naming animals was the evidence, all children possessed the concept, but when clustering in recall or proactive inhibition provided the evidence, many of the same children did not seem to possess the same concept. One rebuttal to this statement is to insist that all 10-year-olds possess a similar conceptual representation of *animal,* but some will not display that knowledge in every assessment context. After all, persons with focal lesions of the temporal lobe do not display signs of that lesion on every relevant diagnostic test. But it is fair to ask if the referential and, therefore, the theoretical meaning of the concept of focal lesion is the same for two patients if one experiences difficulty remembering dates and the other does not, even if both have similar size lesions in the very same place. This question leads to a second, more abstract point.

Contrasts In Description

Most descriptions, whether in scientific journals or newspapers, have an implicit contrast class. When I point to a table laden with Thanksgiving delicacies and say, "That's a pie," I am likely to imply a distinction between the pie and the other foods. But should I say, "That's a pumpkin pie," I am more likely to imply a distinction between two forms of pie. Current theories of cognitive development typically contrast, implicitly, biological preparedness for certain competences with a position that emphasizes the necessary contribution of certain experiences to acquisition of the competence. Piaget's genius was to unite the two by making action on the environment necessary for actualizing a universal cognitive process. When Jensen (1980) writes about level 1 memory skills he intends a contrast with level 2 reasoning abilities and, thus, awards salience to the rote quality of a memory task, rather than the transformations that are part of metamemory. But, when our research group describes the performance of 2-year-olds on a procedure in which the child has to remember the location of a toy placed under one of six cups, our intended contrast is language competence, not reasoning ability. Thus, we make the capacity for sustained attention a primary feature of memory, not its rotelike quality.

When J.J. Gibson theorized about the autochthonous nature of the perception of motion, the implied contrast was learning the cues for motion. As a result, Gibson emphasized the structures of the stimulus arrays that produce a perception of motion. However, when the neuropsychologist Robert Wurtz writes about the perception of motion, the implied contrast is the neural basis for the perception of space, and Wurtz focuses on the brain sites that mediate motion perception. Wurtz and Gibson emphasize different features of the construct "motion perception," even though both use the same descriptive construct and are interested in similar phenomena.

Jean Piaget and Kurt Fischer contrast the infants' sensory-motor actions on objects with representations of those objects, whereas our research, which is concerned with the same developmental period, contrasts the ability to recall a past representation with the ability to anticipate a future event. I do not suggest that one of these contrasts is theoretically more useful than another, only that theorists bring to their observations a small set of a priori contrasts from which description and explanation derive.

Presently, the cognitive scientists interested in artificial intelligence are introducing a totally novel contrast into discussions of mental functioning. When they use terms like *remember, learn,* or *perceive* for the output of a program their contrast is the human mind. But, historically, the contrast for a human cognitive process has always been another human cognitive process (for example, sensation versus perception, perception versus memory, memory versus evaluation). The wholesale borrowing of constructs that have always been used to describe human mental events and applying them to the propositions in computer programs leads to a final idea relevant to the dramatic rise of interest in the field of artificial intelligence.

Equivalent Explanations

Until recently, most psychologists took biology, not physics, as a model for explanation because the historical conditions that mediate biological phenomena are always treated as critical to the preferred explanation. If two qualitatively different conditions lead to the same observable phenomenon (for example, a lesion of the optic nerve and cataracts both produce an inability to see) the two forms of blindness are not regarded as theoretically equivalent, despite the fact that both patients have 20/200 vision. However, the concept of equivalence in physics holds that if the same mathematical description applies to a phenomenon that is produced by very different sets of conditions the two phenotypically identical phenomena are considered equivalent theoretically. The classic example is the concave surface of the water in a bucket that is rotating on a table. However, if one imagines the universe rotating and the bucket standing perfectly still, the surface of the water in the bucket will also appear concave. The mathematics that describes the concave surface is the same for both a rotating bucket and a rotating universe, thus the two instances are considered equivalent.

Theory in cognition and cognitive development has not been friendly to this view. Most investigators have favored the biological premise that phenotypic identity does not imply genotypic identity. For example, the unconditioned nictitating membrane reflex (NMR) in the rabbit to a puff of air involves different brain structures than does the conditioned NMR, even though the reflex appears identical under the two incentive conditions (cerebellar nuclei are necessary for the conditioned reflex but not for the unconditioned one). Thus, no psychologist or physiologist would regard the two phenomena as equivalent. However, increasing numbers of cognitive scientists are showing signs of attraction to the physicists' equivalence. Scholars in artificial intelligence assume that if there is no detectable difference between a solution produced by a program and one produced by a human mind, the two solutions should be considered equivalent, despite the obvious differences in mediating conditions. Thus, the rise of artificial intelligence has created a tension between formalists who treat identity of outcome and imposed explanation as primary and empiricists for whom identity of mediating, historical conditions is primary. Consider an example of this tension from a study on infants.

Starkey, Spelke, and Gelman (1983) reported that infants under 1 year look longer at a picture containing three objects than two objects when they hear a trio of drum beats, but look longer at two objects than three objects when they hear a pair of drum beats. The investigators concluded that young infants possess cognitive structures that appreciate number. In the older child and the adult possession of the concept of number implies the knowledge that numerosity is a feature of every array of objects and that two arrays of physically different objects can have the same numerosity. The investigators assumed that some component of the infant's cognitive structure must be similar to a component in the structure of the 10 year old child's representation of number simply because the infants in this experiment (which, incidentally, could not be replicated; see Moore et al., in press) behaved as if they regarded two sounds and two visual objects as equal.

The persuasiveness of this argument about number representation is derived from the use of the same construct (i.e., number) to explain the phenotypically different, but presumably analogous, behaviors of infants and older children. Some readers may recall that 19th-century theorists believed that the psychological derivatives of the grasp reflex in the newborn could be seen in the adult desire to acquire money and property. Readers who are not persuaded by the conclusions of Starkey and his colleagues (1983) will point to the very different cognitive structures and functions of infants and 10-year-olds; that is, historical facts that imply different mediating conditions. It will be recalled that we argued earlier for a distinction between generalizations that involve schemata and those involving concepts. Unlike a majority of behavioral biologists, a large number of cognitive scientists prefer ahistorical explanations that ignore important differences among infants, children, and adults as long as a feature of a cognitive performance is common to the behavior of persons of varied ages.

Most students of cognitive development remain empiricists rather than formalists, and use similarity in mediating conditions resulting from prior history, not similarity of outcome, as primary bases for theoretical advance.

It is reassuring that Piaget sided with the empiricists, despite his penchant for formalism, for he insisted that a child who conserved because he was tutored in a special way was not the same as one who answered the conservation problem spontaneously because the mediating conditions were different. It will be useful for students of cognitive development to remain acutely self-conscious of this theme as formalists begin to invade a territory that has been dominated by empiricists committed to historical explanations.

This is not an innocent tension, nor is it limited to the social sciences. A similar theme can be detected in evolutionary biology in debates between pheneticists, who argue that the number of contemporary similar features should be the only guide to correct taxonomy, and cladists who insist that an animal's evolutionary history must be part of the taxonomic decision. Scholars who describe contemporary Mexican society would never treat Japan and Mexico as belonging to the same category even though both societies are characterized by an authoritarian relation between husband and wife, avoidance of confrontation in social encounter, and loyalty to the family because each society acquired these characteristics in very different ways. The biology of newborns provides a final example. It is not possible to detect any important differences between newborn mammalian infants conceived naturally and those conceived through artificial insemination. However, theoretical propositions about long-term population trends in animals or humans that contain the concept *reproduction* as a predicate will have very different meanings and validities under the two forms of conception.

Put simply, if a programmed robot's performance on a specific set of problems cannot be distinguished from that of an human adult, is it theoretically useful to assume that the two performances are equivalent theoretically? The influence of 20th-century pragmatism is obvious when the question is phrased in this way. The answer will depend on our purpose. Yes, if we wish to use machines to replace humans on selected tasks, but no if we wish to understand how each form reached its goal. To a pragmatic skeptic who might ask why understanding of mechanism is important, my reply is simply that although coherence is one defensible definition of truth, correspondence between propositions and events in nature remains an equally useful and, I might add, essential second definition.

Scholars in artificial intelligence believe psychological statements about mental functions can be replaced with propositions in a program simulating a cognitive performance. The source of vulnerability in that position differs from the one we noted earlier in the discussion of biological reductionism. One of the most sophisticated attempts at computer simulation of cognitive processes is called PDP—parallel distributed processing (Rumelhart & McClelland, 1986). This effort has the basic assumption that the units activated and inhibited become linked through frequent covariation of certain input events, a premise that does not stray far from David Hartley's 18th-century treatise on associationism. No executive process is represented in the program, consequently knowledge is extremely specific. For example, the program requires just as many trials to learn to recognize the letter *s* in the second position in a word as it takes to recognize the letter *s* in the third position. Moreover, there is no unit in the program that corresponds to a lexical structure. Thus, it is unlikely that the program would predict pro-active interference — one of the most robust phenomena in cognitive functioning.

Investigators in both artificial intelligence and and biology, but for very different reasons, want to replace statements containing concepts like act, representation, symbol, feeling, motive, and self-consciousness with a different language. These territorial invasions seem to me to be motivated primarily by a desire for the greater certainty provided by the logical coherence of a program or the reliable empirical facts of modern biology. The language of modern psychology does rely too often on metaphor and analogy to persuade. For example, the assumption that cognitive development consists of a series of stages in which structures characterizing earlier stages persist into later ones derives neither from data nor coherent argument, but, rather from intuitions about the growth of a tree. The best resistance to these takeovers by either group is generation of robust psychological relations. For those who believe such conquests will advance the behavioral sciences the best help we can offer to the invaders is to tell them what it is they have to explain.

ACKNOWLEDGMENTS

This chapter was supported in part by grants from the John D. and Catherine T. MacArthur Foundation and NIMH. I thank Sandra Waxman for her constructive comments on an earlier draft of this chapter.

REFERENCES

Bachevalier, J., & Mishkin, M. (1986). Visual recognition impairment follows ventromedial but not dorsolateral prefrontal lesions in monkeys. *Behavioural Brain Research, 20,* 249–261.

Boysen, S. T., Bernston, G. G., & Prentice, J. (1987). Simian scribbles. *Journal of Comparative Psychology, 101,* 82–89.

Churchland, P. S. (1986). *Neurophilosophy.* Cambridge, MA: MIT Press.

Diamond, A. (1987, April). *Differences between adult and infant competences.* Unpublished manuscript presented at Fyssen Symposium on "Thought Without Language."

Duhem, P. (1906). *La Theorie' Physique.* Paris.

Flavell, J. H., Speer, J. R., Green, F. L., & August, D. L. (1981). The development of comprehension monitoring and knowledge about communication. *Monograph of the Society for Research in Child Development, 46* (5).

Frege, G. (1979). *Posthumous writings.* Chicago: University of Chicago Press.

Fischer, K. W., & Silvern, L. (1985). Stages and individual differences in cognitive development. In M. R. Rosenzweig & L. W. Porter (Eds.), *Annual reviews of psychology* (pp. 613–648). Palo Alto, CA: Annual Reviews.

Eimas, P. D., & Miller, J. L. (1980). Contextual effects in infant speech perception. *Science, 209,* 1140–1141.

Jensen, A. R. (1980). *Bias in mental testing.* New York: Free Press.

Kagan, J., & Klein, R. E. (1973). Cross-cultural perspectives on early development. *American Psychologist, 28,* 947–961.

Kagan, J. (1981). *The second year.* Cambridge, MA: Harvard University Press.

Kagan, J. (1984). *The nature of the child.* New York: Basic Books.

Kagan, J. (1987). Perspectives on infancy. In J. D. Osofsky (Ed.), *Handbook of infant development* (2nd ed., pp. 1150–1198). New York: Wiley.

Kagan, J., Kearsley, R. B., & Zelazo, P. R. (1978). *Infancy: Its place in human development.* Cambridge, MA: Harvard University Press.

Kuhl, P. K., & Meltzoff, A. N. (1982). The bi-modal perception of speech in infancy. *Science, 218,* 1138–1141.

Lewis, M., & Brooks-Gunn, G. (1979). *Social cognition and the acquisition of self.* New York: Plenum.

McClelland, J. L., & Rumelhart, D. E. (1986). *Parallel distributed ρ⸱ cessing* (Vol. 2). Cambridge, MA: Bradford Books, MIT Press.

Miller, J. L., & Eimas, P. D. (1983). Studies on the categorization of sۡeech by infants. *Cognition, 13,* 135–165.

Mishkin, M., & Appenzeller, T. (1987). The anatomy of memory. *Scientific American, 256,* 80–89.

Moore, D., Benenson, J., Reznick, J. S., Peters, M., & Kagan, J. (in press). The effect of numerical information on infants' looking behavior: Contradictory evidence. *Developmental Psychology.*

Moore, M. J., Kagan, J., Sahl, M., & Grant, S. (1982). Cognitive profiles and reading ability. *Genetic Psychology Monographs, 105,* 41–93.

Oden, G. C. (1987). Concept knowledge and thought. In M. R. Rosenzweig & L. W. Porter (Eds.), *Annual Review of Psychology* (pp. 203–228). Palo Alto, CA: Annual Reviews.

Priel, B., & DeSchonen, S. (1986). Self-recognition: A study of a population without mirrors. *Journal of Experimental Child Psychology, 41,* 237–250.

Rumelhart, D. E., & McClelland, J. L. & PDP research group (1986). *Parallel distributed processing.* Cambridge, MA: MIT Press.

Smith, J. M. (1985). *Science and complexity* (S. Nash, Ed.). Northwood, England: Science Reviews.

Starkey, P., Spelke, E. S., & Gelman, R. (1983). Detection of intermodal numeral correspondence by human infants. *Science, 222,* 175–181.

Stent, G. S. (1987). The mind-body problem. *Science, 236,* 990–992.

Tranel, D., & Damasio, A. R. (1985). Knowledge without awareness. *Science, 228,* 1453–1454.

Tversky, A., & Kahnenon, D. (1973). Availability. *Cognitive Psychology, 5,* 207–232.

Wagner, S., Winner, E., Cicchetti, D., & Gardner, H. (1981). Metaphorical mapping in human infants. *Child Development, 52,* 728–731.

Winner E. (1988). *The point of words.* Cambridge, MA: Harvard University Press.

Author Index

H

Habermas, J., 72, 84, *86*
Hagestad, G., 53, *67*
Hall, G. S., 53, *67*
Haller, E. P., 9, *19*
Hammond, M. A., 7, *19*
Hartman, H., 161, *163*
Harvard University, 131, *135*
Havighurst, R. J., 53, *67*
Hawkins, D., 150, *163*
Haywood, H. C., 166, 171, 175, 176, 177, 178, 182, 183, 187, 188, 189, *190, 191, 192*
Heckhausen, J., 59, *67*
Hinde, R. A., 106, *109*
Hirst, W., 146, *164*
Ho, V., 147, *164*
Hoffman, D. B., 133, *135*
Hoffman, M. B., 133, 134, *135,* 177, 182, 187, 188, *190, 191*
Hoffman, M. L., 102, *109*
Hokoda, A., 9, *19*
Holliday, S. G., 53, 59, *67*
Holmes, F. L., 142, *163*
Horn, J. L., 48, 49, 52, *67*
Hoyer, W. J., 48, *67*
Hymes, D., 78, *86*

I

Inhelder, B., 147, *163, 175, 191*
Irvine, S. H., 13, *19*
Itard, J. M. G., 3, *20*
Izard, C. E., 91, 100, *109*

J

James, W., 8, *20,* 40, *45,* 55, *67,* 91, *109*
Jaskir, J., 99, *109*
Jaynes, J., 89, *109*
Jensen, M. R., 133, *135,* 188, *190*
Jensen, A. R., 228, *233*
Johnson, D. L., 7, *19*
Johnson-Laird, P. N., 74, 84, *87*
John-Steiner, V., 152, *163*
Jones, F. N., 91, *110*
Jones, M. H., 91, *110*

K

Kagan, J., 9, *20,* 213, 222, 223, 226, 230, *233*

Kahneman, D., 84, *87*
Kahnenon, D., 224, *233*
Kamaii, C., 180, *191*
Karmiloff-Smith, A., 74, *86*
Kausler, D. H., 47, 52, 55, *67*
Kearsley, R. B., 222, *233*
Kessel, F., 13, *19*
Kessen, W., 13, *19*
Kihlstrom, J. F., 53, *66*
Kindermann, T., 51, *65*
Kitchener, K. S., 47, 53, *68*
Klein, P. S., 188, *192*
Klein, R. E., 226, *233*
Kliegl, R., 50, 51, *65, 67*
Kohn, D., 142, *163*
Kohn, M. L., 54, 57, *67*
Kuhl, P. K., 219, *233*
Kuhn, D., 28, 29, 41, *45,* 53, *67,* 147, *164*
Kulkin, 145, *163*

L

Labouvie-Vief, G., 48, 52, 53, *68*
Laing, R. D., 98, *109*
Langer, E. J., 9, *20*
Lave, J., 2, *20*
Leadbeater, B., 53, *67*
Leavitt, H. J., 154, *164*
Lehman, H. C., 52, 57, *68*
Lewis, M., 90, 91, 92, 94, 96, 97, 98, 99, 100, 101, 102, 104, 105, 106, 107, *109,* 223, *233*
Lidz, C. S., 188, *191*
Liker, J. K., 54, 58, *66*
Lipman, M., 131, *135*
Lowe, J. C., 53, *68*
Luckmann, T., 48, *65*
Lucy, J. A., 78, *86*
Lukacs, G., 72, *86*
Luria, A. R., 71, 73, 75, 76, 83n, *86*
Lyons, J., 76, 76n, *86*

M

Madsen, R., 73, 74, *86*
Mahler, M. S., 99, *110*
Malkin, C., 79, *87*
Maruyama, M., 143, *164*
Mays, W., 149, *164*
McClelland, J. L., 217, 231, *233*
McNamee, G., 79, *86*
Meacham, J. A., 53, *68*

Subject Index